The Healthful Gourmet

The Healthful Gourmet

Changing our Perception of Food Through Wholesome Recipes and Spiritual and Nutritional Awareness

Jeani-Rose Atchison

Writers Club Press
San Jose New York Lincoln Shanghai

The Healthful Gourmet
Changing our Perception of Food Through Wholesome
Recipes and Spiritual and Nutritional Awareness

All Rights Reserved © 2000 by Jeani-Rose Atchison

No part of this book may be reproduced or transmitted in any form or by any means, graphic, electronic, or mechanical, including photocopying, recording, taping, or by any information storage or retrieval system, without the permission in writing from the publisher.

Published by Writers Club Press
an imprint of iUniverse.com, Inc.

For information address:
iUniverse.com, Inc.
620 North 48th Street
Suite 201
Lincoln, NE 68504-3467
www.iuniverse.com

ISBN: 0-595-09661-1

Printed in the United States of America

*"When Health is Absent....
Wisdom cannot reveal itself, art cannot become manifested; strength cannot be exerted, wealth is useless and reason is powerless."*

*Herophilies,
300 B.C.*

*To my love, Eric,
and our precious little ones,
Rhiannon and Gwendolyn,
who make my heart full....*

Acknowledgments

There are so many people who have helped shape this book, many of whom before I even considered writing it.

My dear friend, Sharon Steele-McGee, who supported and believed in me through my shedding of old identities and the transformation to who I am today.

Arianne and Jean-Claude Koven, who were instrumental in my physical and spiritual paths back to health.

Randy Steer, who trusted my judgment in my change of careers.

Paul Burkett, for his infectious and irreverent sense of humor and friendship.

Sweet Terri Bona, who I had so much fun with searching out answers to our life questions.

Elisabeth Carter, for creating a beautiful atmosphere for me to conduct classes.

Michael and Kim Strickland, for their enthusiastic support of the classes, the feedback on this project, our way of life, and their wide-open embrace of my self and my family, which I treasure.

To those of you at Life Grocery: Lisa, Ronnie, Arlene, Helen, and others who always made me feel like a special part of our wonderful Co-op.

To Myrna and Emery Atchison for never judging, always accepting, and being so supportive in what we do.

To Ronnie Hudson....hey girlfriend! Thanks for the critique and changes made on the text portion of this book.

And to Sue and Neal Tompkins. Especially Sue, whose work on this project was immense. What started out as acquaintances working together, has ended as another beginning. A relationship that is precious to me.

Thank you, all of you.

Contents

Introduction xiii
Suggested Staple List 1
Substitutions 5
Changing Our Perception of Food 9
Feeding Your Children 13
Children's Food List 17
Fats 21
Proteins 27
Dairy 31
Milk Alternatives 37
Carbohydrates 39
Sweeteners 43
Organic Foods 47
Genetically Engineered Foods 55
Irradiated Foods 59
Living Foods 61
Sprouting 63
Appetizers, Dips, and Spreads 67
Condiments 81
Soups 103
Salads 147
Salad Dressings 199
Breads 221
Side Dishes 247

xi

Entrees 271
Desserts 393
Beverages 445
Glossary 461
Dietary Changes 465
The Natural Home 467
Co-Creation 471
References and Resources 475
Index 479

Introduction

In assisting others to transition to a plant-based diet, many people question what my belief system is in regards to the reasons I became a vegetarian.

Prior to changing my diet I had tried many therapies, conventional and complimentary, to heal a myriad of ailments. Some therapies did not work and were discarded, others worked for a period of time, and a few continue to work to this day. Nothing, however, seemed to be "the answer." I was taking care of many aspects of myself, but there was something missing, some piece of the puzzle I had overlooked. In trying to find the missing link, I began to closely examine the food I was consuming and the relationship I had with it.

I grew up on a typical American diet with many missed meals in my preteen and teen years. When a meal was provided, it was eaten with no thought of nurturing, just the primitive notion of survival. My disassociation with food continued into my early thirties. Though I had always loved to cook, it was with a preponderance of rich sauces and gravies and, unbeknownst to me at the time, abominable food combinations.

After I changed my diet, I slowly began to see results. With compromised liver and kidney function, I found that eliminating meat was easier on my body. When I let go of my desire for dairy, I found dramatic results. My body felt more relaxed and I moved easier. My joints were not as stiff, and certain exercises and yoga postures were greatly improved. Eliminating refined foods and eating more raw foods allowed me to breathe easier, as well as feel a greater sense of peace. As I delved into nutritional research, I began to understand why this was happening. Fascinated by the health benefits I was reaping, food became a whole new study, not only the preparation and selection of it, but also the emotional and chemical interactions of it as well.

I had been a Real Estate and Securities Broker during that time and found I was much happier completely letting go of those two careers. With great enthusiasm, I jumped in with both feet to learn as much as possible why food was such a critical player in the physical as well as the emotional and spiritual parts of an individual.

Several years passed. A friend of mine offered me the use of his restaurant to teach cooking classes. Starting out was a little rough, sometimes there were only two students attending classes, but the word got out and eventually others joined. Soon after, interested individuals inquired about private cooking and health consultations. Most of them were working with a specific condition and/or illness. All had the common goal to eat healthy, delicious fare without feeling "deprived." Most clients understood on an intellectual level that the quality, the quantity, and the types of foods was critical to their healing program, but the biggest challenge was to overcome their emotional attachment. Some of my clients could not cross over that barrier, but many others have, and they are enjoying their new life.

Along with my ongoing education on how food acts on the body, I became aware of the ecological and environmental benefits of eating low on the food chain. I felt proud that my family and I could make such a powerful difference in the preservation of our earth.

The sacredness of life is another issue I consider. I strongly believe that all life is precious, whether it is plant, insect, animal or human. Our society has been built without the consciousness of soul and so our intent has been warped as well. Most people who purchase their food at the supermarket are in denial that this was once a living being. The denial is so strong that when an average person finds out how I eat, they become defensive. I am not the type of person who would intentionally make anyone uncomfortable about his or her food or lifestyle choices.

What happens, I believe, is that my beliefs or practices somehow touches their inner most spiritual selves, the consciousness of their soul. Deep inside we know that this is the most natural and correct way to behave, but we are mired in too much confusion created by ourselves and by the food industry that we allow ourselves to become victimized. Blaming the media for the skewed messages sent to the consumer is over simplified since it reflects back to the astronomical advertising budgets of the food industry. Both parties are irresponsible, giving a biased view on the benefits of the products being marketed, all for the sake of profit.

There are cycles of life that are as natural as the air we breathe. One of these cycles includes the lying down of life of one being so that another may live. Many ancient and some present cultures recognize, respect, and honor this exchange of energy. Everyday we all take in life in the food we ingest. Plants are as alive as animals. Through greed, our society has created an industry based on decaying flesh and denatured food products, effectively removing us from the conscious act of nourishment.

Whatever an individual chooses to eat should be respected, as long as that individual comes from a state of awareness. People need to take responsibility for their actions, whether it is how they treat their neighbor, how they use the resources of our earth, or what they choose to eat. Once this consciousness occurs, certain practices such as farm factory animals, genetically engineered food, irradiation, pesticides, and manufactured foods will become intolerable. Intention in life is everything, but how can we have this without awareness?

I am not a religious person, though deeply spiritual. Simple whole foods allow my body to expend energy wisely and without difficulty. I believe this allows a heightened state of awareness within, creating a more receptive heart, mind, and soul. I try to walk with grace and reverence in my daily life and to guide my family in the same manner. My goals in life are very simple—to love, to be happy, to be of service to others, and to be at peace. I hope that this book will be of benefit to you.

*"This is the true joy in life,
the being used for a
purpose recognized by yourself as a mighty one;
the being a force of nature instead of a feverish,
selfish little clod of ailments and grievances
complaining that the world will not devote itself
to making you happy.
I am of the opinion that my life belongs to the
whole community and that as long as I live it is my
privilege to do for it whatever I can.
I want to be thoroughly used up when I die, for the
harder I work the more I live. I rejoice in life for
it's own sake. Life is no "brief candle" to me. It is a
sort of splendid torch which I have got hold of for
the moment, and I want to make it burn as
brightly as possible before handing it on to future
generations."*

George Bernard Shaw

Suggested Staple List

There are many, many products on the market, and new ones coming out daily, so it would be impossible to list them all. I have, though, listed what you might find in my kitchen. There are several items missing in my list that you may find in others, such as packaged convenience foods, seitan, certain sweeteners, cereals, etc. My family thrives on less-processed foods, and so I find no desire or added nutritional benefit in having them there.

I do list certain "cheeses," though the majority of them are not strictly vegan. There is an enzyme, rennet, that is taken from the stomach lining of calves (or other animals) that is used in the cheese making process. Therefore, if your cheese does not specify vegetable enzyme, chances are it is not. There are a few vegan "cheese" products available. Try your local natural foods market. Dairy substitutes should not make up a great portion of your diet, rather it should be used as a condiment to enhance a specific recipe which may have traditionally been made with dairy. For those of you who are ready to give up dairy, there is a great little book called The Uncheese Cookbook by Joanne Stepaniak which is full of vegan renditions of favorite recipes. (See section on "Dairy" for more information.)

Allspice
Amasake
Apple cider vinegar
Arrowroot
Artichoke hearts
Baked chips
Baking powder (non-aluminum)
Baking soda
Barley malt syrup
Basil
Bay leaves
Black mustard seeds
Bread, Sprouted grain bread
Brown rice vinegar
Canned tomatoes (Muir Glen)
Caraway seeds
Cardamom
Carob powder
Chapatis
Chervil
Chili powder
Chipotle powder
Cinnamon
Cloves
Coconut milk
Coconut, shredded unsweetened
Coriander
Corn tortillas
Cumin
Curry
Dill

Dried beans—garbanzo, northern, adzuki, black eyed peas, navy, kidney, pinto, lima, mung, split peas, lentil, soybeans
Dry mustard
Enamel-lined canned beans
Fennel seeds
Garlic powder
Ginger
Grain coffee
Grains—barley (not pearled), oats, rye, brown and wild rice, grits, cracked wheat, quinoa, amaranth, millet, buckwheat, wheat berries
Herbal teas
Ketchup (natural brands)
Kudzu
Lecithin granules
Marjoram
Miso
Mustard (whole-grain, natural)
Non-dairy cheeses
Non-hydrogenated "natural" margarine (or make your own—see "Butter" recipe)
Nut butters—almond, cashew, sesame
Nutmeg
Nutritional yeast
Nuts and seeds—flax, sesame, sunflower, red clover, alfalfa, pumpkin, pine nuts, walnuts, pecans, almonds, cashews (no roasted nuts)
Oils—flax, coconut, olive, sesame, toasted sesame
Onion powder
Oregano
Paprika
Parsley
Peppermint
Pickles

Popcorn
Poppy seeds
Rice cakes
Rice syrup
Rosemary
Sage
Salsa
Sauerkraut (all natural—no chemical preservatives)
Sea salt
Sea vegetables (arame, agar, kelp, dulse, Nori)
Slippery elm powder
Soy milk powder
Stevia powder, liquid, and leaf
Superfoods—Spirulina, chlorella, Kyogreen
Tarragon
Tempeh
Thyme
Tofu (both refrigerated in tubs and aseptic packaged)
Turmeric
Vanilla, maple, lemon flavorings by Frontier
Vegan mayonnaise
Vegan milk
Vogue Vege Base
Wheat-free pasta noodles (try Papadini lentil pasta), soba (try not to eat noodles more than a couple of times a month)
Whole grain crackers

Substitutions

Baking powder—many of the store bought varieties contain harmful ingredients such as aluminum and lime, as well as too much sodium. Here are a few healthier alternatives:
- •Blend 2 parts arrowroot, 1 part baking soda, 1 part cream of tartar.
- •Use low-sodium or non-aluminum brands, such as Rumford.
- •Make a paste with a small amount of yeast, water, and flour. Let sit 30 minutes before using.

Cornstarch—use arrowroot or kudzu.

Cocoa—use carob powder. To help deepen the flavor, add a small amount of grain coffee substitute.

Coffee—there are many grain varieties available. Experiment to find your favorite.

Dairy:
- •**Milk** can be substituted with any soy or grain milk. Another option would be to use seed or nut milks. Simply grind a couple of tablespoons of sesame or sunflower seeds, almonds (blanch and remove skins), cashews, etc., with 1/2 to 2 cups water. Add a pinch of sea salt and vanilla flavoring, if desired. When a recipe asks for milk powder, use soy powder instead.

- **Yogurt, sour milk, and buttermilk** can be substituted with soy milk (1 cup) curdled with 2 teaspoons lemon juice or with soy yogurt.
- **Butter** can be replaced with coconut oil (2/3-3/4 cup for each cup of butter), or other mild-tasting oils, but remember to use less. Natural, non-hydrogenated spreads such as Spectrum or Earth's Balance may be used as well. Try my recipe for "Butter" for a healthy, delicious substitute. Avocado is wonderful on a slice of bread or baked potato instead of butter. If baking sweet breads or cake, you can substitute applesauce, date paste, or prune paste.
- **Cream cheese** in recipes can be substituted with tofu. Or make a thick cashew cream or vegan mayonnaise. There are many faux cheeses on the market today. Experiment with the different types to find the one you like best.
- **Sour cream** is easy—try my Tofu Sour Cream, or use soy yogurt.
- **Heavy cream** can be substituted with my recipe for Cashew Cream.

- **Eggs.** For one egg, use:
  - 1 Tablespoon flax seed ground, mixed with 3 Tablespoons water. This works very well. I favor it in most quick breads and cakes. It has a mild, nutty flavor. When mixed with water it becomes nice and "glooey," similar to eggs. The flax seed has undergone much research and is rated very high, nutritionally speaking. (See flax information in glossary).
  - 1 Tablespoon of any of these: sesame butter, garbanzo flour, lecithin granules, soy flour, or arrowroot mixed with 3 Tablespoons of water.
  - Make a blend of 2 parts arrowroot, 1 part tapioca flour, 1 part slippery elm, and mix 1 Tablespoon with 3 Tablespoons water.
  - There is a product called "Egg Replacer." Follow directions on package.

•Flours

Wheat flour was, once upon a time, a very good food. But ours and other countries have abused the use of wheat to the point that many of us are "wheat intolerant." This has caused me to be wheat defiant. Through refinement, treatment with chemicals and preservatives and a long shelf life, the wheat we purchase is oxidized and rancid (not to mention devoid of a great deal of its nutrients). If you are going to use wheat, then it would be best to grind your own, which is pretty easy to do. An inexpensive spice/coffee grinder is ideal for small amounts.

Reduce or eliminate processed food products, and you will eliminate many allergens, and one of the biggest is wheat. It can be found in a lot of different foods, such as soy sauces, grain vinegar, hot dogs, luncheon meat, beer, catsup, non-dairy creamer, many seasonings, and "hidden" by names such as hydrolyzed vegetable protein, textured vegetable protein, hydrolyzed plant protein, modified food starch, and used as a binder, filler or excipient of a phenomenal amount of packaged foods.

There are many of us who find it difficult to digest gluten, which is the protein found in glutinous grains. These grains include wheat, barley, sweet rice, rye and oats. Oats, however, do not seem to cause the problems that the others do. Since wheat is the prevalent bad guy, I have pretty much rid my diet of it except in the form of sprouted bread on occasion, or sprouted berries (read the section on "Sprouts"). There is no need to feel deprived by removing one or a few from your diet.

When a recipe calls for flour, do not be afraid to substitute some or all of the wheat you would normally use with millet, rice, corn, oat, barley, rye, spelt, kamut, etc. See "Bread" section for more information.

•**Salt.** Use sea vegetables, powdered kelp or dulse, sea salt, miso, Bragg Liquid Aminos, Tamari.

•**Sweeteners.** White sugar or honey for every 1 cup measure:
  •3/4 cup maple syrup, decrease liquids in recipe slightly
  •1 1/2 cups rice or barley malt syrup, decrease liquids in recipe slightly
  •1 teaspoon stevia powder, add 2 Tablespoons liquid to recipe
  •heaping Tablespoon of ground leaf stevia
  •date butter: blend dates in a small amount of hot water until smooth.

Changing Our Perception of Food

The scientific world has come a long way in identifying the roles that specific nutrients play in the way our body functions. They also realize that we have only begun to scratch the surface of understanding how the body works. All components must work synergistically to achieve homeostasis, that is, balance and optimum health.
I sincerely believe that fad diets such as high-protein, low-fat, no-fat, etc., are detrimental to your health and bring you no closer to understanding how your body works. If you want to lose weight, gain clarity of mind, or help your body heal itself, you have to put some effort into it. Most people will not take the first step to health, which is learning what is or is not good for them. Rather, we tend to look towards "experts" to give us a pill or herb or single therapy to cure us. This is because our psyches lean more toward what is the easiest route to take. Man's ego would rather accept that outside influences are responsible for the way we feel, and that it has nothing to do with the hamburger, fries, and cola we had for lunch. We all must realize that healing comes from within. It must also be understood that what we eat and drink, place on our skin and hair, breathe and clean our homes with has a direct effect on how our body will react.

Food manufacturers (now that's a term that should strike fear within us—being as far away from nature as you can get) and major food industries take certain information, revealed by research scientists, out of context and use it for their own monetary gains. One example is fortified packaged foods, which, through processing, lose many nutrients.

Once the nutrients are lost, the powers that be deem which ones are important and process a few back in. Certain food industries campaign heavily in the media to make you aware of the importance of a specific nutrient found in their products without explaining the detrimental effects of other aspects of these "foods."

We are purposely kept in the dark, but we do not mind because it is too difficult to change the mind set of 40-some-odd years of programming that we have received from these industries.

There is considerable research on the effects of poor diet in the development of the unborn child and the young in our society today. Poor health is passed down from generation to generation. I, for one, do not want to leave that legacy behind. I am determined to understand what it is I can do to change this. It would not be a particularly difficult endeavor because learning how to eat and live is natural and instinctual. What does make it difficult, though, is that we have to unlearn many fallacies at the same time. Just think what a precious gift we can give our children if we never introduced these fallacies to begin with.

Often mothers come to me complaining that they cannot change their young ones eating habits because the children refuse to eat anything other than what they are accustomed to eating. My answer is, if you want your children to eat healthier, then every member of the family must change. Throw away the junk from your cupboards, and do not bring it back in the house. If a child requests candy, soda or potato chips, explain to them why you no longer buy these products. Look through this book for healthy snack options that have been kid tested! Even a two-or three-year-old child will understand the explanation that candy has bad sugar and fruit has good sugar. My eldest daughter (now four years old) understands that bad sugar will cause her body to work too hard to try not to get sick and not work hard enough to make her body strong. You do not have to get technical yet. However, you do need to have that knowledge, because children are naturally curious. As they grow older, they will want to know the reasons for your actions.

Your older child will eventually come around as well, especially when you are a good role model. There is also nothing wrong with telling them that you were wrong to bring those foods into the home to begin with—that you were not aware of their bad effects on the body. Include, not exclude, children in food decisions. Soon they will be on their own and will make decisions based on what they learned from you. You cannot stop them from making certain choices outside the home, and neither should you try. Rather, empower them with as much information as you can give and nurture their independence, which will give them the confidence to make decisions for themselves.

A child will not starve to death if she or he skips a meal in protest to the change of menu. Within a short period of time their adulterated taste buds will be cleansed, and they will enjoy with gusto the whole foods placed in front of them. Believe it or not, they will lose the desire for refined, high-sugar, high-salt, and high-fat foods.

Whole foods are more satisfying. They fill you up quicker. The texture is coarser. Full mastication is required. Therefore, a longer amount of time is needed at the dinner table, which invites more familial contact. This is another life practice sorely missing in our society.

Thirst is satiated easily on a whole foods diet, especially when you consume a large amount of fruits and vegetables in their raw state. Large quantities of soda, tea, or water are no longer needed to wash down the food. In fact, you begin to understand that liquid is not important at a meal and how it actually impedes digestion due to diluting the enzymes needed to breakdown the food.

Being conscious of our choices makes us less a victim and more responsible for our actions. Nourishment of the body is a great gift of love, whether to one's self or to one's family—each and every one of us deserves that gift.

Feeding Your Children

The American Academy of Pediatrics stated in 1995, "An American child has viewed about 360,000 advertisements before graduating from high school...In 1750 B.C. the Code of Hammurabi made it a crime, punishable by death, to sell anything to a child without first obtaining a Power of Attorney. In the 1990's selling products to American children has become a standard business practice."

"So what can I feed my children?" or "But my child is such a picky eater!" Sound familiar?

This is so often a source of frustration for a parent as they transition towards a healthier lifestyle. It is certainly easier to feed a child who has always followed a healthy diet than it is for one who has already adulterated their palates and is led by peer pressure. It can be done, however, with persistence and a full explanation as to why.

Each child is so different. My eldest is a mono-diet type, which means she will only eat one thing at a time. My youngest, on the other hand, wants a variety of food. What they both have in common, though, is the desire for simply prepared foods. They do not want fancy dressings, sauces, gravies, casseroles, etc. As I am writing this, it is late spring and the kids have been asking for asparagus and artichokes like crazy. I steam these and let them eat their fill. Shortly after, they want something more and are ready for a heavier food, say a protein or grain. My eldest will also obsess on certain foods, asking for red bell pepper five days in a row. I think this is completely natural and her body knows what is needed. I always offer her two to three choices for a meal and stick with that unless she requests something equal to what I would have given her. I need to bend with my children's desires, but I am still firm about what they will eat throughout the day in regards to a balance of fruits, vegetables, grains, fats, and proteins. Rhiannon understands the importance of eating her vegetables before starting on something else. Most times any conflict on food choices has more to do with emotional control more than it does with taste. That is where patience and the ability to treat your child with respect and as an intelligent individual comes into play. I have never forced her to eat a food with the words "eat because I said so!" Or worse, "eat it or you won't get dessert!" Instead I talk about the reasons why I give her these foods. Number one is because I love her too much not to give her good food. They are never too young to talk to about nutrition, how it works, or where it goes. When Rhiannon was 2 1/2 years old we made a game about where food starts in the mouth and how it ends up. Now, at the age of 4, she has a good understanding on how the digestive system works.

If your child is transitioning to a healthier diet, it is easy to disguise foods into something they will enjoy eating. Shakes are a great way to get sprouts, nuts, and seeds into a child. Use a vegan milk (almond milk is my preference) and add to the nuts, seeds, and/or sprouts, and some frozen raspberries. Whip it up in a strong blender. Cashews work great because they make the shake real creamy. Adding a dash of vanilla and sweetener, such as stevia, adds flavor and masks the sprouts, which will have a distinctive taste. Rhiannon calls this her pink milk and requests it often. If your child is really adventurous, add some green to it, such as spirulina or barley grass. I highly recommend these green foods for children, as well as adults.

Raw cookies are a popular way to get children to eat foods they may not otherwise try. Children love finger foods, probably because it is easier for their little hands and sort of a taboo in most families. Making little balls, patties, or mini shish kebobs on toothpicks are favored.

More exotic foods such as sea vegetables may be a challenge at first due to their unusual appearance. Most children really like the distinctive taste. Dulse can be eaten out of the bag or dry toasted briefly for "chips." Arame and hijiki are fun. Kids like to gross out the parents by telling them they are eating worms! Nori is probably the most accepted, due to the popularity of sushi. I have rolled many combinations of food in a nori sheet with enthusiastic appreciation from young diners. The main thing is to lighten up on how we view food and the dinner table. It should be a joyful experience and a special time for the family to interact. Placing your own expectations on a child will only cause stress between you and your child.

Our perception of food has to change if we want good health for ourselves and our children. Getting connected to the whole cycle of life can be a very empowering feeling. Knowing that we are nourished by the sun, air, water, and earth, directly or indirectly, by eating a food that was, is a spiritual experience. We tend to view life in a more gentle way and journey through the years with more respect to living beings.

The long-term ramifications of this way of thinking are both infinite and awe-inspiring. I am so proud of the fact that my children are being raised in an atmosphere of awareness. Intelligence is not something given to children when they reach a certain age, but rather it is innate. Allowing the information and tools to be readily available to them enables them to sort out and make knowledgeable decisions for their own welfare. The impact that a parent has on their children reaches far past the time they have grown and left home. I believe it is our responsibility to be as informed as possible, and to share this with them. Many of us have unresolved issues from our childhood, which have caused us not to take care of our own bodies. It would be very selfish of us if we did not work on these issues as they most assuredly will affect our children.

Love of self must come before love of another.

Children's Food List

In this section, I have listed all the recipes in my book that children especially like, and included some ideas for meals throughout the day. These are suggestions that will provide a springboard for you and your child's creativity.

Never try to force a child to eat in the morning unless there is hunger. It is not true that a big breakfast is your most important meal of the day. Heavy food actually impedes the body's functioning, making it work harder to break down, assimilate, and remove toxins. This can give a lethargic feeling, headaches, cloudy brain functioning, etc. My children tend to like fruit upon waking, then a couple of hours later ask for something more substantial. There is no reason to feel rushed or pressured in the morning. If you find yourself running out of time, wake up a little earlier and go to bed a little earlier. Planning meals the night before helps tremendously.

The following list is varied, and children will find it difficult to become bored with their meals.

Breakfast:
- Fresh or dry unsulphured fruit and raw nuts or seeds
- Shakes or smoothies (most all of the recipes in the beverage section)
- Baked sweet potatoes
- Yogurt (preferably non-dairy) with or without fruit
- Soups (why not? Leftovers from the night before are great, especially on cool mornings.)

- Creamy rice cereal with oat milk
- Quicky Oats
- Hot millet cereal (1/2 cup rinsed and toasted millet cooked in 2 cups of water or vegan milk)
- Pancakes (measure ingredients the night before and mix dry ingredients into wet ingredients in the morning)
- Waffles (soak grains at night, then blend in morning)
- Cashew French Toast

At home, small children will appreciate a variety of "grazings" for snacks and lunch. Try a large platter or lazy Susan filled with lightly steamed or raw veggies, dips, spreads, etc., and watch as it is devoured throughout mid-morning and afternoon.

Dinner should be more formal, with everyone sitting down together and sharing conversation, food, and laughter....this is a special family connection time.

- Banana Miso Sesame Spread
- Raw or dry toasted dulse chips (see glossary under seaweed)
- Carrot Butter
- Quick and Easy Hummus
- Dulse Gomacio
- Fresh Tomato Sauce
- Vegan Sour Cream
- Broccoli Soup
- Fresh Tomato Soup
- Lemon Soup
- Pea and Carrot Soup
- Spinach Soup
- Tomato Carrot Soup
- Cashew or Almond Butter and Shredded Carrot Sandwiches

- Vegetable Sandwiches
- Carrot Salad Sandwiches
- Quinoa and Lentils (rinse 1/2 cup quinoa, add to 1 3/4 cups boiling water with 1/4 cup lentils. Cook until liquid is absorbed. If lentils are still too chewy, add a little more water and cook a few more minutes.)
- Sprouted chickpeas and brown rice in vegetable broth
- Potato, Corn, and Cherry Tomato Salad
- Coleslaw
- Sesame Carrot Salad with Arame
- Tabbouleh
- Chopped Main Salad Rolled in Nori
- Mock Egg and Chicken Salads (serve with baked corn chips).
- All recipes in the Bread section
- Nori Rolls and Rice Balls
- Potato quarters with Vegan Sour Cream and Dulse Gomacio
- Wilted Spinach
- Spaghetti Squash and Green Beans
- Coconut and Cashew Veggies
- White Beans with Tomato and Sage
- Any plain beans and rice dish
- Bean Croquettes
- Asian Spring Rolls
- Polenta Pizza
- Italian Beans 'n Greens
- Spinach and Rice Casserole with Toasted Almonds
- Squash and Bean Casserole
- Veggie Rolls
- Mediterranean Stuffed Collard Greens
- Squash and Leek Turnovers
- Cashew Burgers
- Earth Burgers

- Millet Nut and Seed Balls
- Rosemary Tofu Sauté
- Tempeh Millet Loaf
- All Dessert recipes

Other snacks may include avocado (my youngest daughters favorite), frozen berries as finger food, toasted pumpkin seeds with or without a splash of Braggs, cashews or almonds....and on and on. Don't forget lots and lots of water throughout the day!

Fats

One U.S. study showed that from 1991 to 1998, obesity increased in every state. The authors of the study said: "Rarely do chronic conditions such as obesity spread with the speed and dispersion characteristic of a communicable disease epidemic."

Many dieters cringe when they see my family and I enjoying avocados, nuts and other full fat whole foods. Most shake their heads in disbelief when I explain these are good fats, essential for optimum body functioning. I grin and add that eating fat actually helps maintain my weight.

It is important to know what a fat is and understand how it works in your body. Fats are as important as protein and carbohydrates. In fact, the basic composition of all foods includes these three components in differing degrees.

A lettuce, tomato, and cucumber salad has fat and so does a handful of almonds. This is natural and the way it should be, with the food also having the proper balance of nutrients needed for it to metabolize into the body.

Fats are similar in makeup as carbohydrates, composed of hydrogen, carbon, and oxygen. The difference between the two is that there is less oxygen and more carbon and hydrogen in fats. So, though they will be broken down similarly, it takes more bodily energy to metabolize fat.

Fats in humans and animals come from two sources—from the food we eat, and from excess carbohydrate intake (and the body's need to break down and store this excess as fat).

Fats are composed of glycerin and fatty acids. Glycerin is broken down into sugar, which may be used as fuel by the body. Fatty acids are described as chains of oxygen, carbon, and hydrogen atoms. These chains have links within where additional atoms may be attached.

If hydrogen is attached to these links, the fat becomes solid as in products like shortening and margarine. If oxygen is attached, the fat turns rancid.

Unsaturated fats are fatty acid chains with one or more carbon atoms missing their hydrogen atom accompaniment. Open links in these fatty acid chains are desirable. This is the way our body can combine certain nutrients with the fatty acids, allowing them both to be transported through the body where they can be used. Nuts and seeds are our chief sources of unsaturated fats, while animal fats contain very little.

Polyunsaturated fats (P.F.'s) are those that have a larger number of fatty acids with two or more open links in their chains. Polyunsaturated fats have harmful effects as well as saturated. It is generally known that P.F.'s lower the cholesterol level in the blood. What is not generally known though is that P.F.'s will move the cholesterol from the blood stream into the tissues where it is more harmful. Researchers have also shown that P.F.'s will inhibit white blood cells.

The hydrogenation process of fats destroys any nutrients that may be present. These added hydrogen atoms fill the empty links on the fatty acid chain and blocks additional nutrients as well.

Saturated fats are found mainly in animal products and coconuts (though fats from coconuts have a different chemical makeup). Saturated fats act like hydrogenated fats and do not allow nutrients to bond onto the fatty acid chains.

The good fat found in whole foods is used by your body as a source of essential fatty acids, as a source of heat and energy, as padding for organs and nerves, as well as a regulator of the fat soluble vitamins A, D, E, and K.

The bulk of fat in your diet should be derived from whole food and not cooking oils. If you do sauté or stir fry, try adding a little water. Baked goods containing oil should be looked at as occasional treats and not as a daily addition to the diet. Do not use low-fat, non-fat food products. They could be detrimental to your health, being deficient in nutrients needed for proper assimilation.

If foods are cooked in high heated oil, they become carcinogenic. That means healthy cells may become cancerous.

In order for fats to be digested, they must be emulsified. High heated oil cannot be emulsified. Your body will try to expel what it cannot use. If your body cannot expel all of it, the body will store it in areas where it will cause the least harm, or will wall it off by creating a tumor around it.

You have to be aware of this even when you shop in health food stores. Potato chips, doughnuts, french fries, etc., are not healthier for you when purchased at these establishments! If you really want something like this, try baked chips, which may be a better selection.

Any food value found in oil will be lost when heated. The heated oil breaks down, and the fat-soluble vitamins will not be absorbed as well. So not only is the heated oil devoid of nutrition, it contributes to nutrient starvation of the body.

Eating whole foods lets go of the need to count calories and fat, and your body will feel satiated with a smaller intake. There are built-in safety factors in the natural food provided for us which prevent us from becoming obese.

Benefits of eating avocados, raw nuts, seeds, and legumes include: protection from cancer, heart disease and arthritis, immunity enhancer, weight loss, mental clarity, hormonal balancing, smooth skin, strong nails, and lustrous hair.

The essential fatty acids found in whole foods are necessary for adults and children for brain and nerve functioning. I make sure my daughters have ample fat daily. I know I am doing well by how they glow with good health!

Coconut oil is an exception to the rule. It is one of the few plant foods that contain saturated fat. The critical difference between coconut and animal fat is that coconut is comprised of medium-chain and not long-chain saturated fatty acids. Medium-chain saturates digest easily and are used for fuel and energy, whereas the long-chain saturates are stored as fat in your body.

Coconut oil has many attributes, a few of which are:
- It contains almost 50% lauric acid in its makeup, which is a disease fighting fatty acid, ideal for immune-suppressed individuals.
- It is a source of medium-chain triglycerides which enable your body to digest fat efficiently
- It is very stable and contains no harmful trans-fatty acids. This makes it a desirable oil for sauté and stir frying. No oil is good for deep-frying.
- Less is needed. Use approximately 1/4 measure less in any recipe.
It has a mild taste, complimenting all types of cooking and ingredients.
- It adds a richness of texture and taste to baked goods.

The food processing industry would like you to believe that coconut oil is unhealthy, mainly because if you choose to use this oil over one of theirs then theirs will no longer be wanted. Secondly, they will have to admit that most of the oil in today's markets is harmful. If this were to happen, it would alert the average Joe to the fact that perhaps other processed foods need to be questioned.

Some tips on oil:
Buy small bottles of cold or expeller pressed
Never buy hydrogenated
Do not fry
Do not let oil smoke in pan
Refrigerate after opening

Keep away from direct light
Smell your oil—if it smells rancid, do not use it
Keep intake to a minimum

My personal choices:
Olive
Sesame
Coconut
Flax—not for cooking

What we need to always keep in mind is a fractionated food of any kind will never be healthier than a whole food. When using oils, do so wisely…a little bit can go a long way.

Roughly 25% of U.S. children are overweight or obese. Children who are overweight turn into adults who tend to be overweight as well.

Proteins

There are many different proteins functioning in our bodies. All proteins are composed of amino acids, which are, simply stated, the building blocks of proteins.

Our body cannot use protein in its original state. Instead, it will break it down into separate amino acids. Once this takes place, the body will then construct the specific protein it needs. When a protein is broken down, it is used immediately or absorbed by our liver and stored for future use. We have in each of us a reserve, or pool, of amino acids from which the body can draw upon at any time. There is no need, therefore, to try and consume foods or combinations of foods to achieve a "complete protein." When we think of protein needs, we should realize that an understanding of amino acids is what is important in evaluating the true ultimate value of a food.

There are two ways our body receives protein. One is by diet—what we consume. The other is by catabolic cell processes, where other cells digest an expired cell. The waste is broken back down into amino acids and then used again to synthesize their own protein.

Of the twenty-three recognized amino acids, eight are considered essential because they must be found in a food source. With a varied whole food diet, you will have no problem attaining these.

Quality of protein is more important than quantity. Too much will wreak havoc in the body. It was originally recommended that people consume approximately 120 grams of protein a day. This conclusion was based on the misconception that since muscles are composed chiefly of protein, then protein must supply energy to the muscles. (Today, it is understood that plant-based food supplies the best fuel for muscular activity.) This recommendation was supported by further research in the late 1800's when experiments on dogs were done to determine safe amounts of protein intake. Unfortunately there was no adjustment made on differences between humans and dogs. At around the same time, experiments in Germany showed that 40 grams of protein was sufficient. However, since the old standards were so well fixed in the minds of the medical establishment, it remained at that level until even more research forced them to lower it to 60 or 70 grams, twice the amount considered safe by the aforementioned experiments.

In the past sixty years, independent researchers have concluded that only 24 to 30 grams of protein are necessary to maintain good health. A study done by Dr. Jaffe at the University of California at Berkley showed diets of large healthy groups of people around the world to be 15 to 35 grams. Today, a typical American meat eater consumes over 90 grams of protein a day.

So, is too much protein detrimental? Definitely!

A high protein diet will eventually destroy the entire glandular system. Protein metabolism leaves waste products such as uric, sulfuric, and phosphoric acids. This causes your body to become highly acidic which forces your body's buffer systems to work very hard at trying to get rid of these substances. Buffer systems are those organs that maintain normal body pH, the major ones being your liver and kidneys.

Back in the early 1950's, scientific research showed that breast milk contained 60% less protein than the infant needed, according to RDA standards. A formula was created with 2 1/2 to 3 times the amount of protein in breast milk, plus salt was added. Disastrous results from using this new formula began to appear. Symptoms included kidney damage, hyperacidity with osteoporosis, dangerously high phenylalanine and tyrosine content in the blood, poor protein metabolism, and increased acceleration of physical growth without mental growth.

Potassium and magnesium are deficient in the typical American diet. Magnesium deficiency syndrome is apparent in arteriosclerosis, high blood pressure, migraine headaches, eclampsia, the leaching of calcium from teeth and bones, liver damage, and disturbance of the neuro-muscular vessel system. The kidneys are deeply impacted by all the above factors. The athletic medicine services in the USA have had to treat an extraordinary number of kidney injuries and breakdowns after athletic competitions due to high protein intake. The American Heart Association concluded that almost all of these diseases—arteriosclerosis, high blood pressure, and coronary disease—are significantly related to kidney function and, therefore, more than half of the population die of kidney disease.

Points to remember:
- The more protein you ingest, the more calcium is excreted from your body. Remember: Dairy is a protein as well, so it would be best if you did the opposite of the popular milk campaign!
- If your calcium levels are low, your body will extract from the bone to use in other functions.
- One in four women have lost 50 to 75% of original bone material by age 65.
- If our blood becomes too acidic, the body extracts calcium, an alkaline mineral, from the bones to balance our pH. Meat, eggs, and fish are the most acid-forming foods.
- Eskimos have the highest dietary calcium intake of any other people (more than 2,000 milligrams per day from fish flesh and bones). They have the highest protein intake, 250 to 400 grams a day. They also have the highest rate of osteoporosis in the world.
- Protein exists in all whole foods in varying degrees. There should be no concern in where we can find it, but rather in the quality and the ease in which our body utilizes it. Especially good sources are whole

grains, such as quinoa, millet, and amaranth, sea vegetables, kale, spinach, broccoli, nuts, seeds, beans, lentils, tofu and tempeh.
•If you eat a wide spectrum of whole-foods, you receive ample amounts of protein and calcium. In fact, it would be difficult not to.

Dairy

When first transitioning my diet to a plant-based one, I still relied heavily on dairy for protein and calcium, predominately with cheese. I was never a milk drinker. As a child I found it unappealing and I never felt good after drinking it. I did, however, enjoy buttermilk on occasion. Becoming more in tune with my body allowed me to connect how I felt from the effects of dairy, usually immediately upon ingestion. Symptoms included constipation, edema, abdominal pain (nausea and gas), difficulty breathing, excess mucus, and others. The most surprising symptom I was not even aware of until I eliminated dairy completely, was the stiffness I felt in my joints and muscles, which I had considered normal. Movement is now more fluid and without discomfort. I feel wonderfully free of any constriction and my yoga postures have improved dramatically.

I weaned myself from dairy several years ago and have not brought it into my home or made it available to my children. I consider it not to be a healthy option.

My eldest daughter, Rhiannon, breastfed for the first couple of years of her life. It was her sole source of nutrition for the first year. My youngest, Gwendolyn, is still going strong after her first year.

Cow's milk and human milk are so completely different in makeup that it boggles my mind how much we rely on it as a food source. A human child grows slower, lives longer, and has the most rapidly growing brain of all animals. A calf has a smaller brain and rapid body growth.

Human milk contains lecithin and high amounts of taurine, an amino acid, both of which are needed for proper brain development. Cow's milk is deficient in these. Human milk also contains much more cystine and tryptophan (two more amino acids). Cow's milk is also deficient in iodine, iron, phosphorus, and manganese. Human milk contains six times more selenium and twice as much Vitamin E.

The Composition of Foods, Agriculture Handbook No. 8, showed that 100 grams of human milk provides 1.1 grams of protein and 9.5 grams of carbohydrates, whereas cows milk provides 3.5 grams of protein and 4.9 grams of carbohydrates. During the most rapidly growing period of our life, we only need modest amounts of protein, and the proper kind!

Rennin is a curding enzyme important in the digestive processes of infants where it prevents the too-rapid passage of milk from the stomach. It starts to diminish when a child reaches approximately two years of age and begins to secrete the enzyme ptyalin, which is necessary for starch digestion. This is your body's way of signaling that it is ready to be weaned.

What is listed above refers to both pasteurized and raw milk. Additionally, pasteurized has its own set of problems, mainly that heating the milk will make it even more difficult to digest. The casein is coagulated and toughened, and the vitamin and mineral components are spoiled and made unavailable to your body. The lactic acid bacilli, which are beneficial intestinal flora, are destroyed. Milk is subjected to many other processes before it reaches your table. These processes are never put on the label.

Those knowledgeable about milk state that it has become more of an excretion of the cow than a secretion, due to the fact that the milk today also contains alarming amounts of drugs, including antibiotics, and concentrated levels of pollutants from the environment, such as pesticides. It has been shown that one dose of penicillin given to a cow will appear in the milk after being milked four to seven milkings. Cows are given hormones for greater milk output. The average cow produces one-and-a-half to two gallons of milk per day. With hormone use they can produce eight to nine gallons!

Bovine growth hormone is another big issue with many health risks. An article in The Los Angeles Times on March 20, 1994, stated the following:
- Growth hormone is not destroyed by pasteurization or digestion and is readily absorbed across the intestinal wall;
- Growth hormone induces rapid division and multiplication of normal human breast epithelial cells in tissue cultures; and
- "the breast tissues of female fetuses and infants are sensitive to hormonal influences. Imprinting by IGF-1 (insulin-like growth factor-1), may increase future breast cancer risks and sensitivity of the breast to subsequent unrelated risks such as mammography and the carcinogenic and estrogen-like effects of pesticide residues in food, particularly in pre-menopausal women." (*A Needless New Risk of Breast Cancer*, by Samuel S. Epstein).

The protein content of human milk is mostly albumin, while cows milk is mostly casein. Casein forms large, difficult-to-digest curds which humans have problems with but a cow (which has a 4-stomach digestive system) can handle it just fine. A wonderful book to read is *Don't Drink Your Milk* by Frank Oski, M.D.

The Nutrition Committees of the American Academy of Pediatrics and the Canadian Pediatric Society, jointly issued a report in 1979 strongly favoring breastfeeding, giving the following reasons:

1 The fats obtained from human milk are more easily absorbed by the human infant than those found in cow's milk.
2 The cholesterol in mother's milk serves a valuable purpose in the development of the infant.
3 The protein in mother's milk is a near-perfect source for infants—much better than cow's milk!

4 Infants are able to absorb about 50% more iron from mother's milk than from cow's milk. Infants on cow's milk for extended periods are at risk for iron deficiency, whereas full-term breastfed infants receive sufficient iron from mother's milk until their birth weight has tripled.

5 Mother's milk also provides important protective factors not available from any formula. Two substances, lactoferrin and transferrin, prevent potentially harmful bacteria from growing in the intestinal tract. In addition, the infant is provided with important immunities by a fluid (colostrom) secreted by the breast during the first few days following birth. Finally, breast milk contains lysozymes, enzymes that attack and break down harmful bacteria, as well as a substance known as the bifidus factor, which promotes the growth of protective bacteria in the infant's body.

Mother's milk is the optimal food for mammals during the period of their most rapid growth, not for adults.

Some people react more severely than others when consuming dairy. Anyone who has asthma, allergies, frequent colds, bronchitis, etc., should get off milk immediately. Other problems connected with dairy consumption include heart disease, colic, cramps, skin rashes, acne, gastrointestinal bleeding, diarrhea, iron deficiency, anemia, arthritis, ear infections, diabetes, osteoporosis, cataracts, ovarian cancer, and autoimmune diseases such as MS.

Babies who are breastfed are 74% less likely to develop symptoms of asthma. American children miss 10 million school days every year because of asthma.

Some 50% of all grain grown in the U.S. is consumed by livestock. The standards for the spraying of pesticides for the grain eaten by livestock is less than the standards for the grain eaten by humans. Thus, pesticides are found in high concentration in cow's milk.

A study conducted on 1422 Norwegian individuals who drank two or more glasses of milk per day had 3.5 times the incidence of lymphatic cancer. (British Medical Journal, 1990).

The use of cow's milk can contribute to juvenile diabetes and autoimmune diseases by interrupting the ability of the pancreas to produce insulin. (The New England Journal of Medicine, 1992).

Europe and New Zealand have banned the importation of rBGH milk. Several states in the U.S. now require labeling on packaging of rBGH products.

So, how do we get calcium if we should not ingest milk? By eating a varied plant-based diet you will never fear of getting too little. Dark greens, such as kale and collards, are my favorite way. Sea vegetables, almonds, sunflower seeds, broccoli, figs, and parsley are all good sources. Plant source calcium is also much more readily utilized by our bodies.

There is another factor essential for absorbing and utilizing calcium. All the minerals in the body are in a delicate, dynamic balance. If a deficiency in calcium exists, other minerals will also be out of balance.

Remember this as well. Digestion of meats result in acids that must be neutralized by calcium (an alkaline mineral). Meat eating contributes to a phosphorous/calcium ratio in Americans that is four times greater than desirable. Phosphorous is essential to calcium utilization, but too much will deplete it. Sulphur, which is concentrated in meat, limits calcium absorption and saturated fats combine with calcium to form a soap-like compound that is eliminated by the body. Simply put, the more meat and dairy consumed, the more calcium is excreted out of the body.

Traditional people in many countries have used dairy in their diet, usually by boiling it or fermenting it into yogurt and cheese. These were enjoyed in small amounts in addition to a plant-based diet. Americans, on the other hand, have over-used dairy in all of its forms, including butter, milk, cheese, and ice cream. Over consumption is something we have done in all areas of our lives, but I am specifically interested in addressing this issue in our diet. Over consumption has affected our health in dramatic ways. Americans look at gluttony as acceptable, and we are paying a heavy price.

Milk Alternatives

There are so many milk alternatives to choose from. I have used soy in the past exclusively, but began to feel uneasy about eating and drinking it in excess (Remember: too much of a good thing can be bad).

There is some research that indicates that the protein in cooked soy products becomes denatured, and thus is not properly absorbed in the body. Whether or not that is true, I have not come across enough data to say. However, I do know that the alternatives are equally delicious. Here are a few:

•**Soy Milk**—The number one milk substitute on the market. Available in full-and low-fat, as well as fortified. Available in plain, vanilla, carob, and cocoa flavors.

•**Rice Milk**—This is thinner and sweeter than regular soy milk. Another very popular drink. Available in plain, vanilla, carob, and cocoa flavors.

•**Multigrain Milk**—Has a rich, creamy texture. My husband favors this. Available in plain or vanilla.

•**Oat Milk**—This is the type preferred by my children. Available in plain or vanilla.

•**Almond Milk**—This has a light texture, with just a hint of almond flavor. This is my preference. Available in plain or vanilla.

•**Other Nut/Seed "Milk"**—These can be made with coconut, sesame seeds, cashews, etc. Whatever your choice, you can whip them up and enjoy them in just minutes!

Carbohydrates

Only 25% of U.S. Medical Schools require future doctors to take nutrition courses.

Carbohydrates are poorly understood. They are a critical component of the foods we eat. Yet, in an extracted or fractionated form, they can create many imbalances in your body. Refined carbohydrates (such as sugar, flour, and cereals) are, I believe, more detrimental to your health than meat or dairy.

All refined carbohydrates are an incomplete food. Most of the nutrients are processed out. In the case of sugar, the body must take vital nutrients from healthy cells to metabolize it. Sodium, potassium, magnesium, and calcium are drawn from various parts of the body to make use of the sugar.

When sugar enters the stomach, glutamic acid and other B vitamins are denied to the body. The loss of these specific vitamins result in a confused mental state and there is a tendency to become sleepy during the day. Since refined sugars are removed from their natural sources, which contain the necessary nutrients for their metabolism, eating sugar causes the body to rob itself of already present vital elements.

For those of you who think you don't eat a lot of sugar products, think about this. Most of the sugar consumed today (about 75%) is hidden in processed foods. This means you, the consumer, are responsible for only about 25% of our sugar intake, meaning what you are physically adding to your food.

We, on an average, eat approximately 130 pounds of sugar each year. Sugar is used extensively in packaged foods to prevent spoilage, to retain moisture, to maintain texture and appearance, and, of course, as a sweetener.

In the new food pyramid, carbohydrates are the heavy favorite. The problem with that is there is no differentiating a good carbohydrate from a bad one. Refined grains, like white rice, grits, couscous, wheat flour, etc., are not recommended. Most flours, breads, cereals, noodles, and pastries fall into this category. They are acidic in nature, devoid of natural fiber, and low in water content, making them constipating.

It is a sad statistic that 75% of American's food comes from factories and not farms. We are so far removed from a natural-foods diet, and it will just continue to worsen because of the increased domination and control of a few giant food companies. Their only concerns seem to be how they can create cheaper large-scale production and increased shelf life. There is very little thought given to the nutritional value of these nonfoods, and then, only when they are pressed by the media to do so. Even then, their attempts are feeble, just enough to satisfy the immediate outcry. But if someone were to go beyond the feeble attempts, they may come up with some very upsetting facts.

Such findings may be something like this: The mineral cadmium always exists along with the mineral zinc in foods. Zinc acts as a balancing mineral for the cadmium and prevents it from being absorbed in large quantities by the body. Cadmium, in excessive amounts, is hazardous to human health. It is one of the poisonous elements in cigarette smoke. When grains are refined, zinc is destroyed, but the cadmium is not.

Both iron and copper are destroyed when grains are refined. Copper is necessary for the utilization of iron by the body to build a healthy bloodstream. The food industry was pressured into adding inorganic iron back to the stripped flour, but of course the copper is not.

Any refining quickly destroys B vitamins. Interestingly enough, the body requires B vitamins to metabolize or use the grains, which is why they are present in the food in the first place. If these vitamins are removed, then the body must once again rob from the current supply of B vitamins in the body so that these refined grains can be digested.

Two of the most popular ways of eating refined grains are in the form of bread and cereals. It is appalling what can be found in a typical store bought loaf of bread. The real scary part is that it is not mandatory to list these added substances on the label. Chlorine gas may be blown into the flour to bleach it white. Hundreds of chemicals may be used, which have not been adequately tested (such as Bht). Other additives include raising agents, preservatives, emulsifiers, yeast stimulators, coloring agents, acids, and more. In order to make these products more palatable to the consumer, large amounts of salt and sugar are added.

What can we do? Stop buying cereals and make your own bread. Or go to a reputable health food store to buy good-quality bread, such as the sprouted variety. Children and adults do not need boxed cereals. Reading through this book will give you many fresh and innovative recipes for the first meal of the day—without spending much time on preparation, which always seems to be the biggest argument. It is not difficult to change. You just need to want to change.

All told, if each American consumes five to ten pounds of chemicals a year in their food, it may not seem like a lot. But remember, most of these chemicals have been inadequately tested or not tested at all. Our bodies are not able to cope with this. When all of these chemicals and refined foods are eaten together, a multi-toxic effect occurs that has never been thoroughly studied. What we do know, however, is that most of our lives are spent gradually dying, and that every day we create new illnesses to die from. This unsettlingly parallels the degeneration of our diets. The ultimate shame is, that it is so very easy to correct.

Sweeteners

The average American eats only 129 pounds of fresh fruit every year, yet consumes 130 pounds of refined sugar every year.

Almost everyone loves sugar in one form or another. It is natural.

What is not natural, however, is the way our society has destroyed and abused this once healthy food component. Refining and processing are just part of the story. Excessive use is the other part of the story. On an average, Americans consume approximately 38 teaspoons of sugar a day!

We were meant to thrive on whole foods containing sugar. That is indicated by the sweetness of mother's milk and by the availability and natural inclination to succulent fruits. Over the past two hundred years though, we have gradually replaced the good sugars in our diet, such as grapes, melons, or apples, with corn syrup, refined cane sugar, or aspartame. Unfortunately, our metabolism cannot handle sugars devoid of all nutrients. Instead it depletes our own reserves.

Though there are many substitutes for white sugar, some should never be used, and others only in small amounts. Nothing will replace whole fruits as the optimum "sweet" food. Here is a partial list:

Aspartame (Nutrasweet) contains methyl alcohol, a poison that converts first to formaldehyde and then to formic acid. Another component is phenylalanine, which breaks down into DKP, a brain tumor agent. Many symptoms are associated with its use, a few of which are memory loss, vision problems, chronic fatigue syndrome, birth defects, and heart and respiratory conditions. For more information, read the book Excitotoxins—The Taste That Kills by Dr. Russell Blaylock, Neurologist.

Stevia, a small shrub native to South America, is extremely sweet, ranging from 10 to 300 times sweeter than sugar. It regulates blood sugar so is safe to use by those with blood sugar imbalances. It has been shown to arrest the growth of plaque in your mouth and regulates blood pressure. A non-caloric herb, it is the only sweetener safely used for candida and yeast-type conditions. Many countries such as China, Japan, South America, and Germany use it extensively with no known adverse reactions. Here in the United States it can only be marketed as a supplement and is available in powdered, leaf, and liquid form. Other than whole fruit, I favor this herb.

Agave Nectar is extracted from a cactus-like plant. It is comprised of 93% fruit sugar. When used to replace sugar or honey decrease amount in recipe by 25%.

Honey is highly refined by bees and has more calories than white sugar. Honey is made by bees eating pollen, then regurgitating several times. While in the stomach, it is mixed with formic, manite, and other acids. Unlike bees, humans lack the enzymes to break down these acids. Acid forming foods need alkaline minerals to neutralize them, thus they are decalcifying.

Raw honey is better than heated and filtered honey, but the minute amount of mineral material found in it provides minimal nutritional value. It acts like white sugar in the body, and is assimilated directly into the bloodstream very quickly. Most health claims stem from the fact that it does have minerals and can be had with little processing. When held up with longer-digesting foods, (which is the norm, since most people do not eat it alone) honey and all other sweeteners, except stevia, readily ferments. Honey is a dehydrated "food," which when ingested, immediately begins to reabsorb moisture from the stomach and stomach flora. This will destroy the bacterial population (the "good" along with the "bad"). The arguments for the use of honey are weak. I prefer to use other sweeteners that, in my opinion, are better utilized by the body.

Maple syrup undergoes high heat processing, which concentrates it beyond its natural strength. There are some nutritional benefits, though not enough for me to even classify it as a minor food source, though you will occasionally see it in my recipes. Be careful of your source. Most supermarkets rarely carry it in its pure form. Sugar, corn syrup, and other refined sugars, can be used to stretch out the more expensive maple syrup. Also, it may be contaminated by paraformaldehyde, which is used during the tapping process. Water, stevia powder, and alcohol-free maple extract may be a good substitute for those who want to eliminate maple syrup from their diet, yet still want a maple flavor in their food.

Blackstrap Molasses is one of the most highly heated and processed sweeteners. It is touted for its high mineral content, though it may contain many impurities, being the final dregs of sugar production. Some of the impurities it contains may be carbon dioxide, sulphur dioxide, phosphoric acid, bone char, and chlorine. If you choose to use this product, only purchase organic and unsulphured brands.

Rice Syrup and Barley Malt Syrup, whether in the form of syrup or powder, are not as highly processed. They are processed by fermenting and/or sprouting techniques. Only about a third as sweet as white sugar, there are still many nutrients intact, as well as complex sugars that take much longer to digest than simple sugars. These sweeteners are primarily composed of maltose and are less destructive to the body's mineral balance. I favor these after stevia.

Unrefined cane juice powder is made simply by evaporating the water from cane juice. It retains a great deal of its mineral and other nutrient content, though it is not recommended due to its high sucrose level. Note though that many food producers are aware of the marketing advantage of not listing sugar as an ingredient. Instead, cane juice or dried cane juice, etc., may be used. Make sure the label reads unrefined cane juice if you choose to use this product.

The most important factor to remember when using sweeteners is to look at quantity as well as quality. Do not trick your self into eating more than small amounts just because you chose a healthier option. Too much of a good thing is not a good thing. Eating sweets should be for special occasions, not a daily occurrence.

Organic Foods

"The word *'organic'* on the label stands for a commitment to an agricultural production system which strives for a balance with nature, using methods and materials which are of low impact to the environment."
 •Katherine DiMatteo, Executive Director, Organic Trade Association

What is the big deal about organic? This is a very common question. Many of us are in agreement that we would rather not have pesticides in our food. But most of us are not aware of the other contaminants used that affect our health, the soil, and the air. Herbicides, weed killers, synthetic fertilizers. . .the list goes on. Interestingly, even after something is grown, chemicals are used in storage or transportation! We are inundated with poisonous substances wherever we turn. This is not said to strike fear, it is only said to bring about an awareness so that we all can make educated decisions regarding our food and health choices.

The organic farmer sees beyond the use of chemicals. They are always looking to give back to the soil as much, if not more, of the nutrients used to produce our food.

Growing a wide selection of crops is one way in which organic farmers work. Typically, non-organic farmers focus on growing only one type of crop. This depletes the soil of nutrients and makes the land unfit to grow any other type of crop.

I was speaking to a student of mine who lived in a small farming community. She remembers how the children, including herself, would run through fields that had just been sprayed or powdered with pesticides. She recalled how they would run behind the trucks that sprayed the chemicals, splashing their feet in the puddles left behind. She is in her early forties right now and says that more than three quarters of the dozen people she grew up with either has cancer now or has died from cancer. It is rather depressing that someone's livelihood can also be his or her destruction.

Agriculture is the largest source of sewage in the United States today. This not only comes from the high volume feeding of production facilities (beef, dairy, pigs, chickens, and turkeys), the processing plants and slaughter houses, but also the nitrates from agricultural runoff. Pesticides for agriculture account for 75% of the 1.1 billion pounds of pesticides produced in the United States.

Once crops are sprayed, the chemicals do not just disappear either. There is a considerable amount of runoff due to irrigation/watering systems. This in turn gets into our water supply. The techniques used by organic farmers not only protect our water supply, but also conserves it.

Though some produce may not be as aesthetically pleasing as those from conventional farmers, the flavor and the quality is dramatically different. I always tell people to try a tomato test. Slice into a tomato and see, smell, and taste why organic is superior.

A study from the Center for the Study of Biological Systems at Washington University in St. Louis found "a five-year average shows that the organic farms yielded, in dollars per acre, exactly the same returns. In terms of yield, the organic farms were down about 10%. The reason why the economics came out is that savings in chemicals made up for the difference."

One other point to consider. Over 70% of farmland is used to feed livestock. So, if we lower our intake of meat, we could cut our yield in half and still have more than enough food at an affordable price for everyone.

After taking all of this into consideration, why wouldn't we support organic farmers?

Why indeed?

Pesticides, Children and Aggression
by Peter Montague
(Excerpted and reprinted with permission from
Rachel's Health & Environment Weekly (#648).)
For a complete, foot-noted copy, or for subscription information,
call (410) 263-1584

For the past 25 years, tens of millions of Americans in hundreds of cities and towns have been drinking tap water that is contaminated with low levels of insecticides, weed killers, and artificial fertilizer. They not only drink it, they also bathe and shower in it, thus inhaling small quantities of farm chemicals and absorbing them through the skin. Naturally, the problem is at its worst in agricultural areas of the country.

The most common contaminants are carbamate insecticides (aldicarb and others), the triazine herbicides (atrazine and others), and nitrate nitrogen. For years government scientists have tested each of these chemicals individually at low levels in laboratory animals—searching mainly for signs of cancer—and have declared each of them an "acceptable risk" at the levels typically found in groundwater.

Now a group of biologists and medical researchers at the University of Wisconsin in Madison, led by Warren P. Porter, has completed a five-year experiment putting mixtures of low levels of these chemicals into the drinking water of male mice and carefully measuring the results. They reported recently that combinations of these chemicals—at levels similar to those found in the groundwater of agricultural areas of the U.S.—have measurable detrimental effects on the nervous, immune and endocrine (hormone systems).[1] Furthermore, they say their research has direct implications for humans.

Dr. Porter and his colleagues point out that the nervous system, the immune system, and the endocrine (hormone) system are all closely related and in constant communication with each other. If any one of the three systems is damaged or degraded the other two may be adversely affected. The Wisconsin researchers therefore designed their experiments to examine the effects of agricultural chemicals on each of the three systems simultaneously. To assess immune system function, they measured the ability of mice to make antibodies in response to foreign proteins. To assess endocrine system function, they measured thyroid hormone levels in the blood. And to assess nervous system function they measured aggressive behavior in the presence of intruder mice introduced into the cages. They also looked for effects on growth by measuring total body weight and the weight of each animal's spleen.

The experiments were replicated many times, to make sure the results were reproducible. They found effects on the endocrine system (thyroid hormone levels) and the immune system, and reduced body weight, from mixtures of low levels of aldicarb and nitrate, atrazine and nitrate, and atrazine, aldicarb and nitrate together. They observed increased aggression from exposure to atrazine and nitrate, and from atrazine, aldicarb and nitrate together.

In the five-year experiment, thyroid hormone levels rose or fell depending upon the mixture of farm chemicals put into the drinking water. Dr. Porter and his colleagues present evidence from other studies showing that numerous farm chemicals can affect the thyroid hormone levels of wildlife and humans. PCBs and dioxins can have similar effects, they note. Proper levels of thyroid hormone are essential for brain development of humans prior to birth. Some, though not all, studies have shown that attention deficit and/or hyperactivity disorders in children are linked to changes in the levels of thyroid hormone in the blood. Children with multiple chemical sensitivity (MCS) have abnormal thyroid levels. Furthermore, irritability and aggressive behavior are linked to thyroid hormone levels.

Interviewed recently by Keith Hamm of the *Santa Barbara Independent*, Dr. Porter explained, Earlier work had shown that thyroid hormone typically changed when exposure to these pesticides occurred. Thyroid hormone not only affects and controls your metabolic rate, that is, how fast you burn food, it also controls your irritability level. For example, Type A personalities are more assertive, more aggressive, more hyper. These people tend to have higher levels of thyroid hormone. Type B personalities—people that are really laid back, really take things very easily—have lower levels of thyroid hormone. We expected that changes in thyroid [would] change irritability levels. This was a concern because there was information that kids are getting more hyper and [that their] learning abilities are going down," Dr. Porter said.

In the interview with Keith Hamm, Dr. Porter expressed concern for the overall effect of pesticides on the nation's children:

Hamm: "I would assume that most people in this country are eating conventionally grown food. If that's the case, wouldn't the problems be more apparent? Why are there not more hyperaggressive dim-witted people with poor immune systems?"

Porter: "If we really looked carefully at what's been happening in this country, you might find exactly that happening."

Because of recent violence in small cities and towns (such as Littleton, Colorado, Laramie, Wyoming, and Jasper, Texas), this is a time when Americans are searching for the causes of violence in their society. Some are blaming a decline in religious upbringing. Others are blaming households with the parents working and no one minding the kids. Some say the cause is violent movies, violent TV, and extremist internet sites, combined with the ready availability of cheap guns. Still others point to a government that has often sanctioned the violence of "gunboat diplomacy" to open foreign markets for U.S. corporations.

No one seems to be asking whether pesticides, fertilizers, and toxic metals are affecting our young people's mental capacity, emotional balance, and social adjustment.

From the work of Warren Porter, Elizabeth Guillette [see below], and others, it is apparent that these are valid questions.

[1] Warren P. Porter, James W. Jaeger and Ian H. Carlson, "Endocrine, immune and behavioral effects of aldicarb (carbamate), atrazine (triazine) and nitrate (fertilizer) mixtures at groundwater concentrations," *Toxicology and Industrial Health Vol. 15, Nos. 1 and 2 (1999)*, pp. 133-150.

Pesticides and Children: A Case Study
by Peter Montague

A recent study of 4-and 5-year-old children in Mexico specifically noted a decrease in mental ability and an increase in aggressive behavior among children exposed to pesticides ("An Anthropological Approach to the Evaluation of Preschool Children Exposed to Pesticides in Mexico," Environmental Health Perspectives, June 1998). Elizabeth A. Guillette and colleagues studied two groups of Yaqui Indian children living in the Yaqui Valley in northern Sonora, Mexico. One group of children lives in the lowlands dominated by pesticide-intensive agriculture (45 or more sprayings each year) and the other group lives in the nearby upland foothills where their parents make a living by ranching without the use of pesticides. The pesticide-exposed children had far less physical endurance in a test to see how long they could keep jumping up and down; they had inferior hand-eye coordination; and they could not draw a simple stick figure of a human being, which the upland children could readily do (see diagram).

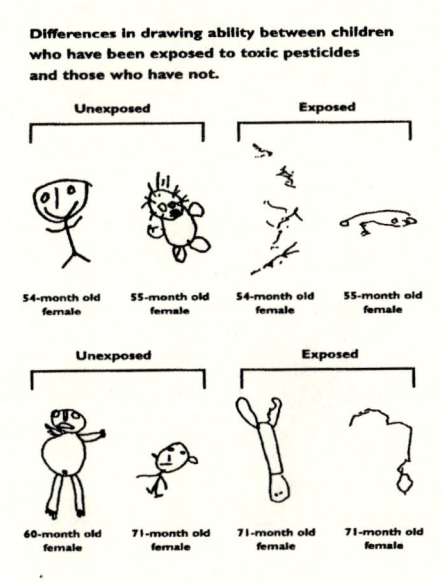

Differences in drawing ability between children who have been exposed to toxic pesticides and those who have not.

Unexposed	Exposed
54-month old female / 55-month old female	54-month old female / 55-month old female
60-month old female / 71-month old female	71-month old female / 71-month old female

Notably, in the Guillette study we find this description of the behavior of pesticide-exposed children: "Some valley children were observed hitting their siblings when they passed by, and they became easily upset or angry with a minor corrective comment by a parent. These aggressive behaviors were not noted in the [pesticide-free] foothills [children]." –P. Montague

Genetically Engineered Foods

Genetically engineered foods are just one more factor to consider in selecting what we put on the table. Some 70% of the food in our supermarkets are altered and the FDA projects that 100-150 new genetically engineered foods will be available by the year 2000. None of these foods are labeled at this time. There are some foods that are now being labeled as not genetically engineered or GMO free, though.

Genetic engineering is the cutting, splicing, and recombining of genes. Each gene in a DNA strand is responsible for a particular feature or function, such as whether a person will be born with blue or brown eyes. By taking a desired characteristic of one organism and injecting it into another, scientists can create what some consider a new and improved product. So far, some of the "successes" include combining a flounder "antifreeze" gene with a tomato to prolong the growth season, as well as creating potatoes that don't brown, corn that produces its own pesticide and soybeans that are resistant to herbicides.

Some of these genes are derived from insects, bacteria, viruses, and other sources that have never been a part of our diet in the past. No one knows if these are safe, as there has never been any long-term studies performed.

Most genetically engineered crops are not segregated from non-genetically engineered crops, which means they are stored and processed together. Certain food manufacturers are attempting to identify and separate ingredients due to consumer demand, but it is an overwhelming job to track down each distributor from an ingredient list.

The dangers of genetically engineered organisms are many, with mutations and side effects being two of the concerns. Not only can genetically engineered food lower the nutritional quality of a food, but it may also create new or higher amounts of toxins and allergens as well, resulting in untreatable conditions and even death by anaphylactic shock.

This science is alarming on an environmental level as well. A great portion of research is focused on the development of plants that can tolerate a greater amount of herbicides, which means more chemicals in our food and water supply. Along with that, insects, birds, and wind carry seeds and pollen great distances and can create new species with unknown dangers to wildlife. Through reproduction, migration, and mutation, these new organisms cannot be recalled. If a mistake is made, it is permanent!

For a more in depth look at this technology and the debate surrounding it contact:

The Natural Law Party and Mothers for Natural Law
P.O. Box 1900
Farfield, Iowa 52556
Website: www.natural-law.org
E-Mail: info@natural-law.org
Telephone: 515-472-2040

I have included a partial list of foods to avoid:

Soybeans: Soy four, soy oil, lecithin, soy protein isolates and concentrates. Products that may contain GE soy derivatives: Vitamin E, tofu dogs, cereal, veggie burgers and sausages, tamari, soy sauce, chips, ice cream, frozen yogurt, infant formula, sauces, protein powder, margarine, soy cheese, crackers, bread, cookies, chocolate, candy, fried food, shampoo, bubble bath, cosmetics, enriched flour and pasta.

Corn Products: Corn flour, corn starch, corn oil, corn sweeteners, syrups. Products that may contain GE corn derivatives: Vitamin C, tofu dogs, chips, candies, ice cream, infant formula, salad dressing, tomato sauce, bread, cookies, cereals, baking powder, alcohol, vanilla, margarine, soy sauce, tamari, soda, fried food, powdered sugar, enriched flour and pasta.

Canola Oil: Products that contain GE canola derivatives: chips, salad dressing, cookies, margarine, soap, detergent, soy cheese, fried food.

Cotton: Oil, fabric. Products that may contain GE cotton or derivatives: clothes, linens, chips, peanut butter, crackers, cookies.

Potatoes: Products that contain GE potatoes or derivatives: unspecified processed or restaurant potato products (fried, mashed, baked, mixes, etc.), chips, Passover products, vegetable pies, soups.

Tomatoes: No plum or roma tomatoes have been genetically engineered. But one cherry tomato has, as have regular tomatoes. Products that may contain GE tomatoes or derivatives: sauces, purees, pizza, lasagna, and all of those wonderful Italian and Mexican foods.

Dairy Products: Milk, cheese, butter, buttermilk, sour cream, yogurt, whey. You have to ask several questions when you are looking at dairy products. Have the cows been treated with rBGH? What kind of feed have they been given? If they are not being fed organic grains, chances are quite likely that they will be eating GE animal feed. What does this do to their milk products? No one knows.

Animal Products: Because animal feed often contains GEOs, all animal products and animal by-products may be affected.

All of this information was provided by Laura Ticciati, Executive Director of Mothers for Natural Law. She and her husband, Robin, have written a powerful little book entitled, *Genetically Engineered Foods, Are they Safe? You Decide*. I strongly recommend this book to all.

One of the primary issues in the health food industry now is that we need verification, even from organic farmers that the seeds they are getting are not GE. There will be pressure applied to organic farmers, as well as other organic products, to label their products as to whether or not they are certified free of GE.

Irradiated Foods

Food irradiation is an FDA approved process which exposes food to radioactive materials in order to kill insects and bacteria and to slow ripening. It has many other capabilities, which proponents for this technology ignore.

To put food irradiation into perspective, a chest x-ray gets a fraction of one rad of radiation, yet FDA permits up to 100,000 rads in our food. It has been shown that irradiated food causes changes in human physiology. It is linked to cancer, kidney disease, and changes in white blood cells and chromosomes.

Along with killing insects and parasites, it also kills bacteria, but not the toxins created by the bacteria which wreak havoc in our bodies. It also destroys up to 80% of the vitamin content, specifically A, B, C, D, and K and almost entirely wipes out Vitamin E.

Most proponents for irradiation seem to be major food manufacturers, which is hardly a surprise since they would be the only ones benefiting, other than the nuclear waste management program from the Department of Energy who recycle their waste into our food supply.

Buying organic is the only answer for those of us wanting to avoid buying genetically altered or irradiated products. Many people complain about the higher prices and the limited availability of organic products. This is changing though. With more and more people becoming aware and switching over to organic, this will increase demand and availability. Ask your supermarket. Most will be happy to bring in the products you request. Also, consider this: the most expensive organic products tend to be the refined and packaged convenience foods that I recommend you do without anyway!

If you are interested in more information, contact: Food and Water at 1-800-Eat-Safe.

Living Foods

On a daily basis, my family's diet consists of between 50 to 75% raw foods. This seems to be a good range depending on the season (having less raw food in cold weather). Fresh, living foods give you the optimum nutrients possible. Heating food destroys a large portion of these nutrients as well as chemically altering a significant part. Enzymes are lost with cooking, therefore, your body will need to use its store of metabolic enzymes. This depletes our reserves, which sets us up for disease and rapid aging, which is, sadly, seen more often than not in our country. There are exceptions however. Certain components in food are made more available only through cooking, so it is important to have a combination of raw and cooked. We are all unique in our dietary needs and experimenting with the proper balance for yourself is important. In general, people are fine with at least 50% raw, deficient or otherwise compromised individuals may need more cooked food initially until they are able to come to balance. Nutrients are also diminished prior to actually eating a meal due to the type of preparation and the length of time it is allowed to sit before ingesting it. A prime example is fresh juices, which need to be consumed immediately for any benefit. If a juice bar is easily accessible to you, that is fine as long as you can see them prepare your selection for you. It is so easy to do your own, though. I cannot imagine going through the trouble of driving or walking to a juice bar. Bottled juice found in the market is not even worth discussing.

My girls enjoy fresh fruits, veggies, nuts, seeds, and sprouts everyday. Although it is easier for children to accept and enjoy a whole foods diet from the beginning, it is not difficult to introduce these foods to older children.

For those of you unaccustomed to eating raw food, it can cause uncomfortable digestive symptoms, such as headaches, gas, and bad breath. This in no way means raw food is bad, rather your body is showing you just how toxic and weak it has become due to past abuse. You must slowly work yourself into it. If you have never eaten a salad, eat one salad a day, or try steaming veggies until they are just tender (do not overcook!) which is better tolerated until your body adjusts.

Be sure to practice correct food combining. Melons should always be eaten by themselves. The reason is quite simple. A melon is made up of mostly water and can be digested very quickly (15 to 30 minutes). If you eat a meal with or before the melon, it is stuck in the digestive tract along with the other food. The sugars from the melon will start to ferment in this warm climate which causes the remaining food to putrefy as well. All sugar has the same type of reaction, so sweetened drinks or desserts should not be ingested with meals either.

If you choose to use dairy, do not have milk with any other food product.

Concentrated protein and grains do not work well together because it takes completely different enzymes to break them down and they need distinctively different atmospheres to do the job. Grains need a more alkaline atmosphere and protein needs an acid state, both of which will be diluted, diminished, or halted when combined. Keep your food choices simple.

We as a nation stuff our bodies with potions and pills to stop heartburn, gas, constipation, diarrhea, etc. This is quite laughable when, if we were combining our food correctly, eating healthier, and eating less, we would not need these products at all. Imagine, a whole industry based on gluttony would disappear!

Sprouting

This is an important part of my daily regime. Sprouting is fun, economical, and also very nutritious. The vitamin and enzyme content increases dramatically with a sprouted food—as much as four to ten times the value. Many people who are allergic to grains, nuts and seeds can tolerate them just fine when sprouted. The reason for this is that the sprouting process predigests the nutrients, which makes it easier for the body to assimilate and metabolize, preventing an allergic reaction.

During sprouting, the starch is converted into simple sugars. Protein is turned into amino acids. Fat is broken down into free fatty acids.

There is much more you can do with sprouts than tossing them on a sandwich or salad. Looking through this book will give you some ideas. Also, remember that sprouts can be added to smoothies or shakes, can be ground and added or used alone for bread making, can be dehydrated and used for cereals or faux meat patties, can be added to soups right before serving, and can even be used in desserts!

Almost any seed will sprout as long as it is in its whole state. My favorites are lentils, mung beans, chickpeas, alfalfa, red clover, barley, and buckwheat. When sprouting certain legumes, such as chickpeas and soybeans, it is desirable to steam them for approximately 15 minutes or until tender. This is so much more convenient than cooking for one to three hours.

How to Sprout

Put one tablespoon of seeds into a wide-mouthed one-pint jar. Cover the seeds with spring water. Place a piece of cheesecloth over the top and secure with a rubber band. Soak overnight and drain in the morning. Continue rinsing and draining the seeds morning and night until sprouts reach the desired length. Be sure to always drain well to prevent mold. Use the sprouts immediately or store in the refrigerator in an airtight container.

Sprouting Chart

Seeds	Sprouting Time (in days)	Optimum Length of Sprouts (in inches)
Alfalfa	3 to 4	3/4 to 1
Buckwheat	3 to 5	1 to 1 1/2
Clover	3 to 4	3/4 to 1
Garbanzo Bean	3	1/2 to 3/4
Lentil	2 to 3	Length of seed
Mung Bean	2 to 3	1/4 to 1/2
Oat	2	Length of seed
Pea	2 to 3	1/4 to 1/2
Radish	3 to 4	1/2 to 1
Rye	2	Length of seed
Sesame	2	1/16 to 1/8
Sunflower	2	1/16 to 1/8
Soybean	3	1/4 to 1/2
Wheat	2	Length of Seed

Sprouting is a no-brainer activity that gives you so much. It would be crazy not to do it. Certain sprouts, such as alfalfa and red clover, can be placed in a sunny spot after the first couple of days to ensure your getting maximum Vitamin A and Chlorophyll.

Almonds and sunflower seeds need only to be soaked over night to start the germination process and increase nutritional value. These can easily be added to your fruit in the morning or blended into shakes or smoothies.

Everybody benefits from sprouted foods. It is one of my first suggestions to an individual who wants to transition over to a healthier diet.

Appetizers, Dips, and Spreads

*"In music, in the sea, in a flower,
in a leaf, in an act of kindness....
I see what people call God
in all these things."*

•Pablo Casals

Babaghanoush

*For a smoky tasting dip, roast the eggplant whole.
Peel and puree.*

1 1/2 pounds eggplant
1/4 cup sesame butter
juice of one lemon
1/3 cup parsley, minced
2 large garlic cloves, minced
Bragg Liquid Aminos to taste

Peel eggplant. Cut into 1 1/2-inch cubes.

Steam eggplant until tender, approximately 5 minutes.

Blend in blender.

Add remaining ingredients. **Puree.**

Serve warm or at room temperature.

Garnish with olives, if desired.

Banana-Miso-Sesame Spread

1 banana
1 1/2 Tablespoons sesame butter
1 teaspoon barley or rice miso

Combine all ingredients thoroughly.

Cheddar, Sunflower Seed, and Olive Spread

*Try this spread on thick slices of fresh rye bread,
or make a wrap sandwich with chapatis, sprouts, cucumber and tomato.*

4 ounces firm tofu
1/2 pound Cheddar-style vegan cheese, chopped
1/2 cup pimento-stuffed or herbed green olives, patted dry
1 roasted red bell pepper, chopped
1/3 cup plain vegan yogurt
1/4 cup sunflower seeds, toasted lightly
sea salt to taste

Blend all ingredients except sunflower seeds in food processor.

Stir in sunflower seeds until combined.

Add salt if needed.

Guacamole

3 ripe avocados (*preferably Haas*)
2 cups tomato, seeded and chopped
1 red onion, chopped fine
1/4 cup coriander, finely chopped (*or to taste*)
1/3 cup fresh lemon juice
ground chipotle pepper or cayenne to taste
sea salt to taste

Halve and pit the avocados. **Scoop** flesh into bowl. **Mash** coarse with a fork.

Stir in remaining ingredients.

Serve.

Lentil Spread

This makes a fabulous sandwich spread, or use as a dip with daikon and carrot sticks.

2 cups lentils, cooked
1/4 cup sunflower seeds, toasted
1 Tablespoon fresh oregano, minced
1 Tablespoon whole-grain prepared mustard
1 Tablespoon red wine vinegar
sea salt to taste
water

Process all ingredients in blender.

Add water as needed to achieve a spreadable consistency.

Spinach Cheese Logs

1 pound vegan-style cheddar cheese
1 cup spinach, finely chopped
2 Tablespoons Bragg Liquid Aminos
1 teaspoon lemon juice
1 teaspoon dill weed (*optional*)
scant 1/4 teaspoon onion powder

Grate cheese into large bowl.

Add remaining ingredients. **Mix** well.

Press together. **Form** into roll. **Cut** into slices.

Roasted Garlic and Mushroom Spread

Garlic and mushrooms are a heavenly combination!

1 pound mushrooms, chopped
1/2 cup onion, minced
2 Tablespoons olive oil
3 Tablespoons parsley, chopped
1 teaspoon whole-grain prepared mustard
1 Tablespoon miso
1 head Roasted Garlic (*see recipe in Condiments*)
sea salt to taste

Sauté mushrooms and onion in 1 Tablespoon oil until soft and mushrooms release liquid.

Add parsley, mustard, and miso.

Squeeze out garlic pulp. **Add** to mushroom mixture.

Stir in another tablespoon of oil. **Add** sea salt, if using.

Spread on toast triangles.

Quick and Easy Hummus

3 Tablespoons olive oil
juice of 1 lemon
1 medium garlic clove
1/4 cup sesame butter
2 cups garbanzo (chickpeas), cooked

Blend oil, lemon, garlic, and sesame butter in blender or food processor until smooth.

Add beans. **Blend** until creamy. **Add** 1 to 2 Tablespoons of water, if needed.

Seed Spread

Use as dip or sandwich spread.

1/4 cup sesame seeds, coarsely ground
1/4 cup pumpkin seeds, coarsely ground
1/4 cup sunflower seeds, coarsely ground
2 Tablespoons flax seed
1 large celery stalk, chopped fine
2 Tablespoons oil
1 Tablespoon apple cider vinegar
2 teaspoons Bragg Liquid Aminos

Combine seeds. **Add** celery.

Whisk together oil, apple cider vinegar and Braggs.

Add to seed mixture.

Spinach-Mushroom Dip

1 clove garlic, crushed
1 cup onion, chopped
1/2 pound mushrooms, cleaned and chopped
2 Tablespoons olive oil
1 1/4 cups spinach
1/2-3/4 cup broth
1/2 cup sesame butter
1 teaspoon sea salt
1/4 cup nutritional yeast flakes
3 Tablespoons lemon juice
1/2 teaspoon dill weed, dried

Sauté the garlic, onion, and mushrooms in oil over low heat until soft.

Stir in spinach.

Combine all ingredients in a blender. **Puree** until creamy. **Chill. Serve.**

Tzatziki

Yogurt, Cucumber, and Garlic Dip

1 32-ounce container of vegan yogurt
2 cucumbers, peeled if not organic, seeded, grated coarse
3 garlic cloves, minced
2 Tablespoons olive oil
1 Tablespoon apple cider vinegar
1-2 Tablespoons fresh dill, minced
sea salt to taste

Drain yogurt in a very fine sieve set over a bowl. **Cover. Chill** overnight. (You can also scoop out a hole in the center of the yogurt container and let sit overnight. Drain excess water.)

Squeeze cucumber to remove as much excess liquid as possible.

Stir together all ingredients in a bowl. **Add** salt.

Serve Tzatziki with bread, crackers, or veggies.

Brilliant Green Dip

1 10-ounce package frozen peas
1 Tablespoon butter
1 Tablespoon vegan mayonnaise
1 teaspoon ground cumin or crushed mint leaves
1/2 teaspoon lemon juice
1/2 teaspoon sea salt

Place peas in a pot with 1" boiling water. **Cover.** **Heat** 2 to 3 minutes. **Drain.** Place all ingredients in blender. **Process** until smooth.

Carrot Butter

I like this best when carrots are still warm!

2 1/2 cups steamed carrots
2 Tablespoons cashew or almond butter
1 1/2 teaspoons Bragg Liquid Aminos
pinch of sea salt

Process all in blender until smooth. **Add** water, if needed.

Condiments

*"What would you attempt to do if
you knew you could not fail?"*

•*Dr. Robert Schuller*

Almonnaise

1/2 cup raw almonds
1/2 cup water
1/4 teaspoon garlic powder
3/4 teaspoon sea salt
1 cup flax or olive oil
1/4 cup lemon juice
1/2 Tablespoon apple cider vinegar

Blanch almonds. **Remove** skins.

Blend almonds, water, garlic powder, and sea salt until smooth.

Add oil slowly. **Add** lemon juice and apple cider vinegar.

Store in covered jar in refrigerator.

Cashew/Sunflower Mayonnaise

1/4 cup sunflower seeds
1/4 cup cashews
1/2 cup water
1/4 cup lemon juice
1/2 teaspoon sea salt
1/4 teaspoon garlic powder
1/4 teaspoon dry mustard
1/2 cup olive oil

Grind seeds and nuts. **Place** in blender. **Add** water and lemon juice. **Add** seasonings.

Pour in olive oil while blender is still running.

Process until thickened.

Butter

Coconut oil is a natural saturated vegetable product that is made up of mostly medium-chain fatty acids. The body can metabolize this efficiently. Coconut oil does not elevate your LDL cholesterol levels.

1/2 cup water
1 small carrot
2 Tablespoons powdered soy milk
1 teaspoon sea salt
1/2 cup flax, sesame or olive oil
1 Tablespoon lecithin granules
1/2 cup coconut oil

Process water and carrot in blender until smooth.

Add soy milk and sea salt. **Blend** well.

Add flax oil and lecithin granules slowly while blender is still running.

Add coconut oil.

Blend until just thickened.

Pour into container. **Chill** to harden. **Keep** refrigerated.

Dulse Gomacio

My daughter dips carrots and other veggies in sour cream ,then gomacio. This can also be used as a table condiment in place of salt. High mineral content, especially calcium.

2 parts sesame seeds, toasted
1 part dulse, toasted

Grind seeds in seed grinder. **Repeat with** dulse. **Mix together.**

Corn and Sun-Dried Tomato Relish

This is an awesome relish to serve along side grilled veggie patties or along side the Rio Grande Tempeh Meatloaf. Also great with baked corn chips.

1/2 cup sun-dried tomatoes, reconstituted
2 cups raw fresh corn
1/4 cup red bell pepper, finely chopped
1/4 cup green bell pepper, finely chopped
1 teaspoon fresh jalapeno pepper, minced and seeded
1 1/2 Tablespoons cilantro, minced
2 Tablespoons fresh lemon juice
1-2 Tablespoons apple cider vinegar
1 Tablespoon olive oil
sea salt to taste

Soak sun-dried tomatoes in hot water until softened. Drain.

Toss together all the ingredients in a bowl.

Add salt, as needed.

Cover. Chill for at least 1 hour or overnight.

Sesame Sauce

*Great served with falafel or hummus wrap sandwiches,
over steamed broccoli,
or as a dip for a variety of fresh veggies.*

Juice of 1 lemon
1 Tablespoon miso, blonde or mellow white
2 Tablespoons sesame butter
water

Mix all ingredients well.

Cranberry Chutney

1/2 cup dried apricots, chopped fine
1/2 cup raisins
3 cups cranberries, picked over and rinsed
1 apple, cored, diced 1/4-inch (*try gala jona gold or macintosh*)
1 teaspoon freshly grated lemon rind
1/4 cup fresh lemon juice
1 Tablespoon fresh ginger, grated
1/2 teaspoon dried hot red pepper flakes
1/4 teaspoon stevia, or to taste

Soak apricots and raisins in 1 cup water overnight. **Drain. Reserve** water.

Place all ingredients in food processor. **Pulse** just to chunk—do not puree!

Add reserved soak water to desired consistency. **Adjust** seasonings, if necessary.

Let sit for a few hours before serving.

Cranberry, Orange, and Ginger Relish

This sure beats the canned cranberry gel my Mom used to serve!

2 teaspoons fresh gingerroot, peeled and chopped
1 large navel orange, including rind, chopped
1 12-ounce bag of cranberries, picked over
stevia to taste (*start with 1/4 teaspoon*)

Chop fine gingerroot and orange in a food processor.

Add cranberries. **Pulse** motor until berries are chopped fine.

Transfer mixture to a bowl. **Sprinkle** in stevia. **Stir** well. **Cover**. **Chill** for at least 30 minutes.

Eggplant, Tomato, and Bell Pepper Relish

This would also taste great over soba Noodles or spaghetti squash.

3/4 pound eggplant, peeled and diced 1/4-inch
1 teaspoon salt, plus additional to taste
2 Tablespoons olive oil
1 teaspoon garlic, minced
1/2 cup yellow bell pepper, finely chopped
2 plum tomatoes, seeded and chopped fine (*about 2 pounds*)
1/4 cup red onion, finely chopped
2 Tablespoons fresh basil, minced
1 Tablespoon fresh parsley, minced
2 Tablespoons balsamic vinegar
3 Tablespoons fresh lemon juice

Toss the eggplant with the salt. **Place** in a colander. **Cover** with a plate that will fit inside the colander. **Weight** the plate. **Drain** eggplant for 20 minutes. **Rinse** eggplant. **Pat** dry.

Heat oil over moderately high heat in a large, heavy skillet until it is hot, but not smoking.

Sauté eggplant. **Stir** 2-3 minutes, or until eggplant is just cooked through.

Add garlic.

Cook mixture. **Stir** 1 minute.

Cool to room temperature.

Toss together eggplant mixture in a bowl with remaining ingredients.

Add additional vinegar and lemon juice if desired.

Fresh Tomato Sauce

I believe it is totally unnecessary to cook your tomato sauce. This recipe bursts with flavor.

2 tomatoes, diced
juice of 1 lemon
1 1/2-2 teaspoons fresh oregano, minced (*or dried to taste, starting with 1/8-1/4 teaspoon*)
1 teaspoon fresh thyme, minced (*or dried to taste, starting with 1/8-1/4 teaspoon*)
balsamic vinegar, if desired

Place all ingredients in bowl. **Add** a splash of balsamic.

Toss with noodles, or try as relish to spinach fritters.

Tomato Salsa

Serve with tortilla chips or on a legume, nut, or grain patty.

2 garlic cloves
1 lime, peeled
2 scallions, chopped coarse
1 serrano chili, seeded (*wear rubber gloves*)
1 Tablespoon fresh lime juice, or to taste
6 large plum tomatoes, seeded and chopped
3 Tablespoons flax or olive
2 Tablespoons cilantro, chopped

Chop all veggie ingredients fine by hand or by processor.

Stir in oil and cilantro.

Garam Masala

*Can be added to your favorite Indian dishes.
A traditional recipe from a friend of mine*

2 Tablespoons cumin seed
2 Tablespoons black cardamom seeds
5 teaspoons black peppercorns
4 1/2 teaspoons green cardamom, ground
1 Tablespoon, plus 1/4 teaspoon whole coriander
2 1/4 teaspoons fennel seeds
1 3/4 teaspoons cloves
2 1/2 teaspoons cinnamon
2 1/4 teaspoons ground mace
2 teaspoons black cumin seed
4 bay leaves
1 3/4 teaspoons ground ginger
1/2 whole nutmeg, chopped coarse
2 Tablespoons dried rose petals (*optional*)

Grind all ingredients as fine as possible in coffee/spice grinder.

Store in covered container.

Roasted Garlic

1 large garlic bulb

Preheat oven to 350 degrees.

Remove as much of the outer skin as possible without breaking the bulb apart.

Place in covered casserole dish.
Bake for 30 minutes or until pressing a finger against a clove shows that it is soft.

Mushroom-Onion Gravy

My husband loves gravy and potatoes (don't all men?).

3 Tablespoons olive oil
1 onion, diced
1 clove garlic, minced
2 cups mushrooms, coarse chopped (*shiitake are nice*)
1 1/2 cups button mushrooms, sliced
2 Tablespoons flour (*oat, barley, or spelt*)
3 Tablespoons nutritional yeast
2 Tablespoons Vogue Vege Base
1 Tablespoons Bragg Liquid Aminos
1 1/2-2 cups water

Sauté onions, garlic, and mushrooms in olive oil until just tender. **Add** flour, yeast, and Vogue. **Cook** for 2 minutes.

Add water slowly. **Stir** with a whisk until smooth.

Add Braggs.

Adjust seasonings.

Tofu Sour Cream

A simple recipe and very versatile.
I love it on baked potatoes sprinkled with dulse flakes.
My daughter scoops it right out of the bowl with carrot sticks.
Also makes a good salad dressing base.

1 package of Mori-Nu silken firm tofu
1 Tablespoon oil
1 Tablespoon apple cider vinegar
1 teaspoon rice syrup
1 Tablespoon lemon juice
1/2 teaspoon sea salt

Process all in blender. **Cover. Refrigerate** until ready to use.

Orange, Fig, and Pine Nut Relish

Serve with my Salisbury Steaks, a legume or nut loaf, or with traditional holiday sides, like stuffing.

1 cup dried figs, stemmed and cut into 1/3-inch pieces
1 Tablespoon freshly grated orange zest
1/2 cup water
2 navel oranges, peel cut away with serrated knife and sections chopped (about 1 cup)
pinch of taste
2 teaspoons shallot, minced
1 teaspoon rosemary leaves, minced (or 1/4 teaspoon dried, crumbled)
1/2-1 teaspoon fresh lemon juice, or to taste
1/4 cup pine nuts, toasted lightly

Soak figs and zest in water over night. **Drain.**

Stir in orange, rice, syrup, shallot, rosemary, and lemon juice.

Let mixture stand for at least 30 minutes and up to 2 days.

Stir in pine nuts.

Creamy "Mozzarella"

1/4 cup onions, diced
1 Tablespoon olive oil
1 cup water
1/4 cup nutritional yeast
3 Tablespoons rolled oats
1 Tablespoon sesame butter
2 Tablespoons arrowroot
2 Tablespoons lemon juice
1/2 teaspoon sea salt

Sauté onion until browned. **Place** onions in blender. **Add** remaining ingredients. **Process** until smooth. **Pour** into saucepan. **Cook** over medium heat. **Stir** constantly until very thick.

Pesto Dressing

1 cup parsley, chopped
1 cup basil leaves, chopped
2 Tablespoons olive oil
1/2 head Roasted Garlic (see recipe in Condiments)
2 Tablespoons pine nuts
1 Tablespoon lemon juice
1 teaspoon lemon rind, finely grated
1 teaspoon balsamic vinegar
1 teaspoon mellow white or blond miso

Process all in blender until well combined.

Basic Cream Sauce for Steamed Vegetables

Basic Sauce:
1 Tablespoon oil
2 Tablespoons flour (*millet, rice, or wheat*)
1 cup vegetable broth, heated
1 Tablespoon miso
dash of nutmeg

Heat oil in heavy saucepan. **Stir** in flour. *Whisk* 1—2 minutes over low heat. **Remove** from heat.

Add heated vegetable broth. **Bring** almost to a boil. **Turn** to low heat. **Simmer** until thickened.

Stir in miso and nutmeg.

Serve.

*Oil can be omitted. Just dry-toast flour.

Variation 1:
Sauté shiitake mushrooms and 1 chopped onion. **Add** to sauce. **Simmer** a few more minutes.

Variation 2:
Add 1-2 teaspoons herbs to sauce while simmering. **Include** combinations such as thyme, nutmeg, garlic; thyme, sage, parsley; coriander, cumin, ginger.

Variation 3:
1 Tablespoon peanut butter
1 onion, minced
1/4 cup orange juice

Combine all ingredients. **Add** to basic sauce. **Omit** oil in basic sauce recipe. **Simmer** 5-8 minutes.

Soups

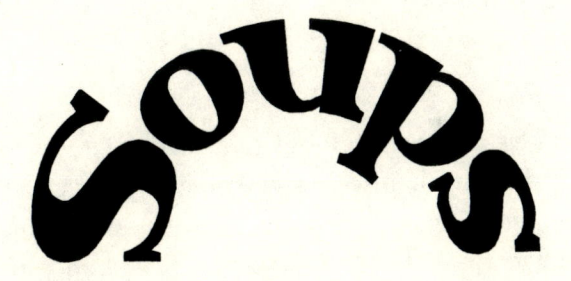

*"Nothing in life is to be feared.
It is only to be understood.*

• Marie Curie

"Cream of ____" Soups

Cooler weather begs for comfort foods and what better way to warm yourself from the inside out than with a steaming bowl of creamy soup? But what about the high fats and cholesterol in our favorite recipes that we have been trying to avoid? Try the following delicious and nutritious alternatives. I think you and your family will be pleasantly surprised!

Suggested "Cream" Alternatives

Oat or soy milk instead of milk or cream
Nutritional yeast (1/4-1/2 cup); 2 Tablespoons sesame butter; 1/4 cup quick cooking rolled oats; 2 Tablespoons lemon juice; Braggs Liquid Aminos to taste. Blend all until smooth.
One potato, 1 Tablespoon sesame butter, 1 Tablespoon miso
Pureed starchy veggies or beans
One package silken tofu
One-eighth to one-quarter cup ground rice

Have fun! Experiment with different seasonings. Soups are not easily ruined—so be daring!

Try leftover cream of soups as a topping on rice, pasta, or other grains for a hearty main-course meal. Sprinkle with raw or toasted nuts and seeds for added nutrition and texture, if desired.

Autumnal Glory Squash, Aduki, Corn Chowder

1 1/2 cups aduki beans
1 Tablespoon oil
2 medium leeks, including greens, rinsed and thinly sliced
4 cups vegetable stock
1 1/2 pounds butternut squash, scrubbed, seeded, and cut into 2-inch chunks (*peeling unnecessary*)
2 teaspoons dried tarragon
2 cups corn kernels, fresh or frozen
1/4 cup scallion greens, thinly sliced
Bragg Liquid Aminos to taste

Rinse beans. **Soak** 4 to 8 hours in water to cover.

Drain and **rinse** beans. **Set** aside.

Heat oil. **Sauté** leeks for 2 minutes. **Add** stock, beans, squash, and tarragon.

Boil. Reduce heat. **Simmer**, covered, until beans are tender, about 60 to 90 minutes.

Stir in corn, scallions, and **Braggs** to taste.

Adjust seasonings, if necessary.

Broccoli Soup

5 cups water
1 onion, coarsely chopped
1 celery stalk, coarsely chopped
2 cloves garlic, chopped
4 cups broccoli, chopped
1 potato, coarsely chopped
2 Tablespoons olive oil
2 Tablespoons light miso
1 heaping Tablespoon sesame butter
1 heaping Tablespoon Vogue Vege Base

Boil all vegetables in a large soup pot. **Reduce** heat. **Cover. Cook** until veggies are tender, 8-10 minutes.

Puree in batches in a blender. **Add** miso, sesame butter, and Vogue.

Adjust seasonings to taste.

Celery Soup

1 onion, chopped
1 carrot, chopped
1/2 fennel bulb, including green top, chopped
2 cups celery, chopped
oil
4 cups vegetable stock
1/2 cup cashews
2 Tablespoons arrowroot
1/4-1/2 teaspoon sea salt

Sauté veggies in oil for 5 minutes.

Add stock. **Boil. Simmer** over low heat until carrots are just tender.

Process half of soup in blender with cashews, arrowroot, and salt.

Pour into remaining soup. **Stir. Serve.**

Chilled Curried Carrot Soup

1 onion, sliced thin
4 carrots, sliced thin
1 Tablespoon oil
1 teaspoon curry powder
1 cup vegetable broth
chopped fresh chives, for garnish

Cook onion and carrot in oil until onion is soft.

Add curry. **Add** broth.

Simmer until carrots are just tender.

Puree in blender.

Cool. Chill before serving.

Fresh Tomato Soup

5 cups water
2 Tablespoons fresh ginger, grated
4 cloves garlic, minced
1 jalapeno, minced
sea salt to taste
6 medium tomatoes, cored
1 Tablespoon cumin seed, toasted
2 Tablespoon cilantro, chopped
"Butter" (see recipe in Condiments)

Boil water, ginger, garlic, jalapeno, and salt. **Lower** heat. **Simmer** 5 minutes.

Pour into blender. **Add** tomatoes. **Process** until smooth. **Add** cumin seeds and cilantro. **Stir** in a small amount of "Butter" into each bowl before serving.

Cilantro Soup

Chipotle Peppers are worth the hunt to find them. They impart a wonderful flavor.

1 Tablespoon oil
1 onion, diced
8 cloves garlic, minced
1 teaspoon cumin seeds
4 medium potatoes, peeled and diced
4 cups water
chipotle peppers, ground (*start with 1/8-1/4 teaspoon; adjust to your heat tolerance**)
1 cup cilantro leaves, minced
lemon juice
sea salt to taste

Sauté onion, garlic, and cumin seeds in oil in a large pot until softened.

Add potatoes, water, and chipotle peppers. **Simmer** until tender.

Process in blender with cilantro leaves.

Return to pot. **Add** lemon juice and sea salt to taste.

*Chipotles are dried and smoked jalapenos. Very potent! If you cannot find them in dried form, you can usually find canned chipotles in adobo sauce.

Cold Zucchini and Red Bell Pepper Soup with Cumin

This is a delightful, late-summer soup

3 cups zucchini, chopped
5 cups vegetable broth
4 red bell peppers, roasted*
1 cup plain yogurt (*preferably soy-based yogurt*)
1 1/2 teaspoons cumin seeds
sea salt to taste

Combine the zucchini and broth in a large saucepan. **Boil. Simmer** for approximately 15 minutes. **Cool.**

Puree the mixture in a blender with the roasted peppers and yogurt.

Dry **toast** the cumin seeds in a clean pan, heated until quite hot. **Shake** the pan, being careful not to burn the seeds.

Pour seeds into a spice or coffee grinder. **Grind** coarse. **Add** to the soup.

Transfer soup to a bowl. **Use** sea salt, if necessary.

Chill, covered, for at least 1 hour and up to 8 hours.

If desired, more cumin seeds can be toasted and sprinkled on top for garnish.

*To roast peppers, slice peppers in half and scoop out seeds. Flatten with your hands onto a broiler or cookie sheet and place under a preheated broiler about 2 inches from the heat, until the skins are blistered and charred. Transfer the peppers to a bowl and let them steam, covered, until they are cool enough to handle. The skin should peel away easily.

Corn and Rice Soup

1/4 cup brown rice
1/4 cup wild rice
5 cups veggie broth
1 cup onions, diced
1 Tablespoon olive oil
5 garlic cloves, minced
1 teaspoon salt
1 teaspoon cumin seeds
1/2 teaspoon thyme
1 teaspoon curry
1 cup tomatoes, peeled and chopped
1 cup corn
1/2 cup red bell pepper, chopped
small handful cilantro, minced
1/4 cup green onion, minced

Simmer rice in broth until tender.

Sauté onions, cumin, and garlic in oil until soft. **Add** to rice and broth.

Add additional spices. **Simmer** 5-10 minutes.

Stir in tomato, corn, and pepper.

Serve in bowls.

Sprinkle with cilantro and green onion.

Creamy Mushroom Soup

1 large onion, diced
2 large celery stalks, diced
2 medium potatoes, diced
2 medium carrots, diced
2 cups mushrooms, chopped
2 Tablespoons Vogue Vege Base
2 Tablespoons raw sesame butter
2 Tablespoons red miso
water

Place all veggies in a large pot. **Fill** with water until water covers veggies.

Bring to a boil. **Simmer** until potatoes are just tender. **Add** remaining ingredients.

Puree in blender, in batches if necessary.

Adjust seasoning to taste. **Serve.**

Lemon Soup

5 cups vegetable broth
1/2 cup rice
2 Tablespoons lemon juice
1/2 cup carrot, shredded
1/2 cup green onion, shredded
1 cup spinach leaves, chopped
1 cup tofu, diced
Bragg Liquid Aminos to taste
lemon slices

Boil broth. **Add** rice. **Cook** covered until rice is tender.

Add remaining ingredients. **Remove** from heat. **Float** a very thin slice of lemon in each bowl of soup for a pretty effect. **Serve.**

Curried Broccoli, Watercress, and Spinach Soup

2 cups vegetable broth
3 cups broccoli, chopped
1 cup parsley, chopped
1 cup spinach leaves, firmly packed, washed thoroughly
1 cup watercress, stems discarded
1/4 cup green onions, sliced
2 cups celery, including leaves, chopped
1/2 cup cucumber, sliced
1/3 cup green bell pepper, chopped
1 cup plain vegan yogurt
1/4-1/2 teaspoon curry powder
sea salt to taste
fresh dill

Simmer broth with broccoli in large saucepan until just tender. **Add** remaining veggies. **Simmer** 5 minutes.

Puree mixture in batches in a blender. **Transfer** to cleaned pan.

Stir in yogurt and curry powder. **Heat** soup over moderately low heat.

Add sea salt, if desired.

Garnish with minced fresh dill.

Serve.

Curried Coconut Noodle Soup

1/2 pound rice or soba noodles
2 Tablespoons oil
2 garlic cloves, minced
2-3 Tablespoons curry powder
2 cups vegetable broth
3 1/2 cups coconut milk, unsweetened
1 cup water
2 lemon grass stalks, outer leaves discarded, trimmed, and 5 inches of lower stalks minced
10 slices fresh gingerroot, peeled, sliced 1/8-inch thick
1/2 pound frozen, defrosted tofu squeezed of water and cubed
2 Tablespoons dulse flakes
Bragg Liquid Aminos to taste
6 Tablespoons fresh lime juice
1/3 cup fresh coriander, chopped

Cook noodles according to package directions. Set aside.

Cook garlic in oil in a heavy saucepan over moderately low heat until fragrant. **Stir** constantly.

Add curry powder. **Cook** mixture for 30 seconds. **Stir** constantly.

Stir in broth, coconut milk, water, lemon grass, and gingerroot. **Bring** to boil. **Simmer** 15 minutes.

Add tofu, dulse, Braggs, and lime juice.

Divide noodles among 6 bowls. **Ladle** soup over noodles.

Sprinkle soup with coriander.

Serve.

Curried Sprouted Lentil Stew

2 Tablespoons olive oil
2 medium potatoes, diced
1 onion, diced
2 carrots, diced
2 celery ribs, diced
2 Tablespoons Vogue Vege Base
1-2 teaspoons curry powder
1/2 teaspoon thyme
2 cups sprouted lentils
3-4 garlic cloves, minced
1/2 red bell pepper, diced (or 1/3 cup sun-dried tomatoes, minced)
1/2 bunch spinach, cleaned, stems removed and chopped

Sauté potatoes, onion, carrots, and celery in oil for 5 minutes.

Add Vogue, spices and enough water to cover vegetables.

Simmer until potatoes are just tender.

Add lentils, garlic, bell pepper, and spinach.

Stir until spinach is wilted.

Remove from heat.

Adjust seasonings, if necessary. **Serve.**

Dal Soup

My friend, A.J., creates excellent Indian cuisine.

1/2 pound black dal
4 ounces chana dal
1/2 cinnamon stick
2 teaspoons turmeric powder
2 teaspoons paprika
2 curry leaves
2 teaspoons garam masala
sea salt to taste
2 teaspoons olive oil
1 teaspoon whole cumin seed
1 teaspoon whole mustard seed
1 medium onion, chopped
1 teaspoon garlic, minced
2 teaspoons ginger, minced
1 jalapeno pepper, finely minced
1 large tomato, diced
cilantro to taste, finely minced (*start with 2 Tablespoons*)

Wash black and chana dal thoroughly. **Add** both dals to a 4-6 quart pot. **Add** water (6x by volume).

Add cinnamon stick, turmeric, paprika, curry leaves, garam masala, and salt. **Boil. Simmer** until dal is tender.

Separate dal from water. **Puree. Pour** back into water.

Heat a skillet. **Pour** in olive oil. **Sauté** whole cumin and mustard seed. **Add** onions. **Sauté** until golden brown.

Add garlic, ginger, and jalapeno. **Sauté** for 2 minutes.

Pour contents of skillet into simmering soup. **Simmer** for additional 30 minutes over low heat. **Remove** from heat. **Add** tomato and cilantro before serving.

Fragrant Oriental Soup

6 cups vegetable broth
1 teaspoon lemon peel, grated
1 Tablespoon fresh ginger, grated
1 cup shiitake mushrooms, stems removed and caps sliced thin
2 slender carrots, sliced on diagonal, approximately 1/8-inch thick
1-2 jalapenos, seeded and minced
2 cups cabbage, shredded (*napa or bokchoy are nice if available*)
1/2 package firm tofu, rinsed and cubed
Bragg Liquid Aminos to taste (*start with 2 Tablespoons*)
1—2-inch x 2-inch piece of kombu
1/4 cup scallion greens, thinly sliced
1/4 cup fresh cilantro, minced

Simmer all ingredients, except scallions and cilantro for 10-15 minutes.

Remove from heat.

Chop kombu into bite size pieces. **Return** to pot.

Stir in scallions and cilantro. **Adjust** seasonings, if needed.

Serve immediately.

Oriental Gazpacho

4-6 vine-ripened tomatoes (*approximately 1 1/2 pounds*)
1 lime peel, finely grated or minced
2 Tablespoons cilantro, chopped
4 green onions, chopped
1 teaspoon fresh ginger, finely grated
1 heaping Tablespoon Vogue Vege Base
1 Tablespoon Bragg Liquid Aminos
1 1/2 cups water mixed with 2 Tablespoons miso
1 celery stalk, diced
1 cucumber, diced
Thai curry paste to taste
sea salt to taste
juice of 1 lime

Cut tomatoes in half. **Chop** flesh coarsely. (You should have about 4 cups).

Place cilantro, green onions, ginger, Vogue, and Braggs in a saucepan. **Simmer** over low heat for 20 minutes.

Pour mixture in blender. **Add** tomatoes, water/miso, celery, and cucumber. **Puree** in blender.

Add curry paste and salt to taste.

Stir in a small amount of grated peel, and the juice of 1-2 limes to taste.

Chill thoroughly before serving.

Serve in chilled bowls.

Gazpacho

3 large ripe beefsteak tomatoes (*about 1 1/2 pounds*), quartered
1 large cucumber, peeled and halved
1 rib celery, cut in chunks
1 small green bell pepper, seeded and cut in chunks
1 small red bell pepper, seeded and cut in chunks
2-3 Tablespoons Spanish or Vidalia onion, finely chopped
3 Tablespoons fruity olive oil
approximately 1/2 cup tomato juice or water
3 Tablespoons parsley, finely minced
2-3 Tablespoons fresh cilantro, finely chopped (*optional*)
1 small garlic clove, peeled and finely minced
1 teaspoon apple cider or balsamic vinegar
sea salt to taste
croutons (*optional*)
tomato juice (*optional*)
avocado (*optional*)

Place all ingredients in a blender. **Process**, using the pulsing action, to create a coarse puree.

Thin soup by using tomato juice or water, if needed.

Adjust seasonings, if necessary.

Chill. Serve in chilled bowls.

Garnish with croutons or slices of avocado, if desired.

Gingered Butternut Squash Soup

2 Butternut squash (*about 3 1/2 pounds*) peeled and halved
1 cup onion, chopped
3 Tablespoons olive oil
1 Tablespoon fresh gingerroot, peeled and grated
1 apple, peeled, cored, and chopped
1 teaspoon fresh nutmeg, grated
1-2 Tablespoons white miso
sea salt to taste

Discard the seeds and strings from the squash. Cut into 1/2-inch pieces.

Combine the squash with enough water to just cover it in a kettle.

Bring to a boil. **Simmer** squash, covered, stirring occasionally, for 30 minutes, or until the squash is tender. **Drain**, reserving the cooking liquid.

Sauté onion in oil in kettle over moderately low heat. **Stir** until soft. **Add** gingerroot, apple, nutmeg, and squash. **Cook** and **stir** mixture for 1 minute.

Add enough water to the reserved cooking liquid to yield 3 cups liquid. **Add** liquid to the squash mixture. **Simmer** 30 minutes. **Stir** occasionally.

Puree the soup in a blender in batches. **Transfer** to a bowl as it is pureed. **Add** the miso to the last batch.

Pour the soup into the kettle. **Heat** over low heat until it is heated through. **Stir** constantly. **Adjust** seasoning either by adding more miso or sea salt to taste.

Lentil and Brown Rice Soup

1 1/2 cups lentils, picked over and rinsed
5 cups vegetable broth
1 cup brown rice
3 carrots, diced
1 onion, chopped
1 celery stalk, chopped
3 garlic cloves, minced
1 Tablespoon basil, minced (*or 1/2 teaspoon dried*)
1 Tablespoon oregano, minced (*or 1/2 teaspoon dried*)
1 teaspoon thyme, minced (*or 1/4 teaspoon dried*)
1 bay leaf
1/2 cup parsley leaves, minced
3 medium tomatoes, diced
2 Tablespoons apple cider vinegar
sea salt to taste

Soak lentils in water overnight. **Sprout** until tails are approximately 1/2-inch long (about 2-2 1/2 days).

Combine broth, rice, carrots, onion, celery, garlic, basil, oregano, thyme, and bay leaf in a heavy kettle. **Bring** liquid to boil. **Cover**. **Simmer** for 45 to 55 minutes, or until rice is tender. **Stir** occasionally.

Stir in lentils, parsley, tomatoes, vinegar, and sea salt. **Discard** bay leaf.

Thin soup with additional water, if necessary.

Muligatawny

olive oil
2-3 dried red chilies
3 garlic cloves, mashed
1/4 cup onion, diced
2 teaspoons fresh ginger, minced
2 teaspoons Madras curry
2 Tablespoons chickpea flour
2 Tablespoons coconut, ground
2 bay leaves
small handful of cilantro leaves
3-4 cups of mixed vegetables
3-4 cups of vegetable stock

Sauté red chilies, garlic, onion, and ginger in olive oil until tender.

Add curry, chickpea flour, and ground coconut. **Stir** briefly.

Add bay leaves, cilantro, and vegetables. **Stir** 2 minutes.

Add stock slowly. **Simmer** until vegetables are just tender.

Remove vegetables. **Discard** chilies and bay leaves. **Puree** in blender until smooth.

Add back to broth.

Serve as is, or pour through a sieve, discarding any solids. (You must discard chilies and bay leaves.)

Pea and Carrot Soup

4 large carrots, sliced
1 large onion, chopped
1/4 teaspoon thyme
5 cups rich vegetable stock
2 1/2 cups peas
1/2 cup almonds or cashews, ground

Boil carrots. **Simmer** until just tender.

Add onion, thyme, and stock. **Bring** almost to a boil.

Add peas and almonds or cashews.

Process in blender until smooth.

Pour back into pot. **Add** sea salt to taste.

Red Bell and Fennel Soup

2 Tablespoons olive oil
1 large red bell pepper, seeded and chopped
1 large onion, diced
2 large stalks celery, diced
2 medium red potatoes, diced
1/2 bulb fennel *(whole if small)*, diced, green top included
1/2-1 teaspoon rosemary, crushed
1/2 teaspoon sea salt
1 1/2 cups plain vegan milk
1 cup water

Sauté veggies in oil until onion is softened.

Add remaining ingredients. **Simmer** until just tender. **Puree** until smooth. **Serve.**

Roasted Garlic and Mushroom Soup

1 medium yellow onion, diced
1 carrot, diced
1 large celery stalk, diced
1 potato, diced small
approximately 5-6 cups vegetable stock
olive oil
1 pound mushrooms, sliced
Bragg Liquid Aminos to taste
2 Tablespoons fresh parsley, minced
1 Tablespoon fresh marjoram, minced (*or 1/4 teaspoon dried*)
1 Tablespoon fresh thyme, minced (*or 1/4 teaspoon dried*)
1 Tablespoon fresh sage, minced (*or 1/4 teaspoon dried*)
1 bulb Roasted Garlic (*see recipe in Condiments*)
1/4 cup sun-dried tomatoes, reconstituted and minced
1-2 Tablespoons miso
sea salt to taste

Boil onion, carrot, celery, and potato in stock. **Simmer.**

Sear mushrooms in oil on high heat until liquid is released. **Add** Braggs.

Add to soup mixture once the liquid is cooked out, and the mushrooms begin to brown.

Add spices. **Simmer** until veggies are just tender.

Squeeze each garlic clove. **Discard** the skin. **Add** roasted garlic, tomatoes, and miso. **Adjust** seasonings, if necessary.

Serve immediately.

Soba Soup with Spinach, Tofu, and Arame

1/2 cup dry arame
1/2 pound dried soba (*look for 100% buckwheat*)
7 cups vegetable broth
2 carrots, sliced thin
1/4 cup Bragg Liquid Aminos
1 Tablespoon rice syrup
10 ounces firm silken Mori-Nu tofu, cut into 1/2-inch cubes
1/2 pound spinach, discard coarse stems, washed, drained, cut crosswise into 1 1/2-inch wide strips
3-4 Tablespoons miso, or to taste
2 scallions, minced

Soak arame in hot water 15 minutes. Rinse. Drain. Set aside.

Cook soba according to package directions. Drain. Rinse under cold water. Set aside.

Boil broth, carrots, arame, Braggs, and syrup for 5 minutes in saucepan.

Stir in tofu. Simmer 1 minute.

Stir together 1/2 cup soup broth and miso in a small bowl. Pour into pan.

Stir in spinach.

Divide noodles among 6 large bowls. **Ladle** soup over noodles. **Sprinkle** each serving with scallions.

Spicy Kale and Chickpea Stew

Sprouting chickpeas greatly reduces cooking time, increases nutritional value, and makes bean easier to digest

1 1/2 cups dried chickpeas*
10 cups water
2 large onions, chopped coarse
3 large garlic cloves, minced
2 green bell peppers, chopped coarse
1/4 cup olive oil
1 1/2 pounds kale, coarse stems discarded and leaves washed well and chopped
2—28-ounce cans plum tomatoes, including the juice, chopped (*preferably Muir Glen*)
1—6-ounce can tomato paste
2 1/2 Tablespoons chili powder
1 teaspoon dried thyme
1 teaspoon dried oregano
1 teaspoon dried hot red pepper flakes
1 teaspoon ground cumin
1 bay leaf
sea salt to taste

If you are not using sprouted chickpeas, **soak** chickpeas overnight in enough water to cover them by 4 inches. **Drain. Rinse.**

Simmer chickpeas in a large saucepan, covered partially in water, for 1 1/2 hours, or until tender. (Alternatively, sprout chickpeas first,* and reduce water to 6 cups.)

Cook onions, garlic, and bell pepper in a heavy kettle in oil over moderate heat until vegetables are golden. **Stir** occasionally.

Add the chickpeas with the cooking liquid, kale, tomatoes (including juice), tomato paste, and spices. **Bring** to boil. **Simmer** stew for one hour. **Stir** occasionally. **Discard** bay leaf. **Season** with sea salt. **Serve** over grains.

To sprout chickpeas: soak chickpeas over night in a large jar. Rinse. Place cheesecloth or screen over top and tilt 70-85 degree angle. Set in corner, away from direct light. Rinse once in the morning and once at night (3 times in summer) for approximately 36-48 hours or until sprouts are 1/4-inch to 1/2-inch long. Then sauté veggies as above. Add chickpeas. Add remaining ingredients. Simmer 5-8 more minutes. Add sea salt to taste.

Spinach Soup

1 Tablespoon oil
1 small onion, diced
2 medium potatoes, diced
3 cups water
2 cups spinach, finely chopped
1 Tablespoon Bragg Liquid Aminos
1 Tablespoon miso *(preferably mellow white)*
1 Tablespoon flax oil or "Butter" *(see recipe in Condiments)*

Sauté onion in oil until translucent.

Add potatoes and water. **Cook** until just tender. **Mash** potatoes in water (or puree in blender). **Stir** in spinach, Braggs, miso, and flax oil.

Serve immediately.

Squash and Sweet Potato Chowder

1 cup carrots, diced and steamed
1 cup sweet potatoes, diced and steamed
2 cups butternut squash, diced and steamed
2 cups vegetable broth
1 bell pepper, diced
1 onion, diced
4 cloves garlic, minced
1/2 teaspoon thyme
1/2 teaspoon marjoram
1 Tablespoon oil
1/2 cup nutritional yeast
1 cup vegan milk
sea salt or Bragg Liquid Aminos to taste
1/4-1/2 teaspoon cinnamon

Blend carrots, sweet potatoes, and squash in broth. Set aside.

Sauté remaining veggies in oil with spices until softened. **Add** pureed veggies, nutritional yeast, milk, and seasoning to taste.

Tomato Carrot Soup

2 leeks, white portions, washed well and chopped
1 1/2 cups carrots, peeled and sliced
3 Tablespoons olive oil
5 cups vegetable stock
1-2 teaspoons fresh thyme, minced
2 pounds plum tomatoes, chopped
1/4 cup sun-dried tomato puree (*after soaking tomatoes, process in mini food processor or blender until smooth*)
sea salt to taste

Sauté leeks and carrots in oil over moderately low heat until softened. **Stir** in stock and thyme. **Simmer** until carrots are tender.

Add remaining ingredients. **Puree** in blender. **Season** with sea salt, if desired.

Serve immediately.

Old Country Cabbage Soup

2 Tablespoons olive oil
2 cups leeks, sliced
1 onion, sliced
2 carrots, diced
1 medium cabbage, chopped
1/2 teaspoon caraway seeds
1 teaspoon thyme
7 cups water
2 Tablespoons Vogue Vege Base
2 Tablespoons white miso
3 Tablespoons lemon juice
1 Tablespoon rice syrup or pinch of stevia
2 medium tomatoes, chopped

Sauté leeks, onion, carrot, caraway, and cabbage in oil until softened.

Add thyme, water, and Vogue. **Simmer** for 10 minutes. **Stir** in miso, lemon juice, and sweetener. **Stir** in tomatoes before serving.

Wild Rice and Shiitake Mushroom Soup

1 cup wild rice
1 onion, chopped
1/4 cup olive oil
1 cup shiitake mushrooms, chopped
1 cup white mushrooms, sliced
1/2 cup celery, thinly sliced
1/4 cup oat flour
6 cups vegetable broth
1 teaspoon curry powder
1/2 teaspoon dry mustard
1 1/2 teaspoons thyme, minced (*or 1/2 teaspoon dried*)
2 Tablespoons miso
1/4 cup parsley, minced

Rinse rice in a sieve under cold water until water runs clear.

Simmer rice in boiling, salted water, covered, for 35 minutes, or until tender. **Drain** in a sieve.

Cook onion in oil in a kettle over moderately low heat until softened. **Stir** occasionally.

Add mushrooms and celery. **Cook** until tender.

Stir in flour.

Stir in rice, broth, and seasonings.

Bring mixture to boil Stir. **Simmer** for 5 minutes.

Scoop out approximately 1/2 cup broth. **Stir** miso into broth. **Pour** back into soup.

Stir in parsley.

Serve.

Winter Greens Soup

[handwritten: Good, but needs more flavor]

1 Tablespoon olive oil
1 large onion, thinly sliced
4 garlic cloves, minced
1 medium potato, thinly sliced
1 large carrot, thinly sliced
Approximately 4 cups vegetable stock
1 bunch kale, stems removed and chopped
1 bunch green chard, chopped
1 bunch spinach, chopped
1 Tablespoon lemon juice
2 Tablespoons white or blonde miso
Bragg Liquid Aminos to taste

Sauté onion, garlic, potatoes, and carrots in oil until just tender.

Add vegetable stock, kale, and chard. **Simmer** at least 5 minutes. **Remove** from heat.

Add spinach, lemon juice, miso, and 1 Tablespoon Braggs.

Process in a blender immediately, until smooth. **Adjust** seasonings, if necessary.

Serve immediately.

Zucchini Basil Soup

1 cup onion, chopped
6 garlic cloves, minced
2 Tablespoons rice
2 Tablespoons olive oil
1 quart vegetable broth
1/2 cup fresh basil leaves, chopped
1 teaspoon fresh thyme, minced
5 small zucchini, scrubbed and chopped
2 heaping Tablespoons of miso *(preferably red)*

Combine onion, garlic, rice, and oil in a large saucepan. **Cook** mixture over moderately low heat until onion is soft. **Stir** often.

Add broth, basil, thyme, and zucchini. **Boil. Lower** heat. **Simmer**, covered, for approximately 25 minutes, or until rice is just tender.

Remove from heat. **Add** miso.

Puree soup in a blender in batches.

Serve immediately.

Salads

*"You must understand the whole of life,
not just one little part of it. That is why
you must read, that is why you must look
at the skies, that is why you must sing, and dance,
and write poems, and suffer
and understand, for all that is life."*

•J. Krishnamurti

Apple and Potato Salad with Mustard Cream Dressing

1 pound small red potatoes, steamed until just tender, cooled
2 red delicious apples
1 celery stalk, sliced thin
1 scallion, sliced thin

Dressing:
1/4 cup dry toasted dulse, crumbled
1 Tablespoon fresh lemon juice
1 Tablespoon whole-grain prepared mustard, or to taste
2 teaspoons fresh parsley, minced
1/4 cup plain vegan yogurt
1/4 cup vegan mayonnaise
sea salt to taste

Steam potatoes until just tender. Cool.

Add remaining vegetables in large bowl.

Prepare dressing:
Whisk together all ingredients. **Toss** gently with vegetables. **Serve.**

Potato, Corn, and Cherry Tomato Salad

1-2 Tablespoons apple cider vinegar
1/2 cup olive oil
1 cup packed fresh basil leaves
sea salt to taste
2 1/2 pounds small red potatoes, diced
Corn kernels cut from 6 ears (*or 2 10-ounce packages frozen, defrosted*)
1/2 pound cherry tomatoes, halved

Blend together vinegar, oil, basil, and salt in a blender until dressing is emulsified.

Steam the potatoes. **Cool. Combine** all ingredients in a large bowl. **Toss** gently.

Collard Potato Salad with Mustard Dressing

Dulse is a great source of minerals.

2 pounds small red potatoes, scrubbed and diced
1 pound collards, stems discarded, leaves washed well, cut into 1-inch pieces
2 Tablespoons whole-grain prepared mustard
2 Tablespoons apple cider vinegar
1/3 cup olive oil
1/2 cup dulse, dry toasted and crumbled
2 green onions, thinly sliced
salt to taste

Steam potatoes until just tender. **Cool. Place** in large bowl.

Place collards in heavy saucepan with 2 Tablespoons water. **Cover. Simmer** for 5 minutes. **Drain. Add** to potatoes.

Whisk together mustard, vinegar, and salt in a small bowl. **Add** oil in a stream. **Whisk** until emulsified.

Pour over potato/kale mixture. **Add** dulse and green onions. **Toss** until well combined. **Serve.**

Warm Potato-Kale Salad

4 large red potatoes, cubed
1 large bunch kale
3 large cloves garlic, sliced or chopped
2 Tablespoons olive oil
1/4 cup vegetable stock
sea salt to taste
1-2 Tablespoons apple cider vinegar

Steam potatoes until just tender.

Remove stems from kale. **Tear** leaves into bite size pieces. **Sauté** with garlic and oil for 2 minutes. **Add** vegetable stock. **Cover** pan. **Simmer** 5 minutes. **Toss** in potatoes, salt, and vinegar. **Serve.**

Potato Salad, My Way

1/2 package firm tofu, cubed in 1/2-inch cubes
3-4 cups red potatoes, cut into 1-inch cubes
2 large stalks celery, diced
1 cup mixed crunchy sprouts (*lentils, peas, etc.*)
1/4 cup parsley, minced

Dressing:
1/4-1/2 cup vegan mayonnaise or Almonnaise (*see recipe in Condiments*)
1/2-1 Tablespoon whole-grain prepared mustard
2 garlic cloves, minced
1-2 Tablespoons lemon juice
1-2 teaspoons kelp powder or dulse flakes
2 Tablespoons dill pickle, minced
1/8 teaspoon turmeric

Wrap tofu in a clean kitchen towel for 30 minutes.

Steam potatoes until just tender.

Mix all salad ingredients in large bowl.

Prepare dressing in a separate bowl. **Stir** into salad.

Serve warm or chilled.

Cole Slaw

Variation 1:
4 cups cabbage, shredded
1 cup carrot, shredded
1/2 cup vegan mayonnaise
2 Tablespoons whole-grain prepared mustard

Mix all ingredients well.

Variation 2:
1/4 cabbage
1/2 beet
1 carrot
1 apple
1 large celery stalk
1 orange, juiced

In processor process beet and carrot.

Pulse with cabbage, apple and celery until just combined.

Add juice and pulse in a couple more times. Serve.

Far East Coleslaw

1 medium cabbage, quartered, core removed and discarded
1 large carrot, finely chopped
1 cup cilantro, minced and tightly packed
1/4 cup green onions, thinly sliced
1 cup cucumber, chopped
1/2 cup pumpkin seeds, toasted
1/4 cup sesame or flax oil
2 teaspoons peanut butter
4 Tablespoons lime juice
3 Tablespoons Bragg Liquid Aminos
1 jalapeno pepper, seeded and finely chopped
sea salt to taste

Shred cabbage by cutting very thin slices along the length of each quarter. **Place** in large serving bowl. **Mix** in carrots, cilantro, green onions, cucumber, and pumpkin seeds.

Whisk oil with peanut butter. **Combine** oil and remaining ingredients in a jar. **Shake** well to blend.

Toss into salad.

Adjust seasonings, if needed.

Chili Slaw

1 medium cabbage
1 1/2 cups red beans, cooked
1 red bell pepper, seeded and diced
1/4 cup scallion greens, thinly sliced
1 cup corn kernels
1/2 cup parsley, minced
2 stalks celery, chopped
1 teaspoon whole cumin seeds
1 teaspoon dried oregano
1 Tablespoon chili powder
1/2-3/4 cup vegan mayonnaise
1 garlic clove, minced
3 Tablespoons lime juice
sea salt to taste

Quarter cabbage. Cut away any hard core. **Shred** cabbage by cutting very thin slices along the length of each quarter.

Place the shredded cabbage in a large bowl or storage container.

Toss in the beans, red pepper, scallion greens, corn, parsley, and celery.

Prepare dressing:
Heat a small heavy skillet for 30 seconds. **Add** cumin seeds. **Stir** constantly until they begin to brown and pop, about 10-20 seconds. **Turn** off heat

immediately. **Stir** in the oregano, and chili powder. **Cool** slightly. **Grind** mixture to a powder in a spice mill or with a mortar and pestle.

Combine the seasoning mix in a small bowl with the mayonnaise and garlic. **Stir** in 2 Tablespoons of lime juice.

Toss enough of dressing into the salad to thoroughly coat. **Add** extra lime juice, if desired.

Sweet Potato Slaw

1 carrot, shredded
1 sweet potato, shredded
1/2 yellow or red bell pepper, chopped
1/2 cup kale, finely minced
2 green onions, minced
1/4 cabbage head, shredded

Dressing:
1/3 cup plain soy yogurt
1/3 cup vegan mayonnaise
1 teaspoon caraway seeds
pinch of stevia powder
2 teaspoons apple cider vinegar
1/4 teaspoon sea salt

Combine dressing with vegetables.

Serve immediately, or slightly chilled.

Celery and Apple Salad

2 Tablespoons vegan mayonnaise
1 Tablespoon whole-grain prepared mustard
1 teaspoon apple cider vinegar
1 teaspoon tarragon leaves, minced, or 1/4 teaspoon dried
sea salt to taste
4 celery stalks, cut into 1 1/2-inch matchsticks, plus celery leaves for garnish
1 crisp tart apple, cut into 1 1/2-inch matchsticks

Whisk together mayonnaise, mustard, vinegar, tarragon, and salt in a bowl.

Toss with celery and apple.

Garnish with celery leaves.

Serve.

South American Jicama and Orange Salad

1/3 cup fresh lime juice
1 teaspoon sea salt, or to taste
1 teaspoon chili powder, or to taste
1/8 teaspoon cayenne
1 pound jicama, peeled, cut into 1/3-inch thick sticks
4 navel oranges, rind and pith cut free, sections cut away from membranes
2 scallions, minced

Whisk together lime juice, salt, chili powder, and cayenne in a large bowl. **Add** jicama. **Toss** to coat well with dressing.

Arrange oranges decoratively around edge of platter. **Mound** jicama with a slotted spoon in center.

Drizzle remaining dressing over oranges. **Sprinkle** scallions over salad.

Cucumbers with Tofu Sour Cream

1 cup Tofu Sour Cream (see recipe in Condiments)
3 cups cucumbers, chopped
1 teaspoon dill, minced

Mix all ingredients well.

Cucumber, Dill, and Wakame Salad

1 12-inch long piece wakame
2 large cucumbers, sliced paper thin
1/4 cup apple cider vinegar
2 Tablespoons green onions or sweet red onion, finely chopped
1 1/2-2 teaspoons dill weed, dried
sea salt to taste

Snip wakame into 1/2-inch pieces. **Rinse** briefly in cold water. **Drain** thoroughly.

Toss all ingredients together. **Cover. Refrigerate** until wakame is tender, about 4-6 hours.

Stir occasionally to make sure the wakame is submerged in juice.

Serve slightly chilled or at room temperature.

Cucumber, Orange, and Aniseed Salad

1/4 teaspoon anise seeds
1 cucumber
1 navel orange
1 Tablespoon apple cider vinegar
1 Tablespoon olive oil
1/4 red onion, sliced thin crosswise
sea salt to taste

Crush the anise seeds lightly with the back of a spoon in a small bowl.

Peel cucumber, if desired. **Quarter** lengthwise. **Cut** crosswise into 1/4-inch thick pieces.

Peel orange. **Cut** pith away with a serrated knife. **Cut** sections free from the membranes. **Slice** thin crosswise.

Combine all ingredients. **Add** salt to taste.

Corn, Kidney, and Cucumber Salad

This tastes best if allowed to rest up to 3 hours.

1 cup bulgur
1 cup raisins
1 1/3 cups water
1 Tablespoon sesame oil
1/3 cup vegetable stock
2 teaspoons orange rind, grated
1 1/2 Tablespoons fresh parsley, minced
1 1/2 Tablespoons fresh mint, minced
1 1/2 Tablespoons fresh chives, minced
1 1/4 cups corn
2/3 cup cooked beans (*kidney or other red bean*)
1 cup cucumber, cut into match sticks
sea salt to taste

Place bulgur and raisins in bowl with water. **Set** aside.

Whisk oil, stock, rind, and herbs in a separate bowl. **Pour** into bulgur mixture. Let sit until all liquid is absorbed.

Fold in corn, beans, and cucumber gently. **Chill** before serving.

Spinach, Fennel, and Pink Grapefruit Salad

1 Tablespoon apple cider vinegar
3 Tablespoons fresh pink grapefruit juice
1/2-3/4 teaspoon whole-grain prepared mustard
1/4 cup olive or flax oil, or both combined
sea salt to taste
1 pound spinach, stems removed, washed well, spun dry
2 pink grapefruits, zest and pith cut away, cut into segments
1 small fennel bulb, sliced thin crosswise

Blend vinegar, grapefruit juice, mustard, oil, and salt until emulsified.

Arrange salad on plates decoratively. **Drizzle** with dressing.

Sesame Carrot Salad

Try adding 1/4 cup of reconstituted arame sea vegetable for an extra boost of flavor and nutrition!

1 garlic clove, smashed
3 Tablespoons oil
1/4 cup sesame seeds
8 medium carrots, grated coarse
2 Tablespoons fresh lemon juice
sea salt to taste

Cook the garlic in oil in a small heavy skillet over moderate heat. **Stir** until garlic is golden.

Add sesame seeds. **Cook**, stirring, until golden.

Toss together carrots, sesame mixture, lemon juice, and salt in a bowl.

Cauliflower Salad

1 cup cauliflower, diced
1/2 red bell pepper, sliced into slivers
1/2 cup daikon radish, sliced into matchsticks
1 cup mung bean sprouts, blanched
olive oil to taste
balsamic vinegar to taste

Combine all ingredients. Mix well.

Chill. Serve.

Broccoli with Cheddar Vinaigrette

1 Tablespoon olive oil
1 teaspoon apple cider vinegar
1 Tablespoon water
pinch cayenne or red pepper flakes
1/2 cup grated cheddar-style vegan cheese, coarsely grated
1/2 pound broccoli, cut into long flowerets
sea salt to taste

Blend together all ingredients, except broccoli, in a blender. **Add** salt, if using.

Steam broccoli until crisp tender, or raw is great.

Serve topped with vinaigrette.

Broccoli Salad Italiano

1 bunch broccoli, cut into bite-size pieces
1/3 cup sun-dried tomatoes, reconstituted in 1 cup hot water
1/4 of a red onion, sliced into thin slivers
small handful sun-dried black olives, chopped

Dressing:
2 Tablespoons balsamic or red wine vinegar
1/4 cup olive oil
1/2 teaspoon basil, dried (*or 2 teaspoons fresh*)
pinch of red pepper flakes
pinch of salt

Steam broccoli until crisp tender.

Drain tomatoes. **Reserve** liquid. **Dice** tomatoes.

Mix broccoli, tomatoes, onion, and olives.

Mix dressing ingredients in a jar. **Shake** well to blend. **Pour** over broccoli salad.

Rice and Broccoli Salad with Sunflower Seed Dressing

2 cups long grain rice, sprouted, or cooked
1 bunch broccoli
1 cup slivered almonds, lightly toasted
1/2 cup scallion greens, thinly sliced
1/3 cup raw sunflower seeds, lightly toasted
4 teaspoons apple cider vinegar
1/2 cup oil
5 teaspoons toasted sesame oil
1 cup vegetable broth
sea salt to taste

Place cooked or sprouted rice in bowl.

Peel stems of broccoli. **Slice** thin. **Cut** flowerets into 1-inch pieces. **Steam** until crisp-tender. **Cool.**

Add broccoli, almonds, and scallion greens to rice. **Combine** mixture well.

Puree sunflower seeds with the vinegar, oils, and sea salt in a blender. **Add** 1 cup vegetable broth in a stream. **Blend** until emulsified.

Toss with salad.

Serve.

Arame-Zucchini Sesame Toss

1/3 cup arame, prepared according to package directions
2 cups zucchini, grated
1/2 red bell pepper, chopped
1/4 cup green onions, minced
3/4 cup sesame seeds, ground
1/2-1 Tablespoon stone-ground prepared mustard
1 Tablespoon Bragg Liquid Aminos
1/4 cup water
1 Tablespoon Vogue Vege Base

Place veggies in a bowl. **Mix** remaining ingredients. **Add** to veggies.

Toss well. Serve.

Moroccan Swiss Chard Salad

1 1/2 pounds Swiss chard
2 Tablespoons oil
1 Tablespoon garlic, minced
1 Tablespoon paprika
2 teaspoons ground cumin
2 Tablespoons fresh lemon juice
sea salt to taste

Trim chard. **Discard** thick stems. **Wash** well. **Chop** coarse.

Heat oil in large skillet over moderate heat until hot, but not smoking. **Cook** garlic briefly, just until golden.

Add chard, paprika, cumin, lemon juice, and sea salt. **Stir** to coat well.

Cook mixture for 5 minutes. **Let** cool.

Serve at room temperature or chilled.

Escarole, Spinach, Hijiki, and Red Onion Salad

1/4 cup hijiki
4 cups packed escarole, rinsed, dried, and torn into pieces
3 cups packed fresh spinach, rinsed, dried, and torn into pieces
1/2 cup red onion, finely chopped
1/2 cup peas
2 Tablespoons sunflower seeds

Dressing:
1 garlic clove, minced and mashed to a paste with 1/8 teaspoon sea salt
1 teaspoon apple cider vinegar
1 Tablespoon fresh lemon juice
1/2 teaspoon whole-grain prepared mustard
1/4 cup olive or flax oil

Simmer hijiki in water for 15 minutes. Rinse well. Chop coarse.

Mix all salad ingredients together.

Process dressing ingredients in blender until smooth.

Combine well with salad.

Serve.

Tabbouleh

1 cup bulgur wheat poured into 2 cups boiling water (*or 2 cups cooked quinoa*)
1 cup parsley, minced fine
2-3 Tablespoons mint, minced fine
1 carrot, diced fine
1 tomato, seeded and diced fine
1 cucumber, seeded and diced fine
2 Tablespoons olive oil
4-6 Tablespoons lemon juice
1/2 Tablespoon whole-grain prepared mustard
1-2 garlic cloves

Let bulgur wheat sit in boiling water 15-20 minutes. **Drain** liquid, if any.

Add vegetables.

Blend olive oil, lemon juice, mustard, and garlic. **Stir** into salad.

Let rest. **Cool** before serving, if desired.

Adjust with lemon juice, if needed.

Tomato and Fennel Salad

5 Tablespoons fresh lemon juice
sea salt to taste
1/2 cup olive oil
2 large fennel bulbs, sliced paper thin
2 pounds tomatoes, sliced

Whisk together lemon juice with some sea salt in a large bowl. **Add** oil in a stream until emulsified.

Add fennel. **Toss** well. **Marinate** for a few minutes.

Arrange tomatoes decoratively on a platter. **Spoon** fennel mixture over them.

Serve.

Insalata Caprese

2 large firm, ripe tomatoes (*about 1 pound*), sliced thin crosswise
1/2 pound mozzarella-style cheese, sliced thin
1/3 cup basil leaves, thinly sliced
2 Tablespoons drained capers
sea salt to taste
1/4 cup olive oil (*Spectrum Organic is my favorite*)

Arrange tomatoes decoratively on platter.

Add mozzarella.

Sprinkle with basil and capers.

Season with salt. **Drizzle** with oil.

Chopped Main Salad

2 avocados
1/2 cup corn
1/2 cup peas
1/2 cup sprouts (*preferably mung or lentil*)
1/2 cup bell pepper (*preferably red*), diced fine
1/2 cup carrot, diced fine
1/2 cup celery, diced fine
1 cup cabbage, diced fine
1 cup ground almonds or sunflower seeds
1/4 cup onions, chopped fine
1/4 cup parsley, chopped fine
3 Tablespoons cider vinegar
3 Tablespoons Bragg Liquid Aminos

Mix all ingredients well. Serve.

Marinated Mushroom Salad

1 pound button and/or crimini mushrooms, cubed
1-2 cups bean sprouts
1 red bell pepper, sliced in slivers
1/4 cup toasted almonds, sliced
1/3 cup fresh parsley, minced

Dressing:
3 Tablespoons apple cider vinegar
2 Tablespoons Oriental sesame oil
2 Tablespoons oil
pinch of red pepper flakes
1/2 teaspoon salt
2 Tablespoons cilantro, minced
2 Tablespoons green onions, minced
1 Tablespoon ginger, minced
2 garlic cloves, minced

Combine salad ingredients. **Mix** dressing ingredients. **Pour** over salad. **Marinate** 30 minutes before serving.

Italian Chopped Salad with Pesto Dressing

1 cup broccoli, chopped
1 cup cabbage, chopped
1/2 red or yellow bell pepper, diced
1/2 cucumber, diced
1/2 cup corn
1 carrot, diced

Place all ingredients in large bowl.

Pesto Dressing:*
1 cup parsley, chopped
1 cup basil leaves, chopped
2 Tablespoons olive oil
1/2 head Roasted Garlic (*see recipe in Condiments*)
2 Tablespoons pine nuts
1 Tablespoon lemon juice
1 teaspoon lemon rind, finely grated
1 teaspoon balsamic vinegar
1 teaspoon mellow white or blond miso

Add dressing to chopped salad, starting with half of the dressing and adding more as desired.

*Any left over dressing can be used over beans, sliced tomatoes, or steamed potatoes.

Spicy Chickpea Salad

1 cup dried chickpeas, soaked over night (*or 2 cup of sprouted chickpeas cooked until tender*)
1 yellow or red bell pepper, diced fine
1 small bunch green onions, sliced thin
1/2 cup cilantro, minced fine

Dressing:
2 Tablespoons lemon juice
1 Tablespoon apple cider vinegar
1 garlic clove, minced
1 teaspoon fresh ginger, grated
3/4 teaspoon cumin, ground
1/4 teaspoon cayenne or chipotle pepper
1/4 cup olive oil

Cook chickpeas until tender.

Combine chickpeas, bell pepper, onions, and cilantro.

Whisk together all ingredients to make dressing.

Add dressing to chickpea mixture. **Stir** well. **Let** rest for at least an hour before serving.

Bean Salad

1 pound green beans, cleaned
1 ripe tomato, diced
1/2 yellow bell pepper, cut in strips
2 Tablespoons red onion, chopped
2 Tablespoons olive oil
2 cloves garlic, minced
1/4 teaspoon thyme
sea salt to taste
1 Tablespoon apple cider vinegar

Steam green beans until crisp tender. **Keep** warm.

Place tomato, pepper, and onion in bowl.

Heat oil in small pan. **Add** garlic. **Sauté** briefly, 1-2 minutes.

Pour over veggies.

Add remaining ingredients.

Toss well. **Serve.**

Sprouted Wheat and Veggie Bowl

2 cups 48-hour sprouted wheat
1/2 cup celery, diced
1/2 red bell pepper, diced
1/2 cucumber, diced
1-2 ears of corn, removed from cob
1/2 cup kale or collard greens, stems discarded, minced

Place all ingredients in a large bowl. Toss with Lemon-Sesame Dressing or my favorite, Dried Tomato, Caper, and Olive Dressing (see recipes in Salad Dressings).

Millet Salad with Apricots, Pine Nuts, and Ginger

1 cup cooked millet
1/2 cup red onion, finely diced
1/4 cup olive oil
1 Tablespoon apple cider vinegar
8 dried apricots, diced small
2 teaspoons fresh ginger, grated
1/4 teaspoon salt
2 Tablespoons pine nuts, toasted
1 celery stalk, diced

Boil water in a small pot. **Place** red onion in water for 15 seconds. **Drain** well.

Toss onion with a few splashes of vinegar to draw out its pink color.

Toss all ingredients together. **Add** salt or vinegar to brighten the flavor, if needed.

Quinoa Salad with Sun-Dried Tomatoes

1 cup quinoa
2 cups water
1/2 cucumber, seeded, skinned if desired, and minced
1/2 cup fresh basil, minced
1/2 cup rehydrated sun-dried tomatoes, minced
2 green onions, minced
2 Tablespoons pine nuts, toasted
1/4 cup olive oil
1-2 Tablespoons whole-grain prepared mustard
2-4 Tablespoons lemon juice
sea salt to taste
1 large garlic clove, minced

Rinse quinoa. **Cook** quinoa as you would rice, simmering for approximately 20 minutes until all moisture is absorbed. **Cool.**

Add cucumber, basil, tomatoes, and onions to quinoa in a large bowl. (The smaller you can dice the vegetables, the better). **Add** pine nuts. **Mix** well.

Blend oil, mustard, lemon juice, salt, and garlic well. **Toss** into salad.

Adjust seasonings, if desired.

Mexican Pasta Salad

1 pound pasta noodles such as rigatoni, elbows or curls (*preferably wheat free*)
Corn kernels cut from 3 ears (*or 1 10-ounce package frozen, defrosted*)
1 small red onion, sliced into 1/4-inch rings, then halved
2 bell peppers seeded and diced (*if available, use red and green*)
2 Tablespoons parsley, minced
2 Tablespoons cilantro, minced
1 cup sun dried olives, sliced
2 teaspoons chili powder
1 teaspoon toasted cumin seeds, ground
1 1/2 cups kidney or pinto beans, drained and rinsed
1 1/2 cups Tomato Salsa (*see recipe in Condiments*), or bottled
1/2 cup Tofu Sour Cream (*see recipe in Condiments*)
sea salt to taste

Cook the pasta according to package directions. **Drain**. **Rinse** under cold water to stop the cooking. **Drain** again. **Place** in a large bowl.

Add the remaining ingredients.

Toss well.

Adjust seasonings if needed.

Pasta and Vegetable Salad with Basil Dressing

I favor Papadini Lentil Pasta. Lundberg Rice or Quinoa Noodles

1 pound pasta shells, fuzilli, or other corkscrew
2 cups basil leaves, firmly packed
1/2 cup olive oil
6-8 sun-dried olives, pitted
2 garlic cloves, minced
1 Tablespoon apple cider vinegar
1/4 cup vegetable stock
sea salt to taste
1 cup carrots, diced 1/4-inch
1 cup fresh or frozen corn
1 cup peas
1/3 cup artichoke hearts, chopped
1/2 cup lentil sprouts
1/4 cup pine nuts, lightly toasted
1 tomato, chopped
vegan-style parmesan (*optional*)

Cook pasta according to package directions. **Rinse. Drain** under cool water.

Blend basil, oil, olives, garlic, vinegar, stock, and salt in blender until dressing is smooth.

Toss all ingredients in large bowl, incorporating the dressing well.

Sprinkle vegan-style parmesan over all, if desired.

Wild Rice Salad

4 cups water
1 1/2 cups wild rice, rinsed and drained
1 medium red or yellow bell pepper, roasted and diced
1/3-1/2 cup sun-dried tomatoes, reconstituted in hot water, drained and chopped
1/4 cup sun-dried olives, pitted and chopped coarse
2 Tablespoons fresh parsley, finely chopped
1/4 cup pine nuts, toasted lightly
1/4 cup olive oil
2 Tablespoons fresh lemon juice
sea salt to taste

Boil 4 cups water in a large saucepan. **Add** the wild rice. **Cover. Simmer** for 40 minutes, or until tender. (Alternatively, sprout wild rice first.)

Drain the wild rice in a sieve. **Transfer** to a large bowl. **Toss** rice with remaining ingredients. **Add** salt, if desired. **Serve** at room temperature or chilled.

Wild Rice Salad #2

(Sprouted rice is a nice substitution for cooked rice.)

1/4 cup wild rice
1/2 cup brown rice
2 cups water
1 cup peas
2 stalks celery, thinly sliced
4 green onions, sliced
1/2 red bell pepper, slivered
1/4 cup orange juice
2 Tablespoons olive oil
1 Tablespoon Bragg Liquid Aminos
2 teaspoons rice syrup
3 Tablespoons sesame seeds, toasted

Cook rice until liquid is absorbed. **Cool. Add** peas, celery, onions, and bell pepper to rice mixture. **Combine** orange juice, olive oil. Braggs, rice syrup, and sesame seeds. **Pour** over rice mixture. **Toss. Serve.**

Mock Chicken Salad

1 package tempeh
1/4 cup vegan mayonnaise
1 celery stalk, finely chopped
2 Tablespoons dill pickle, minced
2 Tablespoons onion, minced
2 Tablespoons parsley, minced
1-2 teaspoons whole-grain prepared mustard
1-2 teaspoons Bragg Liquid Aminos
1/4 teaspoon powdered garlic

Steam tempeh 10 minutes. **Cool. Cut** into small cubes.

Combine with remaining ingredients.

Mock Egg Salad

1 block firm tofu
1/2 cup celery, finely minced
1/4 cup green onion, finely minced
1-2 Tablespoons whole-grain prepared mustard
1/4 cup vegan mayonnaise
1/2 sheet nori, shredded (*or toasted and crumbled dulse*)
Pinch of turmeric
salt and pepper to taste

Crumble tofu. Leave chunky.

Mix all ingredients well.

Mock Chicken

1 Tablespoon Vogue Vege Base
2 Tablespoons Bragg Liquid Aminos
2 Tablespoons tomato sauce
1/2 teaspoon chili powder
1/2 teaspoon cider vinegar
1/4 teaspoon garlic powder
1/4 teaspoon onion powder
1/4 teaspoon sage
1/4 teaspoon paprika
1/4 teaspoon oregano
1 tub of tofu, crumbled

Preheat oven to 350 degrees.

Mix all seasonings together. **Squeeze** into tofu. **Arrange** on an oiled baking sheet.

Bake for 30 minutes, stirring 2 or 3 times. Set aside.

Mock Chicken Taco Salad

1 prepared recipe of Mock Chicken (*see recipe in Salads*)

1 cup tomato, diced
3/4 cup Tofu Sour Cream (*see recipe in Condiments*)
1/2 cup red onion, diced
1/4 cup fresh cilantro, chopped
3/4 teaspoon ground cumin
1/4 teaspoon sea salt (*delete if using salted corn chips*)
tofu mock chicken
4-6 cups salad greens
1 roasted anaheim chili, chopped
1/2 bag baked tortilla chips

Combine all ingredients, except tortilla chips, in a large bowl.

Crush tortilla chips with your hands. **Stir** gently into salad. **Serve** immediately.

Mock Chicken with Spicy Fruit Salad

1 prepared recipe of Mock Chicken (*see recipe in Salads*)
1 mango, peeled and cut into 1/2-inch cubes
1 papaya, peeled, seeded, and cut into 1/2-inch cubes
1 pint strawberries, hulled and quartered
2 Tablespoons rice syrup (*or a pinch of stevia*)
1 red serrano or jalapeno chili, seeded and minced (*wear rubber gloves*)
2 Tablespoons mint leaves, minced
6 cups, approximately, mixed salad greens
1/4 red onion, thinly sliced into half moons
1 carrot, shredded
1 large rib celery, diced
1 Tablespoon fresh lemon juice
1 Tablespoon olive oil

Stir together mango, papaya, strawberries, syrup or stevia, and chili in a bowl. **Let** mixture stand for 10 minutes. **Stir** in mint.

Toss together salad greens, onion, carrot, and celery. **Whisk** together lemon juice and oil. **Combine** well with greens.

Place salad greens on 4 individual plates. **Divide** Mock Chicken. **Place** in center of plates.

Add a large dollop of fruit salsa on top.

Serve.

Egg Salad with Jalapeno and Cumin

*Serve with baked corn chips
for a light, zesty lunch*

1/3 cup vegan mayonnaise or Almonnaise (*see recipe in Condiments*)
1 Tablespoon fresh lemon juice, or to taste
1 Tablespoon Vogue Vege Base
3/4 teaspoon ground cumin, or to taste
1 package firm tofu, rinsed
1/2 cup celery, finely chopped
1/4 cup green onions, white and green parts, thinly sliced
1 1/2 teaspoons jalapeno pepper, seeded and minced
1-2 Tablespoons dill pickle, minced
sea salt to taste

Whisk together mayonnaise, lemon juice, Vogue, and cumin.

Crumble tofu. Add celery, onion, jalapeno, pickle, and salt.

Stir mixture until combined well.

Curried "Tuna" Salad with Coriander

Try this salad on a bed of mixed greens with peas, cashews, nori strips. Rim the plate with cucumber and tomato slices.

1 package tempeh
1/2 cup red onion, finely chopped
1/4 cup vegan mayonnaise or Almonnaise (*see recipe in Condiments*)
1/4 cup plain yogurt (*preferably vegan*)
2 teaspoons fresh lemon juice, or to taste
1 1/2 teaspoons curry powder, or to taste
1/3 cup celery, finely chopped
3 Tablespoons coriander, chopped, or to taste
sea salt to taste

Steam tempeh for 10 minutes. **Cool. Grate.**

Soak onion in bowl of ice and cold water for 10 minutes. **Drain** well.

Whisk together mayonnaise, yogurt, lemon juice, and curry powder.

Add onion, tempeh, celery, coriander, and salt.

Stir mixture until combined well.

Daddy's Favorite Salad

1 pound tofu, frozen
1/2 cup arame
2 cups green beans, sliced into bite-sized pieces
2 stalks celery, diced thin
2 cups red cabbage, shaved
1 bunch romaine
1 cup lentil sprouts
1 yellow bell pepper, diced
2 Tablespoons olive oil
1-2 Tablespoons Bragg Liquid Aminos
1/2 teaspoon dry mustard
1 heaping Tablespoon Vogue Vege Base
2 cloves garlic, minced
1/2 onion, sliced into half moons

Defrost tofu. **Squeeze** or wrap in towel for 30 minutes.

Soak arame in hot water for 15 minutes.

Steam green beans until crisp tender.

Place all veggies and tofu in large bowl.

Whisk oil, Braggs, mustard, and Vogue.

Sauté garlic and onion in a small amount of oil until onion is lightly browned.

Toss all ingredients well. **Serve.**

Ginger Mint "Ceviche"

1 package smoked tofu, cut in 1/4-inch cubes
1 lime, juiced
1 teaspoon lime peel, finely minced
1 Tablespoon ginger, finely minced
1 garlic clove, finely minced
2-4 small chilies, seeded and minced
2 Tablespoons cilantro, chopped
2 Tablespoons mint, chopped
1 green onion, chopped
1/2 red bell pepper, chopped
3 Tablespoons sesame or flax oil
1 teaspoon fresh nutmeg, grated
1/8-1/4 teaspoon curry paste
1/2 teaspoon sea salt
salad greens

Mix all ingredients well, except greens.

Refrigerate for at least one hour before serving.

Serve over bed of greens.

Oriental Salad with Smoked Tofu

*If you cannot find enoki mushrooms,
fresh shiitake would be my next choice,
though plain button mushrooms may be substituted.*

Salad:
3 cups wild rice, cooked or sprouted
1 package smoked tofu, cubed
1 cup fresh mung or soybean sprouts
1 red bell pepper, slivered
1 package enoki mushrooms
1/2 cup sliced almonds, toasted
1/4 cup green onions, sliced

Dressing:
3 Tablespoons red wine vinegar
1 Tablespoon Bragg Liquid Aminos
1-2 Tablespoons Oriental toasted sesame oil
1 Tablespoon rice syrup
pinch of red pepper flakes
1/2 teaspoon sea salt
1 Tablespoon fresh ginger, finely minced
2 teaspoons garlic, finely minced

Mix together salad ingredients.

Toss salad with dressing.

Serve.

Salad Dressings

*"The Earth is the Mother,
a living entity whose milk is
the corn from which the human
body is made."*

•*Ancient Hopi Wisdom*

Basic Vinaigrette Dressing

2 Tablespoons balsamic or red wine vinegar
1/4 cup olive oil
1/2 teaspoon basil, dried *(or 2 teaspoons fresh)*
pinch of red pepper flakes
pinch of salt

Mix all ingredients in jar. **Shake** well to blend.

Herbed Vinaigrette Dressing

2 Tablespoons lemon juice
1/2 teaspoon whole-grain prepared mustard
1/3 cup olive or flax oil
1 1/2 teaspoons parsley, minced
1 1/2 teaspoons snipped fresh chives
1 1/2 teaspoons tarragon, minced
1 1/2 teaspoon chervil, minced
sea salt to taste

Whisk first two ingredients. Add oil slowly, until emulsified. Stir in remaining ingredients.

Miso Vinaigrette Dressing

2 Tablespoons red miso
2 teaspoons Dijon or whole-grain prepared mustard
1 Tablespoon water
1 1/2 Tablespoons fresh lemon juice
1/4 cup sesame or flax oil
1 teaspoon fresh gingerroot, peeled and minced
1 scallion, minced

Mash together miso and mustard in a bowl. Whisk in water and lemon juice. **Add** oil in a stream, whisking. **Whisk** until emulsified. **Whisk** in gingerroot and scallion.

Basil Dressing

2 cups basil leaves, firmly packed
1/2 cup olive oil
6-8 sun-dried olives, pitted
2 garlic cloves
1 Tablespoon apple cider vinegar
1/4 cup vegetable stock
sea salt to taste

Blend all ingredients in blender until dressing is smooth.

Basil, Mint, and Orange Vinaigrette

1/2 cup packed fresh basil leaves, minced
1/2 cup packed fresh mint leaves, minced
1/4 teaspoon orange zest, freshly grated
1 Tablespoon fresh orange juice
1-2 teaspoons apple cider vinegar
1 garlic clove, minced
1/2 cup oil

Blend all ingredients in a blender until emulsified.

Cucumber Dill Sour Cream Dressing

1/2 cucumber, seeded and grated coarse (*about 1/2 cup*)
1/4 teaspoon sea salt
2 teaspoons whole-grain prepared mustard
1 Tablespoon apple cider vinegar or lemon juice
1/2 cup vegan sour cream
1/4 cup plain vegan yogurt
1 Tablespoon snipped fresh dill

Toss cucumber with salt. **Place** in a small sieve. **Set** over a bowl. **Let** sit 10 minutes.

Process remaining ingredients in blender until smooth. **Stir** in cucumber until combined.

Dried Tomato, Caper, and Olive Dressing

1/2 cup vegan mayonnaise or Almonnaise (*see recipe in Condiments*)
1 Tablespoon fresh lemon juice
2 sun-dried tomatoes, reconstituted in hot water and minced
1 Tablespoon bottled capers, drained and minced
1 teaspoon sun-dried olives, pitted and minced
2 Tablespoons water, or enough to thin dressing to desired consistency
sea salt to taste

Whisk together all ingredients in a bowl. **Add** salt to taste.

Sunflower Seed Dressing

1/3 cup raw sunflower seeds, lightly toasted
4 teaspoons apple cider vinegar
1/2 cup oil
5 teaspoons toasted sesame oil
sea salt to taste

Puree sunflower seeds with the vinegar, oils, and sea salt in a blender. **Add** 1 cup water in a stream. **Blend** until emulsified.

Eric's Favorite Dressing

Great over greens with sprouts, avocado, and toasted pumpkin seeds. For a heartier salad, dice up some marinated baked tofu (there are several packaged varieties).

1 heaping Tablespoon Vogue Vege Base
2 Tablespoons Bragg Liquid Aminos
juice of 1 lemon
1/4 cup olive oil
dry mustard to taste (*optional*)

Blend all ingredients well.

Garlic Mint Dressing

1 garlic clove, crushed
2 Tablespoons fresh lime juice
1 teaspoon whole-grain prepared mustard
1 1/2 teaspoons fresh mint, minced (*or 1/2 teaspoon dried*)
1/2 teaspoon rice syrup
1/4 teaspoon sea salt
1/3 cup flax or sesame oil

Process all ingredients in a blender or mini processor until emulsified.

Green Goddess Dressing

1/2 cup vegan mayonnaise or Almonnaise (*see recipe in Condiments*)
1/2 cup yogurt
1 Tablespoon lemon juice
1/4 cup parsley, minced
1 green onion, minced
1 garlic clove, minced

Mix all ingredients well.

Roasted Shallot Vinaigrette Dressing

4 large shallots
2 cloves Roasted Garlic (see recipe in Condiments)
1/3 cup sesame oil
1/3 cup olive oil
4-6 Tablespoons lemon juice
3/4 teaspoon sea salt
1/8 teaspoon dry mustard

Preheat oven to 375 degrees.

Place unpeeled shallots and garlic cloves into a casserole dish. **Cover.** **Roast** until very soft, about 15 minutes. **Cool. Peel.**

Combine remaining ingredients in a blender or food processor until thoroughly blended. **Adjust** seasonings, if desired.

Salad Mix:
Your favorite variety of greens
bell pepper
celery
sprouts (*try buckwheat!*)
Finely shaved red cabbage makes a pretty effect.

Lemon-Sesame Dressing

1/4 cup sesame butter
1/4 cup lemon juice
3/4 cup oil (*part olive and sesame or flax*)
1/4 cup water
1-2 teaspoons Bragg Liquid Aminos
1/4 teaspoon sea salt

Whisk all ingredients until emulsified.

Spiced Sesame Dressing

1/2 teaspoon whole cumin seeds
1/2 teaspoon whole coriander seeds
1/4 cup sesame butter
1/4 cup hot water
1-2 teaspoons apple cider vinegar
1/2 cup silken tofu
1 Tablespoon lemon juice
1 Tablespoon sesame or flax oil
sea salt to taste

Toast cumin and coriander seeds over moderate heat in a dry, small, heavy skillet. **Shake** skillet until spices are fragrant, about 2 minutes. **Cool** completely.

Grind seeds fine in a mortar and pestle or in a spice/coffee grinder.

Whisk together all ingredients in a bowl. **Add** sea salt to taste.

Thin with additional water, if desired.

Spicy Dressing

2 Tablespoons lemon juice
1 Tablespoon apple cider vinegar
1 garlic clove, minced
1 teaspoon fresh ginger, grated
3/4 teaspoon cumin, ground
1/4 teaspoon cayenne or chipotle pepper
1/4 cup olive oil

Whisk together all ingredients.

Raspberry, Orange, and Lemon Dressing

1/2 cup fresh orange juice
1/4 cup fresh lemon juice
1/2 cup raspberries
1/2 cup olive oil
pinch of cayenne or red pepper flakes
sea salt to taste

Process all ingredients in blender until smooth.

Mustard Dressing

2 Tablespoons prepared whole-grain mustard
2 Tablespoons apple cider vinegar
sea salt to taste
1/3 cup olive oil

Whisk together mustard, vinegar, and salt in a small bowl.

Add oil in a stream.

Whisk until emulsified.

Mustard Cream Dressing

1/4 cup dry toasted dulse, crumbled
1 Tablespoon fresh lemon juice
1 Tablespoon whole-grain prepared mustard, or to taste
2 teaspoons fresh parsley, minced
1/4 cup plain vegan yogurt
1/4 cup vegan mayonnaise
sea salt to taste

Whisk together all ingredients.

Mustard Garlic Dressing

1 garlic clove, minced
1/8 teaspoon sea salt
1 teaspoon apple cider vinegar
1 Tablespoon fresh lemon juice
1/2 teaspoon whole-grain prepared mustard
1/4 cup olive or flax oil

Mash garlic and salt to a paste.

Process all ingredients in blender until smooth.

Oriental Dressing

2 Tablespoons rice vinegar
1 Tablespoon oil
1 Tablespoon Oriental sesame oil
1 Tablespoon Bragg Liquid Aminos
1/2 teaspoon dry mustard
2 teaspoons ginger, finely minced
1/2 teaspoon garlic, finely minced
1 Tablespoon green onion, finely minced
1 teaspoon sweetener

Combine all ingredients in a jar. **Shake** vigorously.

Variation:
3 Tablespoons apple cider vinegar
2 Tablespoons Oriental sesame oil
2 Tablespoons oil
pinch of red pepper flakes
1/2 teaspoon salt
2 Tablespoons cilantro, minced
2 Tablespoons green onions, minced
1 Tablespoon ginger, minced
2 garlic cloves, minced.

Breads

"Everywhere people ask, 'What can I actually do?'
The answer is as simple as it is disconcerting—we can,
each of us, work to put our own inner house in order.
The guidance we need for this work cannot be found
in Science or technology, the value of which utterly
depends on the ends they serve; but it can still
be found in the traditional wisdom of human kind."

•E.F. Schumacher
Small is Beautiful
Harper & Row, 1989

Before getting started in this section, please take a few minutes to read these notes:

•*Oil choices*: My personal favorite is coconut oil, though other mild-flavored, unrefined oils can be substituted. Read the "Fats" Section for more information on special oils. If you have problems finding coconut oil in stores, you may order directly from Omega Nutrition at 800-661-3529. Keep in mind that when using coconut oil, slightly decrease the amount used by approximately one-quarter measure.

•*Stevia*: Can enhance the effect of other sweeteners. Adding stevia to recipes as a dietary supplement can help reduce the amount of sweetener you would need. In baked goods I use the ground leaf.

•*Flours:*

> •*Kamut* and spelt are relatives of wheat, though most people tolerate them better.
> •*Amaranth* is used in small amounts with other flours to add flavor. Barley is a flour I usually couple with another flour.
> •*Buckwheat* is very dense. Use in small amounts with other flours. Great in pancakes.
> •*Cornmeal* adds flavor and texture to quick breads.
> •*Garbanzo* is a good wheat replacement, though I would use it with another flour, such as rice.
> •*Oat* flour has a sweet, nutty taste, though dense and should be mixed with another flour.
> •*Quinoa* has a strong flavor and is best used in small amounts.
> *Rice* flour lends wonderful flavor and texture.

- *Rye* flour is dense and hardy. It works well with cornmeal or can be used alone.
- *Soy* flour is dense, so use in small amounts or mix with other grains.
- *Teff* is rich in taste and is good alone, or in combination with other grains. Use in quick breads.

Pumpkin-Apricot Bread

This makes a moist, dense loaf—delicious warm or cooled

2 cups flour (*spelt, pastry, or barley, or combination*)
1 teaspoon baking soda
1 teaspoon baking powder
1/2 teaspoon sea salt
1/4 teaspoon cinnamon, ground
1/4 teaspoon ginger, ground
1/4 teaspoon cardamom, ground
1/4 teaspoon coriander, ground
3/4 cup barley malt syrup
1 teaspoon stevia leaf
1/2 cup dried apricots, coarsely chopped
2 cups pumpkin puree
1 Tablespoon egg replacer, dissolved in 4 Tablespoons water
1/3 cup orange juice
1 Tablespoon orange zest, grated

Preheat oven to 350 degrees.

Lightly grease and flour a loaf pan.

Combine dry ingredients and apricots in a large bowl. **Mix** thoroughly.

Whisk together wet ingredients in another bowl. **Stir** into dry ingredients until liquid is absorbed.

Transfer batter to loaf pan.

Bake for 55-60 minutes, or until a toothpick inserted in center comes out clean.

*If it browns too quickly in oven, cover it halfway through baking.

Apple, Apricot, and Raisin Muffins

3 Tablespoons flax seeds, ground
1/2 cup water
1 3/4 cups spelt, barley, or wheat pastry flour
1 1/4 cups oat flour
1 Tablespoon grain coffee
1 Tablespoon baking powder
1 teaspoon baking soda
1 teaspoon cinnamon, ground
1/8 teaspoon sea salt
1 apple, grated
1/2 cup dried apricots, diced
1/3 cup raisins
1/3 cup barley malt syrup
1/3 cup oil
1 cup apple juice

Preheat oven to 375 degrees.

Stir flax seeds into water. Set aside.

Combine dry ingredients. **Stir** in apple, apricots, and raisins.

Combine wet ingredients in separate bowl, including flax seed mixture. **Whisk** until frothy.

Stir wet ingredients into dry, just until all flour is absorbed.

Spoon into papered muffin tins. **Bake** on middle shelf of oven until tops are lightly browned, and a toothpick inserted in center comes out clean, approximately 15-20 minutes.

Cool muffins on rack for 10 minutes before serving.

Banana Muffins

Light and not overly-sweet

1 1/2 Tablespoons flax seed
1/4 cup water
Approximately 2 1/2 ripe bananas, mashed
2 Tablespoons brown rice syrup
1/3 cup oil
1 teaspoon vanilla
1 1/3 cups wheat pastry, barley, spelt (*or combine with millet or rice flour*)
2 teaspoons baking powder
1/4 teaspoon nutmeg, freshly grated
1/3 cup pecans or walnuts, coarsely chopped

Preheat oven to 350 degrees.

Grind flax seeds. Add to water. **Let** sit for a few minutes.

Add remaining wet ingredients.

Combine dry ingredients into wet until liquid is just absorbed.

Pour into oiled or papered muffin tins.

Bake for approximately 35 minutes, or until a toothpick inserted in center comes out clean.

Cool muffins on rack for 10 minutes before serving.

Banana Date Muffins

3 Tablespoons flax seeds
1/2 cup water
1 3/4 cups oat flour
1 1/2 cups barley flour
1 Tablespoon baking powder
1 teaspoon baking soda
1/2 teaspoon cinnamon, ground
1/2 teaspoon nutmeg, ground
1/8 teaspoon sea salt
1 1/2 bananas
1/2 cup dates
1/4 cup coconut oil
1 cup apple juice

Preheat oven to 375 degrees.

Lightly oil muffin tins or use paper cups.

Grind flax seeds. **Place** in blender with 1/2 cup water. **Let** sit.

Combine dry ingredients in a large bowl.

Process all liquid ingredients in blender until smooth (including bananas and dates).

Stir wet ingredients into dry ingredients until liquid is absorbed.

Pour into prepared tins.

Bake for 15-20 minutes, or until a toothpick inserted in center comes out clean.

Carrot-Date Muffins

Soak overnight:
1/3 cup water
1/4 cup dates, chopped
1/4 cup rolled oats

Next morning, add:
3 Tablespoons flax seed, ground, mixed with 1/2 cup water
1 cup grated carrots
1/3 cup oil
1 teaspoon stevia leaf
1/2 cup walnuts, chopped

Combine in separate bowl:
1 1/2 cups flour (*barley, spelt, or rye*)
1 Tablespoon baking powder
1 teaspoon salt
1/4 teaspoon nutmeg, ground
1 1/2 teaspoon cinnamon, ground
2 Tablespoons soy milk powder

Preheat oven to 350 degrees.

Stir dry ingredients with wet ingredients. **Mix** until barely absorbed.

Pour into oiled or papered muffin tins.

Bake for approximately 20 minutes, or until a toothpick inserted in center comes out clean.

Cool muffins on rack for 10 minutes before serving.

Date and Oatmeal Yogurt Muffins

1/3 cup walnuts
2 Tablespoons flax seeds, ground
1/4 cup water
3/4 cup spelt flour
3/4 cup rolled oats
1 1/2 teaspoons baking powder
1/2 teaspoon sea salt
1/8 teaspoon cinnamon, ground
1/3 cup pitted dates, chopped
1/4 cup barley malt syrup
1/2 cup plain yogurt (*preferably vegan*)
1/2 cup vegan milk
2 Tablespoons oil

Preheat oven to 400 degrees.

Toast walnuts lightly. **Chop** fine.

Stir flax seeds into water. **Set** aside.

Stir together dry ingredients in bowl, including dates and walnuts.

Mix wet ingredients in another bowl.

Stir wet into dry *until just combined*.

Divide batter among 6 paper-lined 1/2 cup muffin tins.

Bake for 30 minutes, or until a toothpick inserted in center comes out clean.

Cool muffins on rack for 10 minutes before serving.

Lemon Cranberry Muffins

Toasted almonds compliment the lemon and cranberries in this recipe wonderfully!

3 Tablespoons flaxseeds, ground
1/2 cup water
1 3/4 cups barley flour
1 1/4 cups oat flour
1 Tablespoon baking powder
1 teaspoon baking soda
1 teaspoon cinnamon, ground
1/2 teaspoon nutmeg, ground
1/4 teaspoon sea salt
2 teaspoon stevia leaf
1/3 cup toasted almonds, coarsely chopped
1 cup cranberries
1/3 cup oil
1/2 cup lemon juice
1/2 cup apple juice
2 teaspoons lemon zest, finely minced

Preheat oven to 375 degrees.

Mix flaxseeds and water. Set aside.

Mix all ingredients, except oil, lemon, and apple juice in large bowl.

Blend together oil and lemon juice.

Mix all liquids (including flax seed mixture) into dry ingredients until just combined.

Pour into oiled or papered muffin tins.

Bake for 20 minutes, or until a toothpick inserted in center comes out clean.

Cool muffins on rack for 10 minutes before serving.

Squash-Corn Muffins

One of my favorites

1/2 cup oil
1/2 cup brown rice syrup
1 1/2 cups squash or pumpkin puree*
1 cup water
2 1/4 cups rye, barley, or oat flour
1 cup cornmeal
1 Tablespoon baking powder
1 teaspoon cinnamon, ground
1/2 teaspoon ginger, ground
1/4 teaspoon cloves, ground
1/4 teaspoon nutmeg, ground

Preheat oven to 375 degrees.

Combine wet and dry ingredients separately. **Blend** together just until liquid is absorbed.

Pour into oiled or papered muffin tins.

Bake for approximately 30 minutes, or until liquid is absorbed.

*I have used butternut, kabocha, or pumpkin with wonderful results. You need to half a squash. Scoop out seeds. Cook cut side down on a baking sheet, at 350 degrees until soft to touch, 30-45 minutes. Cool. Scoop out flesh. Either hand mash or run through processor for a few seconds.

Zucchini Muffins

1 1/2 cups zucchini, coarsely grated, tightly packed
3 Tablespoons flax seeds
1/2 cup water
1 1/2 cups barley flour
1 cup ground oats
1 Tablespoon baking powder
2 teaspoons cinnamon, ground
1 teaspoon ginger, ground
1/4 teaspoon cloves, ground
2 teaspoon stevia leaf
scant 1/2 teaspoon sea salt
1/2 cup nuts, coarsely chopped
1/2 cup raisins
2/3 cup apple juice
1/3 cup oil
1 teaspoon vanilla

Preheat oven to 375 degrees.

Place zucchini on a couple sheets of paper towels to absorb some of the liquid.

Grind the flax seeds in a coffee grinder. **Add** to water. **Let** sit.

Combine all dry ingredients.

Add all liquid ingredients to flax mixture.

Add dry ingredients.

Pour into oiled or papered muffin tins.

Bake approximately 20 minutes, or until toothpick inserted in center comes out clean.

Wheat-Free Muffins

A very versatile batter—be creative!

1/4 cup flax seeds
3/4 cup water
3/4 cup oil
3/4 cup rice syrup
1 cup vegan milk
2 cups barley flour
1 3/4 cups oat flour
1 1/4 cups cornmeal
1 teaspoon baking soda
1 Tablespoon baking powder

Preheat oven to 350 degrees.

Grind flax seeds. Add to water. **Let** sit a few minutes.

Add remaining wet ingredients.

Combine dry ingredients.

Stir into wet.

Spoon into oiled or papered muffin tins.

Bake for 35 minutes, or until a toothpick inserted in center comes out clean.

Variations:
•For a sweet muffin, add 1 teaspoon vanilla to the liquids. And add 2 cups chopped fruit or nuts or a combination of both.

•For a savory muffin, add 2 cups of finely chopped vegetables.

Sesame Biscuits

2 1/4 cups barley flour
1/2 cup soy flour
3 Tablespoons sesame seeds, toasted
3/4 teaspoon sea salt
1 Tablespoon baking powder
1/4 cup coconut oil
2 Tablespoons barley malt syrup

Preheat oven to 425 degrees.

Lightly oil a baking sheet.

Combine dry ingredients. **Stir** in liquids to create a soft dough.

Knead dough briefly. **Dust** a flat surface with flour. **Roll** out to 1/2-inch thickness.

Place on baking sheet. **Cut** into 2-inch squares.

Bake until lightly browned, approximately 14-16 minutes.

Corn Cakes

I love corn muffins, and these are the best whole foods rendition that I've come across.

Mix:
1 1/2 cups brown rice, cooked
2 cups cornmeal
1 1/2 cups boiling water

when cooled,

Add:
3/4 cup oil
3/4 cup rice syrup or barley malt syrup
2 cups vegan milk
1/2 cup plus 1 Tablespoon flax seeds, ground, and added to 1 3/4 cups water

In another bowl, mix:
1 1/2 cups barley flour
4 cups cornmeal
2 Tablespoons baking powder
2 teaspoons sea salt

Preheat oven to 400 degrees.

Combine the dry ingredients with the liquid mixture.

Spoon into muffin tins or square pans (make sure these are well oiled).

For muffins : **Bake** for 25 minutes. *For cakes: Bake* at 375 degrees for 35-40 minutes, or until toothpick inserted in center comes out clean.

This makes 24 muffins or 2, 8-inch square cakes. You can easily freeze these in individual serving sizes. Keeps well. Makes great toast or grilled in a pan with a little oil. You can also split the recipe in half.

Oatcakes

Simple stove-top biscuits—ready in 10 minutes

2 cups oat flour*
1/3 cup oil
1/4 teaspoon sea salt
1 Tablespoon baking powder
1 1/4 cups water

Mix all ingredients.

Lightly oil skillet. **Heat** on medium heat.

Drop spoonfuls of batter into skillet. **Cover** with lid.

Cook until golden on both sides.

Serve immediately.

*Oat flour is simply oats ground in spice or coffee grinder.

Side Dishes

*"Pleasant it looked,
this newly created world
along the entire length and breadth
of the Earth, our Grandmother,
extended the green reflection
of her covering
and the escaping odors
were pleasant to inhale."*

•*Winnebago, p. 238 of Turner
The Portable North American Indian Reader*

Baked Tomatoes

Preheat oven to 350 degrees. **Cut** off tops of tomatoes.

Place in baking pan. **Bake** at 350 degrees for 30 minutes.

Sprinkle with tarragon, parsley and coriander during the last 5 minutes.

Broccoli Stuffed Tomatoes

2 large tomatoes, halved
1 Tablespoon olive oil
1 medium onion, minced
1 small bunch of broccoli, minced (*approximately 3-4 cups*)
2 Tablespoons fresh basil, minced
2 teaspoons Bragg Liquid Aminos
vegan cheese cubes (*optional*)

Dressing:
2 Tablespoons olive oil
1 Tablespoon apple cider vinegar
2 Tablespoon fresh basil, minced
sea salt to taste
tomato centers

Preheat oven to 375 degrees.

Scoop out the centers of tomatoes. **Reserve** centers and shells.

Sauté onion in oil until soft. **Add** broccoli. **Cook** covered for 5-8 minutes.

Add basil and Braggs. Blend in processor or blender until smooth. Add cheese, if desired. Divide mixture between tomato shells.

Place on a lightly oiled pan. Cover. Bake for 10 minutes, or until cheese just begins to bubble.

Process dressing in blender. Serve along side.

Carrots in Orange Sauce

Black sesame seeds make a dramatic presentation

Sauce:
2 cloves garlic, minced
2 teaspoons ginger, minced
1/2 teaspoons orange peel, grated
1 cup fresh orange juice
1 cup vegetable stock
1/3 cup red wine vinegar
1/4 cup rice syrup
1 1/2 teaspoons Bragg Liquid Aminos
1/4 teaspoons sea salt
1/4 star anise (*optional*)

1 pound medium carrots, diced
1 Tablespoon sesame seeds, toasted

Boil sauce ingredients. **Cook,** uncovered, until sauce just begins to thicken, about 15 minutes.

Remove anise if using.

Cook further, until it turns a caramel color. **Sauce** is ready when a spoon leaves a path in it.

Toss in carrots.

Sprinkle with sesame seeds.

Ginger Carrots

4 carrots, sliced
1 teaspoon sesame oil
1 teaspoon ginger, grated
sea salt to taste
1 Tablespoon arrowroot diluted in 1/2 cup water
1 Tablespoon Vogue Vege Base

Sauté carrots for 3 minutes. **Add** ginger and salt. **Cook** 20-25 minutes on low until tender.

Add arrowroot and Vogue. **Stir.**

Simmer for 2 minutes.

Serve.

Citrus Spaghetti Squash Noodles

Spaghetti squash, quartered

Sauce:
1 Tablespoon garlic, minced
2 Tablespoons olive oil
3 Tablespoons Bragg Liquid Aminos
2 Tablespoons brown rice vinegar
2 Tablespoons toasted sesame oil
1 Tablespoon brown rice syrup
pinch of red pepper flakes (*optional*)
2 teaspoons orange peel, finely grated
1/2 cup green onions, minced
1/4 cup toasted sesame seeds*

Preheat oven to 350 degrees.

Scoop out seeds in spaghetti squash. **Place** cut side down on a baking sheet. **Bake** for 30-45 minutes. (Should be soft—but not mushy!—when you press a finger on the skin.)

Cool for a few minutes. **Scrape** out flesh with a fork into a bowl. **Set** aside.

Sauté garlic briefly in a small pan. **Add** remaining ingredients. **Bring** to boil.

Remove from heat. **Add** to squash. **Toss** well.

*To toast sesame seeds, place pan over high heat. Add sesame seeds. Shake pan until seeds start to turn light brown. Careful! They will burn easily. Tip out into a small bowl immediately. Set aside until ready to use.

Lemon Bulgur Mounds with Chives

heaping 1/2 cup scallions, thinly sliced
1/4 cup olive oil
2 1/4 cups bulgur
zest of 1 1/2 lemons, removed with vegetable peeler, making sure no white pith is included, minced fine
3 1/3 cups vegetable broth, hot
1 cup fresh chives, thinly sliced
3/4 teaspoons lecithin
sea salt to taste

Cook scallion in oil in a kettle over moderately low heat. **Stir** until softened.

Add bulgur and zest. **Stir** for 1 minute.

Add broth. **Cover. Let** stand for approximately 10-15 minutes, or until liquid is absorbed.

Fluff bulgur with fork. **Stir** in sliced chives, lecithin, and sea salt.

Cover. Let sit for one half hour before serving.

Nori Rolls

1 package smoked tofu, thinly sliced
4 cups cooked brown rice
umeboshi plum paste (*optional*)
miso or rice vinegar (*optional*)
sesame seeds, dry toasted
Bragg Liquid Aminos
fresh or steamed, thinly sliced vegetables (*such as cucumber, avocado, collard leaves, carrots, broccoli, garlic, green onions, etc.*)
Nori sheets, toasted or not

Place a sheet of nori on a small bamboo mat or heavy cloth napkin.

Spread 1/2 cup of rice over the sheet, leaving a 2-inch edge uncovered at the end of the sheet.

Arrange filling in a line across the middle on the rice.

Roll the nori in the mat.

Place roll with seam down to seal.

Slice 1-inch thick.

Rice Balls:

Shape cooked brown rice into balls the size of ping-pong balls. Dip hands in cold, salted water to prevent sticking. Roll balls in toasted sesame seeds, mashed and cooked beans, or chopped nuts. Wrap in toasted nori sheets.

Oriental Quinoa Pilaf

Quinoa has been a staple food to the natives of the South American Andes since 3000 B.C. The ancient Incas held it sacred, calling it "the mother grain."

2 cups vegetable broth
2 Tablespoons Bragg Liquid Aminos
2 teaspoons orange peel, grated
pinch red pepper flakes
1-2 Tablespoons oil
2-3 garlic cloves, minced
1/2 onion, diced
1 cup quinoa
1/2 cup green onions, chopped
1/2 cup red bell pepper, chopped
1/4 cup raisins, chopped (*optional*)
3 Tablespoons cilantro, minced
1/4 cup sesame seeds, toasted

Combine broth, Braggs, orange peel and pepper flakes. Set sauce aside.

Sauté garlic and onion in oil.

Add quinoa.

Pour in sauce. Cover. Simmer until all liquid is absorbed.

Add sesame seeds, green onions, red bell pepper, raisins, and cilantro to quinoa.

Serve immediately.

Pine Nut, Pinto Bean, and Scallion Pilaf

1 cup brown rice
2 cups vegetable stock
1 cup cooked pinto beans
1/2 cup scallions, including green tops, chopped
1/4 cup pine nuts, lightly toasted
1/4 teaspoon lecithin
sea salt to taste

Cook rice in vegetable stock. **Toss** together all ingredients.

Serve.

Special Mashed Potatoes

5 medium potatoes, diced
1 stalk celery, minced
1/2 onion, minced
1/4 cup parsley, minced
1 bulb Roasted Garlic (*see recipe in Condiments*)
vegan milk
2 Tablespoons olive oil or Butter (*see recipe in Condiments*)
sea salt to taste

Simmer potatoes, celery, onion, and parsley in just enough water to cover. **Drain** when fork tender. **Reserve** broth for future use.

Squeeze the roasted garlic cloves into potato mixture.

Mash the potatoes well, either with a hand masher or mixer, starting with 1/4 cup vegan milk. **Add** olive oil and sea salt as you mash. **Add** more milk to achieve desired consistency.

Serve immediately.

Suzhou Potatoes

3 large potatoes
1 Tablespoon Oriental sesame oil
1 Tablespoon curry powder
1 Tablespoon Vogue Vege Base
1/2 teaspoon sea salt
oil
4 cloves garlic, finely minced
1/2 red bell pepper, cut in slivers
1/2 cup green onions, minced

Wash, dry, but do not peel potatoes. **Cut** into 1/4-inch cubes (enough to make 4 cups). **Rinse** well. **Cover** potatoes with cold water until ready to cook. **Set** aside.

Mix the sesame oil, curry powder, Vogue, and salt in a small bowl. **Set** aside.

Drain and pat dry potatoes.

Heat oil in large pan over medium high heat.

Add the potatoes. **Brown** on all sides.

Add the garlic. **Cook** briefly.

Add sesame oil mixture. **Mix** with a small amount of water to loosen (no more than 1-2 Tablespoons). **Cook** until liquid is absorbed.

Add red bell and green onions.

Serve immediately.

Ratatouille

1/3 cup olive oil
1 pound eggplant, cut into 1/2-inch pieces
4 medium onions, chopped coarse
2 green bell peppers, cut into 1/2-inch pieces
2 garlic cloves, minced and mashed to a paste
1/2 teaspoon dried oregano
1/2 teaspoon dried thyme
1/2 cup packed fresh basil leaves, torn into pieces
2 pounds tomatoes, chopped coarse
sea salt to taste

Heat the oil in a heavy kettle over moderately high heat until it is hot, but not smoking.

Sauté the eggplant. **Stir** until golden. **Reduce** heat to moderately low.

Add remaining ingredients, except basil leaves and tomatoes. **Cook** mixture over low heat for approximately 15 minutes, or until the eggplant is just tender.

Add tomatoes and basil. **Add** sea salt to taste.

Cook until just heated through.

Serve hot or at room temperature.

Spinach and Broccoli

My friend, A.J., gave me this delicious recipe

2 Tablespoons oil
1/2 teaspoon whole cumin
1/2 teaspoon whole mustard seed
1 large onion, chopped
1 teaspoon turmeric
2 Tablespoons fresh ginger, grated
4 cloves garlic, minced
sea salt to taste
4 black cardamom
2 cinnamon sticks
1 teaspoon garam masala
4 curry leaves
1 pound broccoli, finely chopped
1 bell pepper, diced
1/2 bunch cilantro, minced
1 serrano chili, finely minced
2 Tablespoons flour
1 large tomato, chopped
5 bunches of spinach, washed and chopped

Add oil to a large stock pot. **Sauté** whole cumin and mustard seeds.

Add onions and brown lightly. **Add** turmeric. **Sauté** for one minute.

Add ginger, garlic, sea salt, and remaining spices.

Add broccoli, bell pepper, cilantro, and chili.

Add flour. Add just enough water to prevent scorching.

Cook for 30 minutes.

Add tomato and spinach. **Simmer** for 5 minutes.

Discard any spice solids (such as cinnamon stick, curry leaves, etc.) before serving.

Wilted Spinach

*People who ate spinach, collards, and
kale at least once a day cut their
risk of macular degeneration by 43 percent.*

3 large cloves garlic, minced
1 Tablespoon olive oil
2 large bunches spinach, stems removed, washed thoroughly
juice of 1/2 lemon
sea salt to taste, if desired

Sauté garlic in oil until it just begins to brown.

Add spinach. **Cover** immediately.

Remove from heat. **Stir** spinach after 30 seconds.

Add lemon juice and salt.

Serve immediately.

Cooking hardier greens such as kale or collards is not difficult. My daughters favorite method is throwing a handful of kale into a pot with a splash of water. Cover and simmer 5 minutes, splash with a little Braggs before serving.

Winter Vegetables with Horseradish Dill Sauce

3 pounds small red potatoes, quartered and reserved in bowl of cold water
1 1/2 pounds brussel sprouts, trimmed and halved
3/4 pound parsnips, cut diagonally 1-inch thick
3/4 pound carrot, cut diagonally 1-inch thick
3/4 pound small turnips, cut into sixths

Sauce:
3/4 cup oil (*use half olive and half flax with 1/2 teaspoon lecithin granules, or try half oil and half butter from butter recipe*)
3 Tablespoons fresh horseradish, grated (*fresh is best, but bottled can be used*)
3 Tablespoons apple cider vinegar
3 Tablespoons fresh dill, minced
sea salt to taste

Prepare sauce:
Stir sauce ingredients together in a small bowl. Set aside.

Place vegetable steamer over boiling water. **Steam** vegetables separately until they are just tender.

Toss veggies with sauce mixture in a large bowl or pan.

Serve immediately, or keep covered and warm in a 200 degree oven.

Tender Thai Vegetables

1/2 cucumber
oil
1 small eggplant, sliced into 1/2-inch cubes
8 ounces button mushrooms, quartered
1 medium zucchini, diced
1 Tablespoon garlic, minced
1 Tablespoon ginger, finely minced
2 shallots, minced
1/4 cup fresh cilantro, chopped
1/2 cup green onions chopped
1 medium tomato, diced
1 Tablespoon arrowroot
juice of 1 lime

Sauce:
1 cup vegetable stock
1 Tablespoon toasted sesame oil
1 Tablespoon smooth peanut butter
1 Tablespoon Bragg Liquid Aminos
Thai curry paste, red or green (*start with 1/8-1/4 teaspoon; adjust to your heat tolerance*)

Prepare sauce:
Combine vegetable stock with sesame oil, peanut butter, Braggs, and curry paste. Set aside.

Cut cucumber in half lengthwise. **Scoop** out seeds. **Cut** into 1/2-inch cubes.

Sauté all vegetables, except cucumber and tomato, in a small amount of oil in a hot wok or frying pan. **Stir** fry for approximately 2-4 minutes.

Add sauce to vegetables. **Simmer** until eggplant is very tender, approximately 15 minutes.

Add cucumber and tomato. **Stir** in arrowroot mixed with water (just enough to dissolve). **Simmer** until thickened. **Remove** from heat. **Add** lime juice.

Serve immediately.

Spanish Rice

1 large ripe tomato, pureed (*about 1 1/4 cups*)
2 large onions, chopped fine
1 large garlic clove, minced
1 large bell pepper, chopped fine
1 Tablespoon balsamic vinegar
1 teaspoon oregano
1 teaspoon paprika
1/4 teaspoon crushed red pepper flakes
1/2 teaspoon sea salt
1 1/2 cups long-grain brown rice, rinsed
1/2 cup fresh parsley, minced and tightly packed
1/2 cup olives, coarsely chopped

Add tomato puree, plus enough water to make 3 cups of liquid to pan.

Add onion, garlic, and pepper. **Stir** until mixture begins to bubble.

Add vinegar, oregano, paprika, crushed red pepper, and salt. **Bring** to a boil over high heat.

Stir in rice.

Reduce heat. **Cover. Simmer** until almost all liquid has been absorbed, about 45 minutes.

Turn off heat. **Let** stand, covered, for a few minutes.

Stir in parsley and olives.

Entrees

"We are so far removed from the Earth, our Mother, that eating is no longer a conscious act. Nourishment can only be had by awareness, feeding our bodies and souls. Each thought, each action in the sunlight of awareness becomes sacred. In this light, no boundary exists between the sacred and the profane…"

•*Thich Nhat Hanh,*
Peace is Every Step
(New York Bantam, 1991)

Breakfast

1 apple, grated
1 teaspoon lemon juice
1/2 cup vegan yogurt
1 Tablespoon sunflower seeds
1/2 cup cooked grains (*oat, millet, etc.*)

Toss apple with lemon juice.

Add other ingredients.

Serve immediately.

Cream of Rice Cereal

1/2 cup rice
2 cups water
vegan milk (*optional*)

Grind rice finely in a spice or coffee grinder.

Bring water just to boil. **Turn** down water to low. **Whisk** in rice.

Continue whisking for a few minutes. **Stir** often for 5 more minutes. (Cereal will thicken considerably).

Serve hot with or without vegan milk.

Quicky Oats

1/2 cup oat groats or steel-cut oats
1 1/4 cup hot water

Place in thermos. **Let** sit overnight. **Ready** to eat or process briefly in blender.

Cashew French Toast

*This is a delicious alternative to egg-based batters.
Serve with maple syrup or brown rice syrup (my preference).*

1 cup cashews
1 cup water
1/2 teaspoon nutmeg, ground
1/2 teaspoon vanilla
1/4-1/2 teaspoon Bragg Liquid Aminos
1/8 teaspoon stevia powder (adds enough sweetness to where my daughters do not ask for syrup)
8 slices whole grain bread

Process all ingredients, except bread, in blender until smooth.

Lightly oil a non-stick pan. **Place** on a medium-high flame.

Pour cashew mixture onto a pie plate.

Dip a slice of bread into mixture, covering both sides (do not soak bread).

Place in heated pan.

Cook each toast well.

Variation:
Add 1/4 teaspoon maple flavoring, 1/2 teaspoon cinnamon and 1/2 banana.

Do not be tempted to check the side being cooked too soon. Wait at least 2-3 minutes until cashew mixture has sufficiently dried. It will be much easier to flip.

My Favorite Scrambler

1 Tablespoon olive oil
1 medium onion, chopped
4 garlic cloves, minced
handful spinach, chopped
handful mushrooms, sliced
3-4 artichoke hearts, chopped (*optional*)
1/2 red bell pepper, chopped
1 pound tofu, drained and crumbled
1/2 teaspoon oregano
1/4 teaspoon turmeric
1 tomato, chopped
1/2 sheet nori sea vegetable, finely shredded (*or 1 Tablespoon dulse flakes*)
Bragg Liquid Aminos, to taste

Sauté onion, garlic, spinach, mushrooms, artichoke, pepper, tofu, oregano, and turmeric in oil.

Add tomato, along with nori and Braggs.

Serve.

Waffles

I enjoy these with "Butter" (see recipe in Condiments) and sprinkled with stevia and cinnamon.

1 cup millet
1/2 cup brown rice
1/2 cup oat or rye groats
1 1/2 cups water
1 heaping Tablespoon coconut oil
1/4 teaspoon stevia powder
1 teaspoon vanilla (*optional*)
1 cup water

Soak grains in water overnight. **Drain. Place** in blender with remaining ingredients. **Process** until smooth. **Pour** into prepared waffle iron.

Pancakes

1/2 cup oats, ground if desired
3/4 cup buckwheat
1/2 cup cornmeal
1 teaspoon baking powder
1 teaspoon stevia leaf
1/4 cup coconut oil
1 3/4 cups vegan milk

Mix dry ingredients into wet. Let sit for five minutes. **Warm** a non-stick pan on medium heat. **Pour** batter into pan to make the size pancakes you prefer. **Wait** approximately 2 minutes, or until you see bubbles forming on top of pancakes. **Flip** and brown other side. **Serve** with syrup of your choice.

Pancakes #2

These are like a dense, chewy, stove-top muffin.

1/2 cup ground oats
1/2 cup buckwheat
1/2 cup spelt
2 Tablespoons flax, ground
1/4 cup pecan meal
1 teaspoon baking powder
1 teaspoon stevia leaf
1/4 teaspoon nutmeg
1/4 cup coconut oil
1 3/4 cups oat or other vegan milk
1/4 teaspoon maple flavoring
1/2 teaspoon vanilla

Mix dry and wet ingredients separately. **Combine** together. Let sit 5 minutes. **Warm** a non-stick pan on medium heat. **Pour** batter into pan to make the size pancakes you prefer. **Wait** approximately 2 minutes, or until you see bubbles forming on top of pancakes. **Flip** and brown other side. **Serve** with syrup of your choice.

Sandwich Suggestions

vegan mayonnaise or Almonnaise (*see recipe in Condiments*)
cauliflower, chopped
carrot, shredded
red cabbage, shredded
dill pickle, minced
onions, sautéed in BBQ sauce

mock egg or tuna salad
avocado
tomato
mung bean sprouts
cucumber

corn
black beans
cilantro
rice
roasted bell pepper

roasted bell pepper
tofu (*frozen and defrosted*) marinated in Italian Dressing
tomato
soy mozzarella

cucumber
leftover curried vegetables

1 carrot, shredded
1 Tablespoon nutritional yeast
1 Tablespoon vegan mayonnaise
1 small pickle, minced
Combine well and layer on bread with sunflower seeds, 1 sheet of nori, tomato, and sprouts.

cauliflower
rice

vegan mayonnaise or Almonnaise (*see recipe in Condiments*)
avocado
carrot, shredded
tomato, sliced
sprouts
romaine lettuce
pumpkin seeds, lightly toasted
whole grain bread

1 cup sunflower seeds, soaked overnight, drained
1/4 cup both parsley and sesame butter
2-4 Tablespoons lemon juice
1 carrot, chopped
2 green onions
1 teaspoon herb of choice
1 Tablespoon Vogue Vege Base
2 Tablespoons nutritional yeast (*optional*)
sea salt to taste
process until smooth in processor. Roll in Nori sheet or on bread.

Reubens

1 package tempeh
2 Tablespoons apple cider vinegar
1/4 cup water
1 1/2 teaspoons Bragg Liquid Aminos
1/2 teaspoon toasted sesame oil
1/2 teaspoon garlic powder
1/2 teaspoon powdered ginger
whole-grain prepared mustard
4 slices bread
soy, or other mozzarella-or Swiss-style vegan cheese

Coleslaw:
1 carrot, shredded
1/4 head cabbage, shredded
1/3 cup vegan mayonnaise
1 pickle, diced fine
2 Tablespoons sun-dried tomatoes, reconstituted and finely minced

Preheat oven to broil.

Slice tempeh so that you have 2 thin pieces. **Cut** each piece in half. **Steam** for 10 minutes.

Place vinegar, water, Braggs, oil, garlic powder, and ginger in shallow pan.

Add tempeh. **Marinate** for at least one hour.

Sauté tempeh in a small amount of oil until browned on both sides. Set aside.

Prepare coleslaw.

Spread mustard on 4 slices of bread.

Layer with coleslaw, then tempeh. **Top** with a slice of vegan cheese.

Place under a broiler briefly, if desired.

Spaghetti Squash and Green Beans

1 squash, quartered and seeded
1 onion, chopped
1 Tablespoon garlic, minced
1 pound green beans, ends cut and bean halved
2 Tablespoons olive oil
1/4 teaspoon thyme
1/2 teaspoon sage
2 Tablespoons Vogue Vege Base
1/2 cup water
2 Tablespoons lemon juice
1/4-1/2 teaspoon sea salt
2 large tomatoes, chopped
1/2 cup pumpkin seeds, toasted*

Preheat oven to 350 degrees.

Place cut side of squash down on baking sheet. **Bake** for approximately 45 minutes. **Cool. Scrape** with fork to remove flesh. Set aside.

Sauté onion, garlic, and green beans in oil until crisp tender. **Add** squash. **Add** spices, Vogue, and water. **Cook** 3-5 minutes longer.

Stir in lemon juice and salt.

Toss in tomatoes and pumpkin seeds immediately before serving.

To dry-toast pumpkin seeds: Heat a skillet. Add pumpkin seeds. Shake occasionally until seeds have popped. Remove from heat.

Spaghetti Squash with Greens

1 spaghetti squash
1 bunch collards or kale, stems removed, rinsed, and chopped
1 large onion, diced
2 Tablespoons olive oil
1/2 cup arame, reconstituted according to package directions
1 cup cashews, whole or pieces
2 heaping Tablespoons Vogue Vege Base
1-2 Tablespoons apple cider vinegar
1/2 teaspoon sea salt
1/2 cup water

Preheat oven to 350 degrees.

Scoop out seeds from spaghetti squash. **Place** cut side down on a baking sheet. **Bake** for approximately 40 minutes or until softened. **Cool.** **Scrape** out squash into a bowl with a fork. **Set** aside.

Sauté collards and onions in oil until onion is just golden. **Add** squash, arame, and cashews.

Mix Vogue, vinegar, salt, and water. **Pour** into veggies. **Combine** well.

Cover. Simmer 5 minutes. **Adjust** seasonings, if needed. **Serve.**

Ultimate Sandwich with Creamy Mozzarella

You may add or delete any veggie you wish—kind of like a pizza. This is your choice!

Focaccia:
2 teaspoons dry yeast
1 1/4 cups warm water
1 teaspoon brown rice syrup
1 1/2 cups whole wheat or spelt flour
1 1/4 cups barley flour
3/4 teaspoons sea salt
1 teaspoon thyme
1 teaspoon rosemary, coarsely ground
cornmeal
1/3 cup olive oil

Vegetables:
1 head Roasted Garlic (*see recipe in Condiments*)
1 bell pepper, roasted, skin removed, and slivered
1 thinly sliced portabello mushroom
1/2 onion, thinly sliced
1 small eggplant, thinly sliced
1/2 head escarole or other green, rinsed, and torn into pieces

1 recipe Creamy "Mozzarella" (see recipe in Condiments)

Prepare Focaccia:
Dissolve yeast in warm water, along with the rice syrup. **Let** stand until yeast starts to foam.

Combine flours, salt, and spices in a bowl. **Add** 2 Tablespoons olive oil.

Knead dry and wet ingredients together on a lightly floured surface until dough is smooth and elastic (7-10 minutes). **Place** dough into an oiled bowl.

Cover loosely with a towel. **Let** dough rise in a warm, draft-free place until it has doubled in volume (approximately 1 1/2 hours).

Prepare *vegetables while dough is rising*:
Sauté mushrooms, onion, and eggplant in small amount of olive oil until softened.

Preheat oven to 375 degrees.

Roll dough out to form a 12-inch round. **Sprinkle** cornmeal into pizza tin or on a baking sheet. **Slide** sheet under dough. **Pinch** up edges. **Brush** surface with 2 more Tablespoons of olive oil.

Bake for 15-20 minutes.

Spread mozzarella on focaccia layer with mushroom mixture, garlic, pepper slivers, then greens. **Sprinkle** with balsamic vinegar, if desired. **Cut** into squares. **Serve.**

Asparagus-Tofu Stir Fry

1 pound firm tofu
1 bunch asparagus spears
1 small onion, diced
1 Tablespoon garlic, minced
1 Tablespoon ginger, minced
1 small bell pepper, sliced in strips (preferably red or yellow)
oil
1 cup water
1 Tablespoon miso
1/8-1/4 teaspoon Thai curry paste
2 Tablespoons Bragg Liquid Aminos
1 Tablespoon black bean sauce (available in most supermarkets—make sure to select one without preservatives!)
1 Tablespoon arrowroot mixed with 1 Tablespoon water
1/2 cup toasted almonds, chopped coarse

Wrap tofu in kitchen towel for 30 minutes.

Steam asparagus until crisp tender.

Sauté onion, garlic, ginger, and pepper in oil for 3 minutes.

Add water, miso, Thai curry paste, Braggs, and black bean sauce.

Stir in tofu. **Simmer** for 10 minutes.

Add arrowroot/water mixture. **Thicken.**

Toss in almonds and asparagus.

Serve.

O Konomi Yaki

You may bake these patties if desired, on an oiled cookie sheet at 375 degrees for approximately 20-30 minutes, or until lightly browned.

1 small head of Chinese cabbage, thinly sliced
sea salt
1 carrot, shredded
2 Tablespoons fresh ginger, grated
2 Tablespoons Bragg Liquid Aminos
4 green onions, thinly sliced
1/2 pound fresh shiitake mushrooms, sliced 1/4-inch thick
3/4 teaspoon red pepper flakes
1/2 cup flour (*barley, wheat, rice, millet, or oat*)
2 Tablespoons arrowroot
1 package Mori-Nu firm-style tofu
1 teaspoon toasted sesame oil
2 Tablespoons cilantro, chopped
1 Tablespoon sesame seed, toasted

Heat a small amount of oil in a large skillet. **Add** the Chinese cabbage and 1/4 teaspoon salt. **Sauté** cabbage over medium heat until it begins to wilt, about 3 minutes.

Add carrot, ginger, Braggs, green onions, mushrooms, and pepper flakes. **Cook** off excess liquid, if any.

Transfer veggies to a bowl. **Cool.**

Process flour, arrowroot, tofu, and sesame oil in a blender until smooth. **Add** mixture to veggies. **Add** cilantro. **Mix** well.

Spoon mixture into a lightly-oiled skillet (non-stick works best) over medium high heat, making 3-inch cakes. **Brown** on both sides.

Sprinkle with sesame seeds.

Serve immediately.

Coconut and Cashew Veggies with Tofu and Orange Sauce

1 pound tofu, frozen and defrosted
Combination of veggies, steamed crisp tender (*I like carrots, zucchini, sweet potato, and mushrooms; zucchini and mushrooms do not need to be steamed*)
1 teaspoon cayenne
1 teaspoon sea salt
1 teaspoon paprika
3/4 teaspoon black pepper, freshly ground
1 teaspoon garlic powder
1/2 teaspoon onion powder
1/2 teaspoon thyme
1/2 teaspoon oregano
1/2 cup cashews
1 cup water
1 1/2 cups flour (*your choice, spelt, rice, millet, oat, etc.*)
2 cups unsweetened coconut
coconut oil

Sauce:
3/4 cup orange marmalade
2 1/2 Tablespoons Dijon or coarse-ground mustard
2 1/2 Tablespoons drained bottled horseradish or fresh peeled and grated, to taste

Prepare Sauce:
Combine all sauce ingredients well. **Set** aside.

Squeeze tofu. **Wrap** tofu in kitchen towel for 30 minutes. **Cut** into 2-inch squares.

Cube or slice veggies 1/4-inch thick. **Steam** approximately 5 minutes.

Combine spices in a small bowl.

Process the cashews and water in blender until smooth.

Pour cashews into another bowl with 1 cup of flour and 2 teaspoons of the spice blend.

Place coconut in another bowl.

Add 1/2 cup of flour to remaining spices.

Heat a small amount of oil in a non-stick pan to medium high.

Dredge tofu and veggies in flour mixture. **Shake** off excess. **Dip** in batter. **Coat** lightly in coconut.

Sauté on each side until golden brown on each side. **Transfer** to a paper-towel lined bowl. **Repeat** until finished.

Serve with sauce.

White Beans with Tomato and Sage

1 pound dried white beans, soaked over night, rinsed
kombu (*sea vegetable*), one small frond
1/4 cup olive oil
4 large cloves garlic, minced
15 fresh sage leaves, minced
1 bunch collards, stems removed, chopped into 1-inch pieces
2 Tablespoons Vogue Vege Base
sea salt to taste
2 large tomatoes, diced

Cook beans and kombu in kettle with enough cold water to cover by 2 inches at a bare simmer for 1-1 1/2 hours, or until tender.

Heat oil in large skillet until hot, but not smoking. **Add** garlic. **Remove** from heat.

Swirl pan until garlic is just golden. **Stir** in sage leaves.

Add to beans, along with collards, Vogue, and sea salt.

Simmer all for 5 more minutes.

Remove from heat.

Stir in tomatoes. **Serve.**

Bean Croquettes

2 cups cooked beans
1 carrot, diced
1/4 onion, diced
1 Tablespoon chili powder
1 teaspoon cumin seeds, ground
1/2 cup bread crumbs
sea salt to taste
toasted nuts

Preheat oven to 350 degrees.

Mash beans.

Sauté carrot, onion, chili powder, and cumin seeds in a small amount of oil until softened.

Mix all ingredients together.

Bake for 30-40 minutes, or fry until browned.

Lentil-Tomato Loaf

1 pound lentils
1 medium onion, chopped
2 stalks celery, chopped
2 teaspoons salt
4 cloves garlic, minced
1 16-ounce can chopped tomatoes (*preferably Muir Glen*)
1/2 teaspoon thyme
4 slices bread, crumbled (*preferably Ezekiel*)
2 Tablespoons oil.

Cook lentils.

Preheat oven to 350 degrees.

Sauté onion, celery, salt, and garlic in small amount of oil.

Add remaining ingredients.

Mix well.

Bake in a loaf pan for 45 minutes.

Chipotle and White Bean Pasta

Cilantro would make a delicious addition to this dish, if desired.

1 package Pappadini pasta (*or your choice of pasta*)
1 ounce sun-dried tomatoes
1 chipotle pepper (*or scant 1/8 teaspoon chipotle powder*)
1 onion, chopped
4 cloves garlic, chopped
2 Tablespoons olive oil
1 cup corn kernels
1 1/2 cups white beans, cooked
1-2 Tablespoons Vogue Vege Base

Cook pasta according to package directions. **Drain. Set** aside.

Soak sun-dried tomatoes and chipotle pepper in 1/2 cup hot water until softened. **Drain. Reserve** liquid.

Sauté onions and garlic in olive oil until tender.

Chop tomatoes. **Slice** peppers and scoop out seeds to discard (seeds are very hot!). **Mince** chipotle.

Add tomatoes and chipotle to onions and garlic, including liquid from tomatoes.

Add corn kernels, beans, and Vogue. **Heat** through.

Adjust seasonings, if needed.

Toss into noodles.

Serve immediately.

Primavera Pasta

1 package soba noodles (*or spaghetti squash*)
1 bunch kale, stems removed and torn into small pieces
1/4 cup olive oil
4-6 garlic cloves, minced
1 onion, diced
1/2 bell pepper, diced
1 zucchini, diced
1/4 teaspoon fennel, coarsely ground or crushed
1/2 teaspoon rosemary, coarsely ground or crushed
1/2 teaspoon thyme
1/4 teaspoon oregano
1/4 teaspoon red pepper flakes
1 heaping Tablespoon Vogue Vege Base (*or other strong powdered broth*)
3/4 cup water
2 large tomatoes, chopped
1/3 cup parsley, minced

Cook noodles according to package directions.

Rinse kale. **Place** in large preheated pot (temperature should be high). **Cover** immediately. **Cook** in the rinse water that was still clinging to the leaves. **Stir** after a few minutes. **Add** a couple more Tablespoons of water if pan is dry. **Simmer** for a total of 5 minutes. **Remove** from heat.

Heat olive oil in a large sauté pan.

Add garlic, onion, bell pepper, and zucchini. **Sauté** until onion is just transparent.

Add spices and Vogue. **Cook** 2 more minutes.

Add water. **Cover. Simmer** on low for 5 minutes.

Add in kale, tomatoes, parsley, and soba noodles.

Serve immediately.

Primavera Pasta #2

1 package soba noodles
2 leeks, rinsed and chopped
2 cups broccoli, chopped
4 garlic cloves, minced
2 Tablespoons olive oil
1/4 teaspoon marjoram
1/2 teaspoon sage
1 cup almond or other vegan milk
1 Tablespoon Vogue Vege Base
2 Tablespoons arrowroot
1 Tablespoon Bragg Liquid Aminos
1 cup sprouted or cooked garbanzo beans
1 yellow bell pepper, slivered
1 large tomato, diced

Cook noodles according to package directions.

Sauté leeks, broccoli, and garlic in oil until leeks are softened.

Add spices.

Stir in milk, Vogue, arrowroot, and Braggs. Heat through. Remove from heat.

Stir in chickpeas, pepper, and tomato.

Pour over soba noodles.

Noodles in Green Sauce

1/2 pound soba noodles (or cooked spaghetti squash)
1/2 cup shiitake mushroom caps, thinly sliced
2 medium carrots, cut in very thin slivers
1/2 cup pine nuts, toasted

Sauce:
1 1-pound bunch spinach, cleaned, stems removed
2 bunches chives, chopped
1/2 cup cilantro, chopped
1/4 cup basil leaves, chopped
2 cloves garlic, minced
3/4 cup rich veggie stock
2/3 cup cashew cream
1/2 teaspoon sea salt
1/8-1/4 teaspoon Thai curry paste
1 Tablespoon arrowroot mixed with 1 Tablespoon water

Cook noodles according to instructions. (If using squash, quarter and remove seeds. Place cut side down on baking sheet. Bake at 350 degrees for 30-40 minutes. **Cool. Scrape** out flesh.)

Process first 4 sauce ingredients into puree, using blender or food processor.

Add remaining sauce ingredients, except arrowroot. **Puree** again.

Pour into a pan. **Sauté** garlic in a small amount of oil until lightly browned. **Stir** in mushrooms. **Heat** to simmer. **Add** arrowroot to thicken.

Toss with noodles. **Add** carrots. **Sprinkle** with pine nuts.

Serve immediately.

Oriental Noodles with Spicy Ginger and Peanut Sauce

1 package soba noodles (*or cooked spaghetti squash*)
1 broccoli bunch, cut into small flowerets

Sauce:
1/2 cup unsalted peanut butter (*preferably organic*)
2 1/2 Tablespoons fresh ginger, grated
2 small garlic cloves, minced
1/2 cup water
2 Tablespoons Bragg Liquid Aminos
1 teaspoon brown rice vinegar
1 teaspoon maple or barley malt syrup
1/4 teaspoon red pepper flakes

Cook noodles per package instructions. Set aside.

Steam broccoli until crisp tender. Set aside.

Process all sauce ingredients in blender until smooth. **Add** more water, if necessary, to create a medium-thick consistency. **Heat** briefly.

Adjust seasonings, if desired.

Toss into broccoli and noodles.

Serve.

Asian Spring Rolls

1/4 head cabbage, shredded
6 shiitake mushrooms, stems discarded, caps sliced thin (*save stems for broth*)
3 garlic cloves, minced
3 large shallots, minced
1 Tablespoon fresh gingerroot, peeled and minced
1 large carrot, shredded
1/3 cup cilantro, chopped
1/3 cup mint leaves, chopped
1 cup mung bean sprouts, chopped
2 Tablespoons Bragg Liquid Aminos
1 teaspoon sea salt, or to taste
20 spring roll wrappers, or vegan crepes

Dipping Sauce:
1/4 cup Bragg Liquid Aminos
1/4 cup fresh lime juice
2 Tablespoons water
2 garlic cloves, minced and mashed to a paste with 1/2 teaspoon sea salt
2 Tablespoons rice syrup
1 2-inch fresh red or green chili, seeded and minced (*wear rubber gloves*), or 1/4 teaspoon dried hot pepper flakes, or to taste

Preheat oven to 400 degrees.

Combine all ingredients for spring rolls, except wrappers. **Sauté** briefly in small amount of oil in a large skillet. **Wilt** cabbage. **Soften** remaining veggies.

Wrap spring roll wrappers like you would a burrito, making sure ends are tucked in.

Bake crepes and wrappers for approximately 10-15 minutes. **Serve** like a wrap sandwich.

Mix all ingredients for dipping sauce.

Matar Paneer

This is traditionally made with homemade cheese, but I substitute tofu with excellent results!

2 Tablespoons fresh gingerroot, peeled and minced
2 Tablespoons garlic, minced
1/4 cup raw cashew nuts
1/2 onion soaked in 1/4 cup hot water
3 Tablespoons sesame oil
1/2 teaspoon fenugreek seeds
2 1/2 teaspoons turmeric
1 teaspoon chili powder
2 1/2 Tablespoons coriander, ground
3 Tablespoons sesame oil
1 cup cubed tofu
1 cup cooked fresh or thawed frozen peas
1 1/2 Tablespoons garam masala (*store bought or see recipe*)
1/4 cup fresh coriander, minced
1/4 cup gingerroot, peeled and cut into 1 1/2-inch julienne strips
sea salt to taste

Puree minced gingerroot, garlic, cashew nuts, and onion with water.

Heat oil over low heat. **Add** fenugreek, turmeric, chili powder, and ground coriander. **Cook** 30 seconds.

Add gingerroot puree. **Cook** mixture for 5 minutes. **Stir** gravy occasionally.

Heat oil in heavy skillet over moderate heat until hot. **Sauté** tofu for 1 minute. **Stir.**

Add peas and gravy. **Cook** 4 minutes. **Stir.**

Stir in garam masala, half of minced coriander, half of gingerroot, and sea salt.

Transfer to serving dish.

Sprinkle with remaining coriander and gingerroot.

Thai Stir Fry

*Cashews or toasted pumpkin seeds
can be added to this recipe, if desired.*

1/3 cup arame, soaked in hot water for 15 minutes
1/2 pound tofu, cubed (*optional*)
1 onion, chopped
1 carrot, chopped
1 zucchini, chopped
1 cup fresh shiitake mushrooms, sliced
1/2 yellow or red bell pepper, cut in slivers
coconut oil

Sauce:
14 ounces coconut milk
1/2 cup fresh basil, chopped
1/4 cup Bragg Liquid Aminos
1 heaping Tablespoon Vogue Vege Base
1/8-1/2 teaspoon Thai curry paste (*to your tolerance*)

Prep all veggies. Set aside.

Combine sauce ingredients. Set aside.

Sauté veggies in medium hot oil until crisp tender, approximately 2-3 minutes.

Stir in sauce. **Cover. Simmer** approximately 5 more minutes. **Serve** over grains.

Spicy Thai Noodles

**Peanuts are a nice addition and keep this dish more authentic, they are not necessary though.
Please try to buy organic. There are brands out there that are tested aflatoxin free.*

1 package soba noodles
2 cups mung or soybean sprouts
2 Tablespoons roasted peanuts, minced
1/3 cup red bell pepper, minced
1/4 cup green onions, minced
1/4 cup fresh cilantro, minced

Sauce:
2 cloves garlic, finely minced
1 Tablespoon oil
3 Tablespoons Bragg Liquid Aminos
3 Tablespoons tomato sauce
2 Tablespoons lime juice, plus 2 limes
2 Tablespoons brown rice syrup
1/4-1/2 teaspoon red Thai curry paste *(adjust to your heat tolerance)*
1 teaspoon lime peel, finely grated

Prepare sauce:
Combine garlic with oil. Set aside.

Combine remaining ingredients. **Set** aside.

Cut 2 limes into wedges. Set aside.

Last minute cooking:
Bring at least 4 quarts water to a vigorous boil. Add noodles. Cook noodles until they lose raw taste, but are still firm, approximately 5 minutes. Drain immediately. Shake out excess water. Transfer to a large bowl.

Sauté garlic mixture in a small skillet over medium-high heat for about 30 seconds. Add remaining sauce ingredients. Bring to low boil. Remove from heat.

Add sauce to noodles. Add bean sprouts. Toss well.

Turn out onto a heated platter. Sprinkle with peanuts, red pepper, green onions, and cilantro.

Serve immediately, accompanied by lime wedges.

Spinach Fritters

1 medium onion, diced
1 large bunch spinach, rinsed and chopped
1 Tablespoon olive oil
1 package Mori-Nu tofu, firm
1/2 cup flour (rice, spelt, etc.)
2 Tablespoons arrowroot
1 Tablespoon Bragg Liquid Aminos
1/4-1/2 teaspoon nutmeg

Sauté onion until lightly browned. **Place** spinach in pan. **Cover**. **Remove** from heat. **Lift** lid after one minute. **Drain** all liquid.

Process remaining ingredients in a blender until smooth.

Mix into spinach mixture.

Drop by spoonfuls (not too large) onto an oiled and heated non-stick pan.

Cook until golden brown on both sides.

Serve with lemon wedges and/or fresh Tomato Sauce (see recipe in Condiments).

Coconut Curry Melange

Just the thing to clear your sinuses on a chilly day!

1/2 tub frozen, defrosted tofu, cubed
1 Tablespoon Bragg Liquid Aminos
1 Tablespoon arrowroot
1 potato, peeled and diced into 1/2-inch cubes
1/2 head cauliflower, chopped into bite-size pieces
4 cloves garlic, minced
1 Tablespoon fresh ginger, finely minced or grated
1 red onion, diced
1 green bell pepper, diced
1/2 cup peas

Sauce:
1 cup unsweetened coconut milk
1 Tablespoon Bragg Liquid Aminos
2 Tablespoons curry powder
2 teaspoons Oriental sesame oil
1/8-1/4 teaspoon Thai curry paste, red or green
1/4 teaspoon sea salt

Squeeze tofu between 2 plates to remove water. **Cube** tofu. Set aside.

Mix Braggs and arrowroot in small bowl. **Toss** in tofu. Set aside.

Steam potato and cauliflower until just crisp tender. **Place** all other veggies nearby.

Combine ingredients for sauce in a small bowl.

Heat a small amount of oil on high heat in a wok or large frying pan.

Add garlic and ginger first. **Stir** for 30 seconds. **Add** remaining veggies, except peas.

Stir fry until onion pieces separate and green pepper brightens, about 2 minutes.

Add tofu and peas. **Pour** in sauce. **Stir** in a little arrowroot and water mixture to thicken, if desired, when sauce comes to a low boil. **Adjust** seasonings.

Serve immediately.

Italian Beans 'n Greens Over Polenta

1 cup anasazi beans, dried or sprouted
1/3 cup sun-dried tomatoes
1 cup hot water

Polenta:
1 cup yellow corn grits
3 cups water
2 Tablespoons olive oil
1/4 teaspoon salt

1 Tablespoon olive oil
1 onion, sliced into thin half moons
4 cloves garlic
1 bunch kale, cleaned and chopped
2 Tablespoons Vogue Vege Base
Salt to taste

Cook beans until tender.

Soak sun-dried tomatoes in hot water for approximately 15 minutes. **Remove** tomatoes. **Reserve** water. **Mince** tomatoes. **Set** aside.

Prepare polenta. **Pour** grits slowly into boiling, salted water. **Turn** temperature to low. **Stir** constantly. **Add** olive oil as it thickens. **Stir** as it thickens, approximately 3-5 minutes. **Pour** into oiled 10-inch pie pan. **Set** aside.

Sauté onions in oil until translucent. **Add** garlic, kale, Vogue, and water from tomatoes. **Simmer** 5 minutes.

Add beans. **Season. Warm** through. **Pour** over polenta.

Sprinkle with Vegan mozzarella or parmesan, if desired. **Slice** into wedges.

Baked Polenta with Shiitake Ragout

Elegant entree. Great for non-vegetarian dinner guests.

Ragout:
1 large onion, chopped fine,
4 garlic cloves, minced
1 teaspoon dried rosemary, crumbled or coarsely ground
3 Tablespoons olive oil
1 pound white mushrooms, sliced thin
1 pound fresh shiitake mushrooms, stems discarded and, if large, the caps quartered
1 Tablespoon tomato paste
3/4 cup dry red wine (*preferably organic*)
1 Tablespoon arrowroot
1 cup vegetable broth
1-2 Tablespoons red miso

Polenta:
6 cups water
1 Tablespoon olive oil
2 cups yellow cornmeal
1/3 cup fresh parsley, minced
sea salt to taste
1/4 pound mozzarella-style vegan or soy cheese, grated

Preheat oven to 400 degrees.

Ragout:
Cook the onion, garlic, and rosemary in a large, deep skillet in oil over moderate heat, until the onion is softened. **Stir** constantly.

Add mushrooms. **Cook** mixture over moderately high heat. **Stir** until liquid the mushrooms give off is evaporated.

Stir in tomato paste and wine. **Boil** mushroom mixture until most of liquid is evaporated.

Stir arrowroot into broth in a small bowl.

Add mixture to the mushrooms. **Bring** the ragout to a boil, stirring. **Simmer** the ragout for 2 minutes.

Mix the miso in equal part water. **Add** to ragout. **Stir** miso in completely.

Polenta:
Boil water with the oil in a large, heavy saucepan.

Add 1 cup of cornmeal, a small amount at a time, stirring

Reduce heat to low. **Add** remaining 1 cup cornmeal in a slow stream. **Stir** constantly. **Boil** mixture.

Remove the pan from the heat when thickened. **Stir** in the 2 remaining Tablespoons of olive oil, parsley, and sea salt to taste.

Spread 1/3 of the polenta in an oiled 3-quart shallow baking dish. **Top** with half the ragout. **Top** ragout with half the mozzarella.

Spread another third of the polenta quickly over the cheese.

Pour remaining ragout over that. **Top** with remaining cheese. **Dot** the casserole with remaining polenta.

Bake for approximately 30 minutes.

Polenta Pizza

Toppings are unlimited! Try roasted garlic, or sauté mushrooms with onions.
Or marinara, pesto....
Sprinkle with coarsely ground rosemary and oregano and drizzle with olive oil....
etc.!

Polenta:
1 cup yellow corn grits
3 cups water
2 Tablespoons olive oil
1/2 teaspoon sea salt

Topping:
fresh mushrooms
tomato slices
bell peppers
olive slivers
roasted garlic

Preheat oven to broil.

Bring water to a boil.

Stir in grits slowly. **Lower** heat to a simmer.

Stir often, approximately 10 minutes, until creamy.

Pour into oiled baking pan.

Top with veggies.

Add cheese, if desired.

Set under broiler briefly, or if using cheese, until bubbly.

Add fresh Tomato Sauce (*see recipe in Condiments*).

Cashew Nut Casserole

2 Tablespoons olive oil
1 1/2 cups cashew pieces
1 large onion, finely chopped
2 garlic cloves, minced
1 large zucchini, diced small
1 medium carrot, diced small
2 large stalks celery, sliced thin
1 teaspoon chili powder
1 teaspoon cumin, ground and toasted
1 heaping Tablespoon Vogue Vege Base
1 1/2 cups tomatoes, chopped
4 sun-dried tomatoes, minced
2 teaspoons fresh basil, finely chopped
1 1/2 Tablespoons Bragg Liquid Aminos
2/3 cup vegan milk, diluted with 2/3 cup water

Heat 1 Tablespoon oil in large stock pot. **Toast** cashews. Set aside.

Heat remaining oil. **Sauté** onion until soft.

Add garlic, vegetables, and nuts. **Cover. Cook** for 10 minutes.

Add chili and cumin powders.

Mix in Vogue, tomatoes, basil, and Braggs.

Stir in diluted milk.

Season.

Simmer 15-20 minutes.

Creamy Eggplant Casserole

1 cup bulgur
2 medium eggplants, sliced thin
1 Tablespoon olive oil
1 cup onion, diced
2 cups mushrooms, diced
1 large zucchini, diced
4 cloves garlic, minced
1 1/2 Tablespoons Vogue Vege Base
1 Tablespoon fresh basil, minced
1 Tablespoon fresh oregano, minced
3 Tablespoons oat flour
1/2 cup cashews
1 cup water
1 cup "mozzarella" cheese *(optional)*

Preheat oven to 350 degrees.

Soak bulgur in hot water to cover for 10 minutes.

Bake eggplant on an oiled pan until just tender. **Set** aside.

Sauté onion, mushrooms, zucchini, and garlic in oil until crisp tender. **Add** Vogue, basil, oregano and flour. **Cook** 2 minutes.

Process cashews and water in blender until smooth. **Pour** into veggie mixture. **Stir** until gravy thickens. **Add** more water, if needed, to create a smooth sauce.

Pat down bulgur in an oiled 9x13 pan. **Add** half of the eggplant slices. **Pour** veggie and gravy mixture over all. **Top** with remaining eggplant.

Spread generously with cheese, if desired. **Dust** top with paprika.

Bake for 20 minutes.

Let sit 10 minutes before serving.

Portabello Casserole

1/2 cup sun-dried tomatoes
2 very large or 4 medium portabello mushrooms, cleaned, stems removed
1 onion, sliced into half moons
1 zucchini squash, diced
3-5 large cloves of garlic, minced
stems of portabellos, cleaned and diced
2 heaping Tablespoons Vogue Vege Base
1/4 cup olive oil

Preheat oven to 450 degrees.

Reconstitute tomatoes in water. **Drain. Reserve** water. **Chop.**

Place mushrooms in large baking dish, top side down.

Cover with vegetables.

Sprinkle with Vogue. **Drizzle** oil over all.

Add 1/3 cup reserved water to dish. **Cover** tightly.

Bake for approximately 30 minutes.

Spinach and Rice Casserole with Toasted Almonds

1 cup brown rice
2 cups water
olive oil
1 onion, chopped
4 garlic cloves, minced
1/2 package firm-style tofu, rinsed and drained
1 Tablespoon vegetable broth
1-2 teaspoons toasted sesame oil
1-2 Tablespoons Bragg Liquid Aminos
1/3 cup arame, reconstituted according to package directions
1 bunch spinach, stems removed, rinsed well, and if large, leaves torn
1/3 cup almonds, toasted and coarsely chopped*

Simmer rice in water in a covered pot until all liquid is absorbed.

Sauté onion and garlic in a small amount of oil until softened.

Crumble tofu into pan.

Add broth, sesame oil, and Braggs. **Simmer** for a few minutes.

Add rice and arame. **Heat** through.

Remove pan from burner. **Stir** in spinach, allowing the heat of the grain to wilt the leaves.

Stir in toasted almonds.

Serve immediately.

To toast almonds: place on a cookie sheet a few inches from heat source in your broiler. Shake after a couple of minutes. Remove when lightly browned.

Squash and Bean Casserole

*Warming on a cold, winter day.
These three flavors blend well.
Very Native American!*

1 large kabocha, butternut, or acorn squash
3 cups water
1 cup corn grits
1/4 teaspoon salt
2 Tablespoons oil
1 large onion, diced
oil
4 cups cooked beans (*anasazi, pinto, etc.*)
1 Tablespoon Vogue Vege Base
1 Tablespoon chili powder
2 Tablespoons Bragg Liquid Aminos
1/8-1/4 teaspoon chipotle powder (*optional, but nice*)

Preheat oven to 350 degrees.

Quarter squash. **Remove** seeds. **Place** on baking sheet, cut side down. **Bake** for approximately 45 minutes. **Let** cool. **Mash.** **Set** aside.

Bring water to boil. **Add** grits slowly. **Turn** down temperature to low. **Stir** continuously until polenta thickens. **Add** salt and oil. **Stir** briefly. (Total cooking time should be 7-10 minutes). **Pour** immediately into oiled casserole dish. **Set** aside.

Sauté onion with oil in pan until translucent. **Add** remaining ingredients, adding a small amount of water, if needed. **Adjust** seasonings. **Cook** for 5 minutes. **Pour** over polenta.

Layer the mashed kabocha squash over beans. **Sprinkle** with toasted pumpkin seeds, if desired.

Bake at 350 degrees until heated through, approximately 15-20 minutes.

Vegetable Enchilada Casserole

12 corn tortillas

Sauce:
1 Tablespoon olive oil
1 medium onion, diced
sea salt to taste
2 teaspoons cumin seed, toasted and ground
2 teaspoons dried oregano, toasted
8 garlic cloves, finely chopped
1 28-ounce can tomatoes, pureed
pinch of chipotle powder

Preheat oven to 350 degrees.

Heat oil in a large pan.

Add onion, 1/2 teaspoon salt, cumin, and oregano.

Sauté over medium heat until onion begins to soften, about 3 to 4 minutes. **Add** garlic. **Sauté** for 1 minute.

Add tomatoes, chipotle, and 1/4 teaspoon salt.

Reduce heat. **Cook**, uncovered, for 15 to 20 minutes

Filling:
2 Tablespoons oil
1 medium onion, diced
sea salt to taste
1/2 teaspoon cumin seed, toasted and ground
1 red bell pepper, diced
4 medium zucchini, diced
2 medium potatoes, cubed and steamed
5 garlic cloves, finely chopped
3/4 pounds mushrooms, thickly sliced
1 cup roasted walnut pieces (roast in 450 degree oven until golden and fragrant, apx. 15-20 minutes)
pinch of chipotle powder

Heat 1 Tablespoon oil in large pan.

Add onion, 1/2 teaspoon salt and half the cumin. **Sauté** over medium heat for 5 to 7 minutes.

Add pepper, zucchini, potato, 1/2 teaspoon salt, half the garlic, and remaining cumin.

Cook for 10 minutes. **Transfer** to bowl.

Heat remaining oil. **Brown** mushrooms over high heat.

Toss mushrooms and walnuts with other vegetables and chipotle powder.

Place 3-4 corn tortillas in baking dish.

Place filling on top of tortillas. **Pour** sauce over filling. **Repeat** 2 or 3 times, ending with sauce.

Bake 10-15 minutes.

Vegetable Lasagna

Instead of noodles, try using 1/8-inch eggplant slices which have been broiled briefly until just cooked through.

1 large eggplant, sliced thin and briefly broiled

Tofu Ricotta Sauce:
2 onions, chopped
4 cloves garlic, chopped
1-2 Tablespoons olive oil
1 pound firm tofu, drained and diced
2-3 Tablespoons Bragg Liquid Aminos
1/2 cup water
1/2 teaspoon basil, chopped
1/2 teaspoon oregano, chopped
1 Tablespoon parsley, chopped
1/4 cup nutritional yeast

Preheat oven to 350 degrees.

Sauté onion and garlic in oil.

Add tofu, Braggs, water, and herbs. **Cover.**

Simmer 15 minutes.

Blend half in blender and mash other half for a creamy/chunky texture.

*For a meaty texture, add half a package
of crumbled tempeh to marinara mixture
or 1/2 cup of bulgur soaked in 1/2
cup hot water until liquid is absorbed.*

Marinara Sauce:
1/3 cup sun-dried tomatoes
3-4 large garlic cloves, minced
1 large onion, diced
1-2 Tablespoons olive oil
1 28-ounce can chopped tomatoes (*preferably Muir Glen*)
1/2 teaspoon basil, chopped
1/2 teaspoon oregano, chopped
1 bay leaf
1/8 cup balsamic vinegar
pinch of red pepper flakes
sea salt to taste

Soften sun-dried tomatoes in 1/2 cup boiling water. **Remove** from heat. Let sit until cooled. **Drain. Reserve** liquid. **Chop. Set** aside.

Sauté garlic and onion in olive oil until softened. **Add** remaining ingredients, using reserved water from sun-dried tomatoes as needed to loosen mixture. **Simmer** 20 minutes.

Filling:
1 bunch spinach
1 carrot, shredded
6-8 ounces mushrooms, sliced

Remove stems from spinach. **Rinse** well. **Wilt** briefly in covered pan. **Chop.**

Mix spinach, carrots, and mushrooms into ricotta sauce.

Layer a pan with marinara sauce first, then eggplant, ricotta, and sauce. **Repeat** once or twice more. **Finish** with marinara on top.

Cover.

Bake 20-25 minutes until bubbly.

Chestnut, Apple, and Cornbread Stuffed Squash

2 butternut squash

Stuffing:
1 large onion, chopped
2 celery stalks, chopped
1 pound fresh chestnuts, or 3/4 pound canned chestnuts
2 Tablespoons sage leaves, minced (*or 1 Tablespoon dried*)
2 Tablespoons thyme leaves, minced (*or 2 teaspoons dried*)
1 Tablespoon rosemary, minced (*or 1 teaspoon dried*)
1/2 cup parsley, minced
2 Granny Smith apples, cut into 1/4-inch pieces
1/4 cup "Butter" (*see recipe in Condiments*)
1 cup vegetable broth

Cornbread for stuffing:
3/4 cup flour (*spelt, barley, or wheat pastry*)
1 1/4 cups yellow cornmeal
1 Tablespoon non-aluminum baking powder
1/2 teaspoon sea salt
1 cup vegan milk

Preheat oven to 375 degrees.

Cut squash in half. **Clean. Bake,** cut side down, until tender, approximately 30-45 minutes.

Shell and peel chestnuts. **Roast** in a hot oven (400-450 degrees) until tender, approximately 20-30 minutes. **Chop** coarse.

Prepare cornbread:
Mix dry and liquid ingredients separately. **Stir** together. **Pour** batter into greased 8-inch square baking pan. **Bake** in preheated 425 degree oven for 20-25 minutes, or until top is pale golden and a tester comes out clean. **Remove** from pan. **Break** into coarse chunks to cool and dry out completely.

Cook onion and celery with salt and pepper to taste over moderately low heat. **Stir** until vegetables are softened. **Transfer** the mixture to the bowl of cornbread.

Add chestnuts and herbs. **Adjust** seasonings, if necessary. **Toss** mixture gently until combined well. **Let** cool. **Stir** in apples. **Stuff** cooked squash. **Return** to oven. **Pour** vegetable broth over all.

Bake for another 30-45 minutes.

Veggie Rolls

Whole grain bread may tear when you try to roll it. Briefly steaming bread will make it more pliable.

1 onion, chopped
1 cup greens, shredded
1/2 cup carrot, shredded
1/4 cup bell pepper, slivered
1/2 cup mushrooms, minced
oil
1 tomato, chopped
2 Tablespoons flour
1/2 teaspoon sea salt
8 slices bread
olive oil
sesame seeds, toasted and ground
dulse flakes, toasted and ground

Sauté onion, greens, carrots, bell peppers, and mushrooms in a small amount of oil until softened. **Add** tomato. **Stir** in flour and salt. **Cool.**

Preheat oven to 375 degrees.

Mix sesame and dulse on a plate. **Steam** bread briefly. * **Flatten** bread. **Spread** veggies in center of each. **Roll.** **Brush** each with oil. **Roll** in seed/dulse mixture.

Place on baking sheet, seam down. **Bake** for approximately 20 minutes, or until browned.

I have a bamboo steamer which works well, but any medium-sized steamer will work. It only takes 15-30 seconds to soften bread.

Mediterranean Stuffed Collard Greens

I love these little rolls served warm or cold. Try them with hummus and pita or my version of tzatziki for a complete meal.

1 large bunch of collard greens, stems removed.
1/2 cup coarse cracked wheat or bulgur
1/3 cup green lentils
1 1/2 Tablespoons fresh parsley, finely minced
1 1/2 Tablespoons fresh dill, finely minced
1 1/2 Tablespoons fresh mint, minced
1/4 cup raisins, chopped (optional)
1 cup onion, finely chopped
5 Tablespoons olive oil
3 Tablespoons fresh lemon juice
3 Tablespoons olive oil
3 Tablespoons fresh lemon juice
about 1 cup vegetable broth
lemon wedges as an accompaniment

Blanch collard greens, a few leaves at a time, in a large pot of hot (not boiling) water for 15-30 seconds. **Remove. Cool.**

Make the Filling:

Soak bulgur in a small bowl of hot water to cover for 15 minutes. **Drain. Press** hard to extract water.

Simmer lentils in a small pan of boiling water for 20 minutes. **Drain. Add** to bulgur. **Add** parsley, dill, mint, and raisins.

Cook onion in 3 Tablespoons of oil in a skillet over moderate heat. **Stir** until golden. **Add** to grain mixture.

Stir in lemon juice and the remaining 2 Tablespoons oil. **Add** salt and pepper to taste.

Stuff the Leaves:
Spoon a heaping teaspoon of filling on each leaf (if leaves are large, cut in half).

Roll the filling up tightly in the leaf, folding the sides. **Squeeze** the roll to compact the filling (rolls should be about the size of your forefinger).

Line the bottom of a 3-quart heavy saucepan with leftover collard greens. **Arrange** the rolls in layers close together, seams down. **Season** each layer with a small amount of salt, if desired.

Drizzle oil and lemon juice over rolls. **Cover** with an inverted heatproof plate slightly smaller that the diameter of the pan. **Press** down lightly.

Add just enough broth to come up to the rim of the plate. **Bring** to a boil.

Reduce heat to low. **Cook** rolls, covered with the plate and the lid, for 45 minutes, or until most of the liquid is absorbed.

Remove from heat. **Let** cool, covered.

Serve at room temperature or chilled. **Arrange** on a plate with lemon wedges.

Chili and Corn Filled Zucchini

Try guacamole and tomato salsa as an accompaniment on a bed of mixed greens.

6 medium zucchini

Filling:
1 Tablespoon olive oil
1 onion, chopped
1 teaspoon cumin seeds, ground
sea salt (*start with 1/4 teaspoon*)
ground chipotle pepper or cayenne (*start with 1/8 teaspoon*)
3 cups corn kernels
5 garlic cloves, minced
1 teaspoon marjoram, ground
scooped zucchini flesh
2 Tablespoons cilantro, chopped
1 cup cooked adzuki, anasazi or other bean
toasted pumpkin seeds

Cut the zucchini in half lengthwise. **Leave** ends on.

Scoop out centers, leaving about a 1/4-inch shell. **Save** the scooped flesh to add to the filling. **Save** shells.

Preheat oven to 375 degrees.

Prepare filling. **Sauté** all ingredients in oil, except cilantro and cheese, for 5 minutes.

Toss in cilantro and beans. **Adjust** seasonings, if needed.

Mound the filling into reserved zucchini shells. **Sprinkle** with pumpkin seeds.

Place in an oiled baking dish. **Cover.**

Bake for 30 minutes. **Let** rest 10 minutes before serving.

Millet Stuffed Zucchini

6 medium zucchini

Filling:
1/2 cup pine nuts
1/3 cup millet
1 cup water
4-6 cloves garlic, minced
1 heaping Tablespoon Vogue Vege Base
1 onion, chopped
scooped zucchini flesh
1/3 cup sun-dried tomatoes, reconstituted in water and minced
1 Tablespoon fresh basil, minced
1 Tablespoon fresh oregano, minced
sea salt to taste
olive oil

Preheat oven to 375 degrees.

Cut the zucchini in half, length wise, leaving the ends on. **Scoop** out the centers of the zucchini. **Leave** about a 1/4-inch shell. Save the scooped flesh to add to the filling. **Save** shells.

Toast pine nuts. Set aside.

Cook millet in water in a small covered sauce pan until all liquid is absorbed.

Sauté all ingredients, except pine nuts, in approximately 2 Tablespoons of olive oil until onions are softened.

Mix in millet and pine nuts. **Mound** into zucchini boats.

Place in a lightly oiled baking dish. **Cover.**

Bake for 30 minutes.

Savory Stuffed Portabellos

*Great with roasted potatoes,
peppers, and Italian Chopped Salad*

3 portabello mushrooms
small handful parsley
4-5 garlic cloves, minced fine
1/2 onion, minced fine
2 Tablespoons olive oil
2 slices bread, toasted, finely ground
1 Tablespoon nutritional yeast
2 Tablespoons Bragg Liquid Aminos
1/4 teaspoon marjoram, ground
lemon
Creamy "Mozzarella" Cheese Recipe (*optional*) (*See recipe in Condiments*)

Remove stems from mushrooms. **Hollow** partially to stuff. **Set** aside.

Preheat oven to 350 degrees.

Sauté parsley, garlic, and onion in olive oil until soft.

Mix with remaining ingredients.

Stuff mushrooms.

Bake for 30-40 minutes.

Spread "mozzarella" over top. **Sprinkle** with additional parsley. **Serve.**

Stuffed Cabbage Stroganoff

6-8 large cabbage leaves (*or large collard greens, stems removed*)

Filling:
3 cups cooked barley (*not pearled, which is highly refined*)
3/4 cup onion, chopped
1 1/2 cups mushrooms, chopped
3/4 cup almonds, toasted and coarse chopped
1/4 cup parsley, minced
1 Tablespoon Bragg Liquid Aminos
1 cup vegan yogurt

Sauce:
1/3 cup onion, chopped
1 1/2 Tablespoons oil
1 1/2 cups mushrooms, thinly sliced
1/8-1/4 teaspoon red pepper flakes
2 Tablespoons arrowroot
2 Tablespoons Bragg Liquid Aminos
2 Tablespoons nutritional yeast
1 1/4 cups vegan milk

Preheat oven to 350 degrees.

Combine all filling ingredients.

Spoon into cabbage leaves. **Place** in large shallow baking pan.

Sauté onion in oil for 2 minutes. **Add** mushrooms and red pepper flakes. **Cook** for 2 minutes. **Add** remaining ingredients slowly. **Stir** over moderate heat until thickened.

Pour sauce over cabbage.

Bake covered for 20 minutes.

Squash and Leek Turnovers

Filling:
1 1/2 pounds butternut squash
5 garlic cloves, finely chopped
2 Tablespoons olive oil
2 large leeks, white parts only
1/2 teaspoon salt
1/2 teaspoon dried thyme
2 Tablespoons miso
1 Tablespoon fresh thyme, chopped (*or 1/4 teaspoon dried*)
3/4 cup vegan cheese (*mozzarella, Monterrey, jack, etc.*) (*optional*)

Pastry:
3 1/2 cups flour
1/4 cup oil (or 3 Tablespoons coconut oil)
1 1/2 teaspoons sea salt
1 Tablespoon sweetener
1 cup water

Preheat oven to 400 degrees.

Peel, seed and cut butternut squash into 1/2-inch cubes. **Set** aside.

Prepare filling:
Combine 2 cloves of chopped garlic with 1 Tablespoon oil. **Place** cubed squash in baking dish. **Toss** with garlic oil and 1/2 teaspoon salt.

Cover. Bake 25-30 minutes, until squash is tender, but still holds its shape. **Do** not over cook.

Heat remaining oil in large skillet. **Add** leeks, salt, and thyme. **Sauté** over medium heat for approximately 2 minutes, until softened. **Add** remaining garlic. **Cover** pan, allowing leeks to steam until tender, about 5 minutes.

Add miso, mixed with a small amount of water.

Toss the squash, leeks, and thyme gently together. **Add** cheese if desired. **Season** filling well so its flavor comes through the pastry.

Prepare pastry:
Mix flour and oil until crumbly.

Dissolve salt and sweetener in water.

Combine flour mixture and sweetened water. **Mix** to form a dough. **Roll** out dough on floured board. **Cut** into 8-inch rounds. **Place** approximately 1/3 cup filling on each piece. **Wet** edges. **Press** with fork to seal.

Bake for 15-20 minutes, or until light brown.

Sweet Squash Stuffed with Wild Rice

1/4 cup olive oil
2 cloves garlic, minced
1 small red onion, finely chopped
4 ribs celery, minced
1 small zucchini, diced
1/4 pound mushrooms, chopped
1/2 of a 10-ounce bag frozen peas
1/2 teaspoon rosemary
1/2 teaspoon sage
1 1/2 Tablespoons Vogue Veggie Base
5 cups cooked wild and brown rice
sea salt to taste
1/4 cup pecans, chopped
1 large squash (*butternut*) or 2 smaller (*acorn*) cut in half and seeded

Preheat oven to 450 degrees.

Heat olive oil in a large skillet over medium low heat.

Add all veggies and spices. **Cook** several minutes, until softened. **Stir** in rice, salt, and pecans.

Divide the stuffing into each half. **Arrange** in a baking pan. **Pour** water into pan to 3/4-inch. **Cover** pan tightly.

Bake for 1—1 1/2 hours, or until squash is tender when pierced.

Enchilada Pie

Sauce:
1 cup onions, chopped
3 cups tomatoes, chopped
2 garlic cloves, minced
pinch of cayenne
1 Tablespoon chili powder
1 Tablespoon rice syrup
sea salt to taste
1/2 teaspoon ground cumin

8 soft corn tortillas
1 1/2 cups pinto beans, cooked and mashed
1/4 cup black olives, sliced
1/4-1/2 pound cheddar-style cheese, grated
corn kernels (*optional*)
green onions, chopped (*optional*)

Simmer onions, tomatoes, garlic, cayenne, chili powder, rice syrup, salt, and cumin, uncovered, for 30 minutes.

Preheat oven to 350 degrees.

Pour a small amount of sauce on bottom of baking dish.

Begin layering ingredients, starting with tortillas, then beans, olives, cheese (at this point you could add corn kernels or green onions). **Continue** layering.

Finish with sauce and cheese.

Bake until bubbly.

Quick and Easy Soft Tacos

For those nights when you're pressed for time!

2 cups quinoa, cooked
1 cup beans, cooked
1 cup salsa
1/2 cup corn

Corn tortillas

Condiment suggestions:
cheddar-style cheese, grated
salsa
vegan sour cream
avocado slices
chopped tomatoes
mixed salad greens
sprouts
dulse gomacio
pumpkin seeds

Combine first four ingredients well. **Warm** on stove.

Steam tortillas briefly to soften.

Build soft tacos with filling and condiments to taste.

Veggie and Black Bean Tacos

2 cups broccoli, coarsely chopped
1 cup onions, sliced into half moons
1 red bell pepper, cut in strips
1 large portabello mushroom, sliced
1/2 teaspoon ground cumin
2 teaspoons chili powder
1 Tablespoon olive oil
1/4 cup water
1 heaping Tablespoon Vogue Vege Base
2 Tablespoons lime juice
2 cups of cooked and drained beans (*your choice, anasazi, pinto, black*)
2 medium tomatoes, chopped
12 tortillas

Condiments:
vegan cheese (*optional*)
lettuce, shredded
salsa
vegan sour cream
cilantro

Sauté first 6 ingredients in olive oil for five minutes.

Add water and vege base. **Simmer** 2 minutes. **Remove** from heat.

Stir in lime juice, beans, and tomatoes.

Build tacos by using veggie mix. **Use** condiments to taste.

Spicy Sausage and Soba Noodles in Paprika Sauce

*This is a very spicy dish.
For those of you with a low-heat tolerance,
you may cut down on the paprika and cayenne*

2 Tablespoons garlic, minced
1 Tablespoon shallot, minced
3/4 package of vegan sausage, chopped (*store bought or try Tempeh Sausage recipe*)
1/8 cup olive oil
2 Tablespoons sweet paprika
1/4 teaspoon cayenne powder
2 Tablespoons fresh basil, minced (*or 2 teaspoons dried*)
2 Tablespoons fresh oregano, minced (*or 2 teaspoons dried*)
1 cup vegetable broth
1/2 cup plain vegan yogurt (*I use White Wave soy yogurt*)
1/2 cup Tofu Sour Cream (*see recipe in Condiments*)
1 package soba noodles, cooked as per instructions
1/3 cup scallions, finely chopped
1 medium tomato, chopped
sea salt to taste

Cook garlic, shallot, and sausage in a large skillet in olive oil until garlic is golden and sausage begins to brown

Add paprika, cayenne, basil, and oregano.

Stir in broth and simmer mixture until liquid is reduced by half.

Stir in yogurt and sour cream. **Simmer** mixture until liquid is slightly reduced.

Toss the soba noodles, scallions, and tomato into sauce mixture. **Add** salt, if desired.

Chickpea, Eggplant, and Tomato Stew

This is a time intensive recipe...but worth it!

1/2 pound dried chickpeas (or sprouted, which will cut the preparation time dramatically)
1 pound eggplant
1 teaspoon salt, plus additional for sprinkling the eggplant
2 onions, chopped
2 1/2 teaspoons hot green chili, chopped (wear rubber gloves)
1 green bell pepper, seeded and chopped
1/4 cup olive oil
14-16 ounce can whole tomatoes, including juice (preferably Muir Glen)
1/2 cup fresh parsley, chopped
1 1/2 teaspoons garlic, crushed
1 teaspoon dried oregano
1 bay leaf

Soak chickpeas in a large bowl in water to cover by 2 inches overnight. **Drain. Transfer** to a saucepan. **Add** fresh water to cover. **Boil.**

Lower heat. **Cover. Simmer** for 45 minutes, or 15 minutes if using sprouted chickpeas. **Drain** in a sieve. **Reserve** the cooking liquid.

While chickpeas cook, peel eggplant. **Cut** into 1-inch cubes. **Place** in colander. **Sprinkle** lightly with additional salt. **Allow** to stand for 1 hour. **Rinse** eggplant. **Squeeze** dry.

Preheat oven to 300 degrees.

Sauté onions, chili, and bell pepper in a large skillet in oil over moderately high heat for 3 minutes. **Stir** constantly.

Stir in eggplant. **Sauté** mixture for 2 minutes. **Stir** constantly, being careful not to let eggplant brown.

Stir in tomatoes, including juice, parsley, garlic, oregano, and remaining 1 teaspoon sea salt.

Simmer mixture for 10 minutes. **Stir** often.

Stir together chickpeas, 1 3/4 cups of reserved cooking liquid, bay leaf, and eggplant mixture in a 4-quart casserole. **Cover.**

Bake for 2 1/2 hours, or 30 minutes if using sprouted chickpeas.

Sausage and Potato Skillet

4 vegan sausage links, diced (*or 1 recipe Tempeh Sausage rolled into small balls*)
olive oil
1/2 onion, diced
2 cloves garlic, minced
1/2 bell pepper, diced
1/2 tub tofu, crumbled
1-2 Tablespoons strong vegetable broth powder (*preferably Vogue Vege Base*)
1 Tablespoon Bragg Liquid Aminos
2-3 potatoes, cooked and diced*
1 tomato, chopped

Brown sausage links in oil.

Add onion, garlic, and bell pepper.

Cook until veggies are slightly softened.

Add tofu, Vogue, and Braggs.

Stir until combined and just heated through.

Toss in potatoes and tomatoes.

Serve.

*If you have leftover baked potatoes, this would be the time to use them—or steam cubed potatoes.

Cashew Burgers

2 cups cooked rice or moist cooked millet
2 medium carrots, finely diced
2 cloves garlic, minced
1 onion, diced
oil
1 cup cashews
2/3 cup sunflower seeds
1/3 cup sesame seeds
1/2 cup parsley, minced
1 teaspoon sage, minced
2 Tablespoons nutritional yeast
2 Tablespoons Vogue Vege Base
1 teaspoon sea salt

Preheat oven to broil.

Sauté carrots, garlic, and onion until softened in a small amount of oil.

Grind all nuts and seeds.

Mix all ingredients together well. **Form** into patties.

Broil until browned on both sides, approximately 10 minutes total.

Earth Burgers

Use Cashew Burgers recipe above. **Substitute** pumpkin and sunflower seeds for cashews and sesame.

Add 2 Tablespoons tomato paste and 1 teaspoon chili powder instead of sage.

Cook as above.

Nut Burgers In-The-Raw

Serve Burgers with Salsa!

1 cup sprouted wheat
1/4 cup water
1 cup walnuts, ground
1/2 cup sunflower seeds, chopped
1/3 cup sesame or peanut butter
1 small stalk celery, chopped
2 Tablespoons parsley, chopped
2 Tablespoons onion, chopped
1/4 cup water mixed with:
1 Tablespoon miso
1 teaspoon lecithin
1 teaspoon Bragg Liquid Aminos
pinch of marjoram
pinch of dill

Combine all ingredients in a large bowl. **Mix** thoroughly. **Form** into burgers. **Add** more water if too dry. **Serve.**

Tempeh Sausage Patties

1 package tempeh
1/2 cup vegetable broth
1 Tablespoon olive oil
1/2 onion, finely chopped
1/4 teaspoon fennel seeds, crushed
pinch red pepper flakes
1 teaspoon sage
1/2 teaspoon oregano
2 Tablespoons nutritional yeast
1/4 cup rolled oats
1-2 Tablespoons Bragg Liquid Aminos

Simmer tempeh in vegetable broth. **Cool. Grate. Reserve** broth. Set aside.

Sauté onion until golden. Mix ingredients together, using enough reserved broth as necessary to hold patties together. **Brown** in a skillet with a small amount of oil. Serve.

Millet Seed Patties

1 medium onion, diced
1 cup millet, cooked in 3 cups water
1/2 cup rice, cooked in 1 cup water
1 cup pumpkin seeds, ground
1/4 cup almond or cashew butter
3 Tablespoons olive oil
1 teaspoon sea salt
2 Tablespoons Vogue Vege Base
1 teaspoon sage

Sauté onion in small amount of oil. **Cool.**

Mix remaining ingredients well. **Form** into patties. **Brown** in lightly oiled pan.

Serve plain, with gravy, or salsa.

Pecan Patties

These keep well in refrigerator for several days.

1/2 cup oatmeal
1/4 cup water
1 medium onion, diced
1 Tablespoon oil
3/4 cup pecans, ground
1-2 Tablespoons Bragg Liquid Aminos
1/4 teaspoon thyme
1 heaping Tablespoon Vogue Vege Base

Mix oatmeal in water. **Let** sit for a few minutes.

Sauté onion in oil. **Cool.**

Mix all ingredients well. **Form** into patties. **Let** sit for 30 minutes.

Brown lightly in skillet. **Serve** warm or cold.

Millet Nut and Seed Balls

Rhiannons' "Booger Balls"

1/2 cup millet
1 1/2 cups water
1 large stalk kale, stem removed, minced very fine
1/4 teaspoon onion powder
2 Tablespoons Bragg Liquid Aminos
2 heaping Tablespoon Vogue Vege Base
1 heaping Tablespoon cashew butter
1/4 cup raw pumpkin seeds, ground fine

Simmer millet with water until almost absorbed.

Add kale. **Cover.** Let sit for 5 minutes.

Combine onion powder, Braggs, Vogue, and cashew butter well. Mix into millet and kale mixture, along with pumpkin seeds.

Adjust seasonings if needed.

Form into walnut-sized balls (smaller balls for smaller fingers).

Serve.

Baked Tofu with Cabbage and Wild Rice

A large green salad, raw corn and red bell salad, mashed potatoes, and a cranberry relish or chutney would make this a terrific holiday meal!

1/4 cup wild rice
1 1/4 cups water
1/2 package tempeh
1 1-pound package tofu, sliced in 4 pieces
1 cup red cabbage, chopped
1 cup red onion, chopped
1/2 cup apple cider
1/2 teaspoon sage
1/4 teaspoon thyme
1/4 teaspoon marjoram
2 Tablespoons Bragg Liquid Aminos
1 Tablespoon Vogue Vege Base
whole-grain prepared mustard
nutritional yeast

Cook rice in water over low heat for approximately 40 minutes. **Drain.**

Steam tempeh for 10 minutes. **Cool. Grate. Set** aside.

Wrap tofu in clean kitchen towel for 30 minutes.

Preheat oven to 375 degrees.

Combine cabbage, onion, and cider. **Cover. Simmer** until cabbage is just tender. **Add** tempeh, wild rice, sage, thyme, marjoram, Braggs, and Vogue. Set aside.

Spread each slice of tofu generously with mustard on both sides. **Dip** in nutritional yeast. **Place** on a baking sheet. **Bake** for 30 minutes.

Place a scoop of dressing on a plate topped with a tofu cutlet.

Serve with a simple brown gravy (try mine without the mushrooms and finely chop the onions).

Rosemary Tofu Sauté

1 pound extra-firm or firm tofu
1/4 cup nutritional yeast
1 slice of bread, ground in coffee/spice grinder*
1 Tablespoon Vogue Vege Base
1/2 teaspoon garlic powder
1/2 teaspoon paprika
3/4-1 teaspoon rosemary, coarsely ground
1 lemon, juiced
olive oil
kale or spinach, cleaned, stems removed, and chopped

Wrap tofu in kitchen towel for 30 minutes.

Mix yeast, bread, Vogue, garlic powder, paprika, and rosemary. **Set** aside.

Cube tofu into 1/2-inch pieces. **Place** tofu in a bowl. **Stir** in 1 Tablespoon olive oil.

Add dry ingredients. **Toss** to cover. **Let** sit for a few minutes.

Heat a heavy pan over medium high. **Add** 2 or more Tablespoons of olive oil. **Heat** until hot, but not smoking.

Add tofu cubes and any excess breading. **Cook** until browned on all sides.

Add lemon juice. **Stir. Pour** onto a serving platter.

Bring heat to high. **Add** kale or spinach (do not shake off rinse water). **Cover** immediately. If you are using spinach, turn the heat off and let sit for 45 seconds. If using kale, add 1-2 Tablespoons water and bring heat down to low. **Simmer** for 5 minutes until just tender.

Serve immediately.

If you do not have a spice or coffee grinder, let the bread dry out completely (overnight) then crush with a rolling pin. It is not necessary to use dry bread in grinder.

Salisbury Steaks

2 packages tempeh
1/2 tub tofu, crumbled
1/2 cup moist cooked millet or rice
1/4 cup parsley, finely minced,
1/4 cup celery, finely minced
1/4 cup mushrooms, finely minced
1/2 cup onion, finely minced
1 clove garlic, minced
1 teaspoon dry mustard
1 teaspoon paprika
2 Tablespoons Bragg Liquid Aminos
2 Tablespoons Vogue Vege Base

Simmer tempeh in vegetable stock for 10 minutes. **Cool. Grate.**

Mix all ingredients well (this works best with your hands).

Form 3-4 inch patties.

Sauté in small amount of olive oil until golden brown on both sides.

Serve with Mushroom-Onion Gravy (*see recipe in Condiments*).

BBQ Style Tempeh

1 package tempeh
1 Tablespoon olive oil, diced
1 large onion, diced
1 celery stalk, diced
2 large carrots or 1 red bell pepper, diced
1 cup BBQ sauce (*try "Annie's" brand*)
1/2 cup vegetable broth

Steam tempeh 10 minutes. Cut into cubes. Set aside.

Sauté veggies in oil for 2 minutes. **Add** sauce and stock. Stir.

Add tempeh.

Bring to boil. **Reduce** heat.

Cover. Simmer 15 minutes.

Serve over grains.

Deli Style Tempeh

1 package tempeh
1 large onion, diced
2 medium carrots, diced
1 Tablespoon oil
1 bunch of collards, stems removed, chopped
2 cups sauerkraut, rinsed
1-2 Tablespoons whole-grain prepared mustard, or to taste
1/2 cup water
1 Tablespoon Vogue Vege Base

Steam tempeh for 10 minutes. **Cool.**

Sauté tempeh, onion, and carrots in oil until onions are translucent.

Stir in remaining ingredients.

Reduce heat to low. **Cover.**

Simmer 5 minutes.

Serve.

Hot and Pungent Tempeh with Broccoli

1 package tempeh, cubed
1 Tablespoon Bragg Liquid Aminos
2 Tablespoons, plus 2 teaspoons arrowroot
1-2 Tablespoons oil
3 cloves garlic, minced
1 bunch broccoli, cut into small flowerets, blanched

Sauce:
1/4 cup vegetable broth
2 Tablespoons Bragg Liquid Aminos
1 1/2 Tablespoons brown rice vinegar
1 Tablespoon Oriental sesame oil
1 Tablespoon brown rice syrup
1/4 teaspoon sea salt
1/4-1/2 teaspoon red Thai curry paste
2 Tablespoons cilantro, minced

Place tempeh in a bowl. **Add** Braggs and 2 teaspoons arrowroot. **Set** aside.

Combine ingredients for sauce in a small bowl. **Set** aside.

Place wok or pan over medium high heat. **Add** 1 Tablespoon oil.

Add tempeh. **Stir** fry until browned. **Add** more oil if pan dries out. **Remove** tempeh from pan.

Add garlic and broccoli. **Stir** fry just until heated through.

Return tempeh to wok. **Pour** in sauce. **Bring** sauce to a low boil. **Simmer** for several minutes.

Stir in a little arrowroot (mixed with equal water) until lightly thickened.

Serve immediately.

Lettuce Wrapped Tempeh Meatballs

1 package tempeh
1 cup vegetable stock
2 green onions, minced
2 Tablespoons cilantro, minced
2 Tablespoons Bragg Liquid Aminos
2 Tablespoons sesame butter
1 teaspoon orange peel, minced
3/4 teaspoon nutmeg, ground
1/4 teaspoon chili sauce or Thai curry sauce
4 cloves garlic, minced
1 Tablespoon ginger, minced
oil
lime juice to taste
Lettuce leaves

Simmer tempeh in vegetable stock. **Drain. Cool. Grate.**

Mix all ingredients, except oil and lime juice, well.

Form into small balls.

Sauté in a small amount of oil until browned.

Squeeze lime juice over meatballs.

Serve wrapped in lettuce leaves. **Eat** like soft tacos.

Rio Grande Tempeh "Meatloaf"

Serve with salsa if desired or try my Corn and Sun-dried Tomato Relish...yummy!

12 ounces tempeh
1/2 cup onion, chopped
1/2 cup green bell pepper, chopped
1/2 cup fresh cilantro, chopped
2 jalapeno peppers, minced and seeded
1 Tablespoons Vogue Vege Base (*or other strong powdered broth*)
2 Tablespoons olive oil
1/4-1/2 teaspoon sea salt
2 teaspoons cumin, ground
2 teaspoons chili powder
3 large garlic cloves, minced
1 1/2 cups cooked black beans
1/2 cup silken tofu
2 Tablespoons Bragg Liquid Aminos
Approximately 2 cups tortilla chips, crushed
1/2 cup vegetable broth

Preheat oven to 375 degrees.

Steam tempeh for 10 minutes. **Cool. Grate.**

Combine all ingredients well. **Pack** mixture into an oiled loaf pan.

Bake for 50 minutes.

Let loaf stand 10 minutes before serving.

Tempeh Hash

1 package tempeh
2 large potatoes, diced
1 large onion, diced
1 teaspoon cumin seeds
1 Tablespoon olive oil
1 cup veggies, diced (*such as corn, carrot, peas, etc.*)
1/2 yellow or red bell pepper, slivered
1 Tablespoon chili powder
1-2 Tablespoons Bragg Liquid Aminos
pinch red pepper or chipotle pepper (*optional*)

Simmer tempeh in 1 cup of rich vegetable stock. **Cool. Grate.**

Broil potatoes until brown on all sides.

Sauté onion and cumin seeds in oil for 2 minutes. **Add** tempeh. **Brown** lightly.

Add remaining ingredients.

Heat through. **Serve.**

Tri-Grain Hash

1 cup quinoa
3/4 cup millet
1/4 cup amaranth
5 cups water
2 Tablespoons olive oil
1 large potato, diced
1 large onion, diced
1 large carrot, diced
1 roasted red bell pepper, chopped
1-2 heaping Tablespoons Vogue Vege Base
1/2 cup water
1 zucchini, diced
1/2 cup corn
1-2 Tablespoons chili powder
1/2-3/4 cup cheddar-style vegan cheese (*optional*)
1 teaspoon sea salt

Simmer quinoa, millet, and amaranth in water, covered, until liquid is absorbed (approximately 20 minutes).

Sauté potato, onion, and carrot in olive oil.

Add remaining ingredients.

Stir in cooked grain.

Adjust seasonings if needed.

Serve.

Tempeh in Shiitake Cream Sauce

1 medium carrot, shredded
1 green onion, shredded
1 package tempeh
2 Tablespoons olive oil
1/2 cup shiitake mushroom caps, sliced thin
1 Tablespoon ginger, finely minced
1/2 cup cashew cream
1 Tablespoon Bragg Liquid Aminos
1 Tablespoon Oriental sesame oil
1/2 teaspoon orange peel, finely grated
1/8-1/4 teaspoon Thai curry paste

Blanch carrot and green onion by pouring boiling water over them through a sieve. **Set** aside.

Slice tempeh in half. **Slice** again. **Split** them into 4 thin scallops. **Steam** for 10 minutes.

Heat olive oil in pan. **Add** tempeh. **Brown** on both sides. **Remove** from pan. **Add** mushrooms and ginger to hot sauté pan.

Combine Braggs, oil, orange peel, curry paste, and ginger in small bowl to make sauce.

Add sauce. **Bring** to boil. **Simmer** 5 minutes.

Spoon sauce over tempeh slices.

Garnish with carrots and green onions.

Serve immediately.

Tempeh in Red Wine Sauce

*Great served over
mashed potatoes or millet.*

1 package tempeh
1 Tablespoon oil
1 onion, diced small
2 carrots, diced small
1 celery or celeriac root, outer skin discarded, cut into 1/4-inch cubes
1/4 teaspoon thyme
1 heaping Tablespoon Vogue Vege Base
1/4 cup red wine
2 heaping Tablespoons tomato paste
1 bay leaf
1/4 cup Bragg Liquid Aminos
1 cup vegetable broth
1 Tablespoon arrowroot, mixed with 2 Tablespoons water
sea salt to taste

Steam tempeh for 10 minutes. **Cool. Cut** into 1/2-inch cubes. **Set** aside.

Sauté veggies in oil for 5 minutes.

Add thyme, Vogue, and red wine. **Cook** 2 minutes.

Add tomato paste, bay leaf, Braggs, and broth. **Simmer** 15 minutes.

Add arrowroot mixture.

Stir in tempeh.

Simmer 10 additional minutes.

Add salt to taste.

Tempeh Millet Loaf

*Delicious served with
Mushroom Onion Gravy.*

1 package tempeh
1 cup hot vegetable stock
2 cups cooked millet
1 large onion, chopped
2 teaspoons olive oil
1/2 cup parsley, minced
2 teaspoons Bragg Liquid Aminos
2 teaspoons fresh sage, minced
1 teaspoon fresh oregano, minced
2-3 teaspoons whole-grain prepared mustard.

Simmer tempeh in vegetable stock for 10 minutes. **Cool. Reserve** liquid. **Grate** tempeh.

Preheat oven to 350 degrees.

Pour hot stock over millet.

Sauté onion in oil.

Mix tempeh, millet, and onions with parsley.

Mix in remaining ingredients.

Pat into a well oiled loaf pan.

Cover.

Bake for 20-30 minutes.

Serve as is or with Mushroom-Onion Gravy (*see recipe in Condiments*).

Tempeh Skillet Dinner

1 package tempeh
1/2 pound green beans, cut into 1-inch pieces
olive oil
1 onion, diced
2 medium potatoes, diced
2 Tablespoons Vogue Vege Base
2 Tablespoons Bragg Liquid Aminos
1/2 teaspoon dry mustard
2 large tomatoes, diced (*or 1-14 ounce can Muir Glen diced tomatoes*)
water

Steam tempeh 10 minutes. Cool. Cube.

Steam green beans until crisp tender.

Sauté onion, potatoes, and tempeh in oil until lightly browned.

Add Vogue, Braggs, and dry mustard.

Stir in tomatoes and approximately 1/3 to 1/2 cup water.

Cover. Simmer until potatoes are tender.

Mix in green beans.

Serve immediately.

Tempeh with Lemon Ginger Glaze

1 package tempeh
1/2 cup lemon juice
1/4 cup rice syrup
1/4 cup vegetable stock
2 Tablespoons Bragg Liquid Aminos
1/2 teaspoon sea salt
2 teaspoons lemon peel, grated
2 teaspoons fresh ginger, grated
1-2 Tablespoons oil
3 garlic cloves, finely minced
2 Tablespoons arrowroot
2 Tablespoons water

Steam tempeh for 10 minutes. **Cool. Slice** into slender fingers or dice into 1/4-inch pieces.

Place lemon juice, rice syrup, vegetable stock, Braggs, salt, lemon peel, and ginger in a small saucepan. **Set** aside sauce.

Sauté garlic and tempeh in oil until tempeh is golden brown.

Simmer sauce for 5 minutes.

Dissolve 2 Tablespoons of arrowroot into equal amount of water. Stir into sauce until a thick glaze is achieved.

Stir sauce into tempeh.

Serve immediately.

Desserts

*"What is enough?
It's the key to bringing our lives into
alignment with what the Earth can
sustain. It can also be the key to a
personal fulfillment—to a life that
is simpler, less cluttered, yet rich with
purpose and meaning."*

*•In Context,
A Quarterly of Human Sustainable Culture
No. 26, Summer 1990*

*Stevia can enhance the effect of other sweeteners.
Adding to recipes as a dietary supplement can help reduce the amount
of sweetener you would need.*

Agar Fruit Gel

This is a vegan version of jello.

4 Tablespoons Agar flakes
4 cups apple, peach, or apricot juice
2 cups fresh fruit, chopped, pureed, or both
1 teaspoon vanilla
juice of 1/2 lemon

Place agar and juice in a saucepan. Let sit for a few minutes to soften.

Bring to a boil. **Simmer** for 5 minutes.

Remove from heat. **Stir** in fruit and flavoring. **Pour** into a bowl or mold. **Allow** to set.

Sesame Custard

2 cups apple juice
2 1/2 Tablespoons rice syrup
1/4 teaspoon agar powder
2 1/2 Tablespoons arrowroot
2 Tablespoons water
1/4 cup sesame butter

Combine apple juice and syrup. **Bring** to a boil. **Add** agar powder. **Simmer** for 2 minutes.

Make a paste of arrowroot and water. **Stir** into hot juice. **Cook** over low heat until thick.

Stir in sesame butter. **Cook** until smooth.

Pour into large bowl or into 4 individual dishes.

Cool to room temperature. **Chill.**

Carob Pudding

1 package Mori-Nu tofu
2 Tablespoons carob powder
1 Tablespoon grain coffee (*preferably Pero*)
2 Tablespoons cashew butter
1/4 teaspoon stevia or 2-4 Tablespoons rice syrup
1 teaspoon vanilla

Process all ingredients in blender until smooth.

Chill. Serve.

Creamy Fruit Pudding

3/4 cup cashews
1/2 cup water
2 large bananas
2 cups fresh or frozen fruit, chopped
pinch of stevia*
1 teaspoon vanilla

Process cashews, water, and bananas in blender until smooth.

Stir fruit into mixture.

Chill or serve immediately.

If you want a sweeter taste, add more stevia powder or 1 Tablespoon of rice syrup.

Tapioca Pudding

Though not a traditional recipe, this conjures up memories of cold childhood winters spent in a toasty, warm kitchen, my hands warmed by a bowl of freshly made pudding.

1 cup cashews
4 cups water
1/2 cup tapioca pearls
1/3 cup maple syrup or barley malt syrup
1 teaspoon vanilla
1/2 cup unsweetened coconut, shredded
1/2 cup dates, chopped (*optional*)

Blend 1 cup cashews with 1 cup water until smooth.

Pour into saucepan with remaining water.

Add tapioca pearls. **Soak** 15 minutes.

Add maple syrup. **Bring** to boil. **Reduce** heat. **Simmer** 10 minutes.

Remove from heat. **Add** vanilla, coconut, and dates, if desired.

Cool before serving.

Lemon Mousse

1 package Mori-Nu tofu
1 1/2 Tablespoons smooth cashew butter
2 Tablespoons brown rice syrup
1/4 teaspoon stevia powder
1/4 teaspoon sea salt
2 Tablespoons lemon juice
1/2 Tablespoon lemon zest, finely grated
1 teaspoon vanilla extract
pinch of turmeric dissolved in the lemon juice

Blend all ingredients in a food processor or blender.

Refrigerate before serving.

Strawberry Mousse

1/2 cup juice
1 Tablespoon agar flakes
10 1/2-ounce package silken tofu
1/4 teaspoon stevia powder
3 cups strawberries
1 teaspoon vanilla
1 teaspoon lemon rind, finely grated

Simmer juice in a sauce pan over low heat. **Add** agar. **Stir** until dissolved, approximately 5 minutes.

Combine all ingredients in a blender or processor.

Pour into dessert dishes.

Chill about one hour.

Banana Spice Bars

Wet ingredients:
3 Tablespoons flax seed, ground finely
1/2 cup water
2/3 cup rice syrup
1/4 cup oil
1/2 cup plain soy yogurt
1 teaspoon vanilla extract

Dry ingredients:
1 1/2 cups flour (*barley, spelt, rye, or oat*)
1 cup rice flour
1 Tablespoon arrowroot
1 Tablespoon baking soda
1/2 teaspoon sea salt
1 teaspoon stevia leaf
2 teaspoons cinnamon, ground
1/2 teaspoon nutmeg, ground
1 teaspoon allspice, ground

Nut mixture:
1/2 cup pecans, chopped
2 Tablespoons sesame seeds
2/3 cup sunflower seeds
1 1/2 cups bananas, mashed

Preheat oven to 350 degrees.

Mix flax seeds with water. Set aside.

Blend flax mixture with wet ingredients.

Stir dry ingredients together. **Add** to wet ingredients.

Stir in nut mixture.

Pour into oiled 9"-inch x 13-inch pan.

Bake for 30-35 minutes or until done. **Cut** into squares while still warm.

Sesame Crunchies

1/2 cup peanut butter
1/2 cup sesame butter
1/2 cup rice syrup
1 teaspoon vanilla
1/2 cup oil
3/4 cup oats, ground
3/4 cup millet flour
1/2 cup coconut, shredded
1/2 cup sunflower seeds
1/2 cup carob chips

Preheat oven to 350 degrees.

Combine all ingredients.

Drop by spoonfuls on oiled cookie sheets. **Press** slightly.

Bake for 10-15 minutes.

Cool before removing from pans.

Double Dip Fruit Bits

When kids want something sweet and I'm busy, these are fast and satisfying!

Strawberries (*or other fresh or dried fruit, except melons*)
finely ground nuts (*preferably almonds*)
plain vegan yogurt

Dip fruit in yogurt. Dip in nuts. Eat!

Almond Balls

1/2 cup raw almond butter
1 Tablespoon rice syrup
1 Tablespoon oat flour
1/4 teaspoon vanilla
raisins
carob powder

Mix first five ingredients.

Make balls. **Press** raisins inside each.

Roll in carob powder.

Carob Chews

1/2 cup peanut or cashew butter
1/2 cup almond butter
2/3 cup brown rice syrup
1/2 teaspoon vanilla
3 Tablespoons carob flour
1 1/4 cups oats

Combine butters, sweetener, and vanilla. **Mix** well.

Combine dry ingredients. **Add** to wet.

Roll into balls.

Store in refrigerator.

Options: *Add 3/4 cups raisins, or*
1-2 teaspoons grated orange or tangerine peel.
Roll in flaked coconut or crushed nuts.
Place a surprise dry fruit filling in middle (apricots, for example).
Use your imagination!

Fruit and Nut Balls

*Great source of calcium, phosphorus, and protein.
Kids eat them up!*

1 cup cashews
1 cup almonds
1 cup raisins
1/2 cup figs (*or 1 cup dates*)
1/2 cup dates
coconut, shredded (*or carob powder*)

Grind nuts in food processor.

Add dry fruit slowly.

Process until you are able to roll into balls.

Add a small amount of water if too dry.

Roll in shredded coconut or carob powder.

Almond Clusters

1 cup almonds, ground
1/2 cup brown rice syrup
1/2 teaspoon ground cinnamon
1/2 teaspoon vanilla
3 Tablespoons almond or cashew butter
3 cups boxed flake cereal (*preferably Erewhon Corn Flakes*)

Mix all ingredients except flakes.

Stir in flakes. Mix well. Shape into small balls. Chill.

Sunflower-Apricot Patties

1 cup sunflower seeds, ground
1 cup dried apricot, finely chopped
pinch of sea salt
3/4 teaspoon vanilla
carob powder

Combine sunflower seeds, apricot, salt, and vanilla.

Roll and pat into half dollar size.

Coat in carob powder.

Sprouted Wheat Surprises

These freeze well.

1 1/4 cups sprouted wheat (*tail should be 1/8-inch to 1/4-inch long*)
1 cup each, dates and figs, pitted
1/3 cup each, pumpkin and sunflower seeds, chopped
1/4 cup sesame seeds
2 Tablespoons nut butter
2 Tablespoons orange or lemon rind, grated
1/4 teaspoon sea salt
shredded coconut (*optional*)

Put wheat and dates and figs through a food grinder or processor.

Work in remaining ingredients with hands.

Form into balls. **Place** an additional nut half in center of ball, if desired.

Roll each ball in shredded coconut, if desired.

Carob Dessert Fondue

3 Tablespoons Earth Balance spread
10 ounces unsweetened carob chips
1/2 teaspoon nutmeg, grated
1 teaspoon vanilla
1/2 cup maple syrup
3/4 cup vegan milk
2 pints fresh strawberries, or other fruit

Combine all ingredients, except fresh fruit, in a fondue pot over a low flame or on top of a double broiler placed over hot water.

Stir until carob chips are melted, about 15 minutes.

Serve as a dipping sauce.

Carob Frosting

Great on Carob Cupcakes or Peanut Butter Cake!

1 cup cashew or almond butter
6 Tablespoons rice syrup
2 teaspoons vanilla
6 Tablespoons roasted carob powder
3-6 Tablespoons vegan milk

Blend all ingredients well.

Add enough milk to achieve a spreading consistency.

Cashew Cream

Wonderful with Pumpkin or Apple Pie!

1 cup raw, unsalted cashews
Approximately 1/4 cup water
2-3 Tablespoons maple syrup (*or a pinch of stevia, with or without 1/4 teaspoon maple extract flavoring*)
1 teaspoon vanilla

Chop nuts coarsely in a blender.

Add remaining ingredients gradually to the blender with the motor running.

Taste. Add additional syrup, if desired.

Blend to desired consistency. **Add** more water, if needed.

Carob Ganache A Pourable Icing

1/2 cup rice syrup
1/4 cup vegan milk
1 cup non-dairy carob chips
2 Tablespoons "Butter" (*see recipe in Condiments*)
1/2 teaspoon vanilla extract

Heat syrup and milk to a simmer. **Add** chips and "butter." **Cook** until chips melt. **Remove** from heat. **Stir** in vanilla.

Use to dip fruits or pour over cakes.

Vanilla Tofu Cream

This is a wonderful cream to serve over strawberries and shortcake, or as a parfait with carob pudding.

1 pound silken tofu
1/2 cup oil
1/2 cup maple syrup
1 Tablespoon lemon juice
1/4 teaspoon salt
3/4 teaspoon agar powder (*or 4 teaspoons agar flakes*)
1 cup water
1/4 cup arrowroot powder
1 cup vegan milk
1/4 cup vanilla extract

Combine tofu, oil, maple syrup, lemon juice, and salt in a blender.

Combine agar powder and cold water in a heavy bottomed saucepan.

Stir over medium flame until mixture reaches a boil.

Combine arrowroot with milk and vanilla in a separate bowl. **Add** to boiling liquid.

Cook until mixture begins to bubble. **Stir** continuously.

Remove from heat.

Add hot mixture to blender. Blend until smooth.

Pour into container.

Place in refrigerator about one hour to cool.

Serve when cooled.

Coconut Macaroons

1 cup coconut, grated
1 cup oatmeal flour
1/4 cup rice syrup
1/8 teaspoon sea salt
1 teaspoon vanilla
1 teaspoon lemon zest
2 Tablespoons flax meal
water (*enough to hold everything together*)

Mix all ingredients. **Roll** into small balls. **Set** aside for a few hours.

Store in refrigerator.

Ginger Cookies

Fresh ginger is what makes this cookie!

1/2 cup oil
1/2 cup barley malt syrup
Egg replacer for 1 egg
1/2 cup brown rice syrup
1 teaspoon cinnamon, ground
3 Tablespoons ginger, freshly grated
2 teaspoons baking soda
1/4 cup oat bran
2 cups oat flour

Preheat oven to 350 degrees.

Combine wet ingredients in a medium bowl. **Mix** well.

Mix dry ingredients in another bowl.

Combine wet and dry ingredients thoroughly…do not over mix!

Drop by spoonful onto a greased cookie sheet.

Bake for approximately 15 minutes.

Oatmeal Date Cookies In-The-Raw

These may be stored in refrigerator for several days.

2 cups oatmeal, ground
1 Tablespoon flax seed, ground
1 teaspoon lecithin
1/4 teaspoon sea salt
1/2 teaspoon cinnamon, ground
1/2 teaspoon allspice, ground
2 teaspoons vanilla
1/2 cup dates, blended in 1/2 cup apple juice
1/4 cup pecans or walnuts, ground

Mix all ingredients well. (The dough will be stiff.) **Roll** into small balls.

Let sit for an hour.

Quick and Easy Oatmeal Cookies

3 bananas
1/2 cup nuts, chopped
1 cup dates, chopped
1 cup figs, chopped
1/2 teaspoon salt
1 Tablespoon vanilla
2 cups oats

Preheat oven to 400 degrees.

Mash bananas, leaving some chunks. **Add** nuts, dates, and figs. **Beat** well.

Add salt, vanilla, and oats.

Drop from spoon onto ungreased cookie sheet. (You can spread cookie sheet with a small amount of lecithin or oil, if needed.)

Bake approximately 25 minutes.

Sesame Crunch Cookies

If not eaten immediately, refrigerate in an airtight container.

1 cup rolled oats
3/4 cup toasted sesame seeds
1 1/2 cups barley flour
1 teaspoon baking soda
pinch sea salt
3 Tablespoons lemon rind, finely minced
1/2 cup oil
1/2 cup maple syrup
2 Tablespoons lemon juice

Preheat oven to 375 degrees.

Grind oats and sesame seeds coarsely. **Add** flour, baking soda, and salt.

Mix liquid ingredients. **Stir** into dry ingredients, creating a soft dough.

Roll dough into smooth balls about the size of a small walnut.

Place about 2 inches apart on lightly oiled cookie sheets.

Press balls gently to flatten them slightly.

Bake until lightly browned on the bottom, approximately 10-12 minutes.

Cool completely.

Sesame Millet Cookies

1/4 cup millet
1/2 cup water
1 cup barley malt syrup
1 1/2 cups sesame butter
1 teaspoon vanilla
1/4 cup cornmeal
1/4 cup rye flour
1/2 cup toasted sesame seeds

Preheat oven to 350 degrees.

Simmer millet in water in a covered pan until water is absorbed.

Add remaining liquid ingredients.

Mix dry ingredients in separate bowl.

Add wet ingredients to dry ingredients. The dough will be very sticky.

Spoon dough onto oiled cookie sheets. **Flatten** with wet fingers.

Bake for approximately 15 minutes or until browned.

Cool. They will firm as they cool.

Banana Raisin Ice Cream

2/3 cup raisins
1/2 cup water
2 cups cashews, ground
2 pounds very ripe bananas
1 teaspoon vanilla

Soak raisins in water overnight.

Process all ingredients in blender.

Pour into container. **Freeze.**

Banana Chipsicle

1 banana
nut butter
vegan carob chips or raisins
ground nuts or coconut

Cut banana in half. **Insert** popsicle stick

Spread banana with nut butter.

"Stud" banana with chips or raisins.

Roll in ground nuts or coconut.

Crepes

Any of these would be great with a dollop of Vanilla Tofu Cream (see recipe in Desserts)

1 cup barley flour
1 cup spelt, kamut, or pastry flour
1/4 cup nutritional yeast
1/2 teaspoon baking powder
dash of sea salt
3 1/2 cups water
2 Tablespoons oil
1 cup silken tofu
oil to coat pan

Puree all ingredients in a blender until smooth.

Heat a 9-inch nonstick crepe pan (or regular pan) over medium-high heat until a drop of water sizzles.

Coat pan with oil.

Pour in 1/4 cup of batter. Tilt and swirl pan so that batter forms an even layer over the whole surface.

Cook until edges loosen from side of pan and top starts to bubble. **Flip** crepe over.

Cook on other side until flecked with gold.

Stack finished crepes in a dish to cool. (makes approximately 24 crepes).

Fill crepes with your choice of fillings.

Crepe Fillings

Variation 1:
2 apples, chopped
1/4 cup raisins
1/4 cup fruit juice
1/2 teaspoon cinnamon
1 teaspoon lemon juice
1 Tablespoon arrowroot mixed with 2 Tablespoons fruit juice

Simmer all ingredients, except arrowroot mixture, in saucepan until apples are tender.

Mix in arrowroot.

Simmer until thickened.

Fill and roll crepes.

Variation 2:
3/4 pound tofu
1/3 cup carob powder
1/4 cup rice syrup
2 Tablespoons oil
1 1/2 teaspoons vanilla
1 teaspoon lemon juice

pinch of salt

Blend all ingredients until smooth and creamy.

Chill until set.

Roll crepes.

Serve with dollop of tofu whipped cream or cashew cream. **Sprinkle** with nuts.

Variation 3:
1 cup raspberries
2 bananas, sliced
2 teaspoons lemon juice
2 Tablespoons flaked unsweetened coconut

Mix all ingredients well in bowl. **Chill.**

Fill and roll crepes.

Pie Crust

Enough for one 10-inch pie.

1 1/2 cups sunflower seeds
1 1/2 cups almonds
pinch of salt
1 1/2 teaspoons baking powder
2 Tablespoons oil*
3 Tablespoons water

Preheat oven to 375 degrees.

Grind seeds and nuts.

Combine with salt and baking powder.

Stir in oil and water with a fork, adjusting to create a moist dough.

Pat into a lightly oiled pie plate.

Bake for 15 minutes, or until golden brown.

Cool. Fill.

*Variation: you can delete oil and add cashews and walnuts.

Pie Crust #2

3/4 cup barley flour, chilled
3/4 cup spelt flour, chilled
3 Tablespoons coconut oil
pinch of sea salt
1/2 cup ice water

Add oil to flour. **Work** in until it forms a crumbly meal. **Stir** salt into water. **Add** to flour. (Do not worry if dough seems too wet, it will dry up.) **Roll** out each half of dough on a floured surface. **Transfer** to pie plate. **Trim** and crimp edges.

Place in a 400 degree oven for 10-15 minutes if you are pre-baking shell.

Fruit Mousse Pie

*Proper food combining is critical with fruit.
For strict combining, tofu would not be used.
You should not eat this after a meal (unless it is just a light salad),
as it will interfere with the digestive processes.
Instead, enjoy this pie on its own. It is healthy, light, and delicious.*

Crust:
1/3 cup sunflower seeds
1/3 cup cashews
1/3 cup almonds
1/3 cup coconut
1/2 to 1 cup raisins (*enough to hold mixture together*)
1 cup soft dates

Grind seeds, nuts, and coconut to a fine meal in a food processor.

Add the fruit. **Process,** adding additional raisins as necessary.

Press into a lightly-oiled 9-inch pie plate.

Fill crust.

Filling:
1 bag frozen berries
1-3 Tablespoons brown rice syrup
1 package Mori-Nu tofu

1/2 cup cashews

Blend all ingredients in blender until smooth.

Pour into pie crust.

Refrigerate immediately until ready to serve.

Lemon Pie

1 Tablespoon agar flakes or 3/4 teaspoon agar powder
1/4 cup boiling water
1 1/2 cups water
1/2 cup lemon juice
1 cup apple juice
2/3 cup cashew nuts
2/3 cup rice syrup
1/3 cup coconut
6 Tablespoons arrowroot powder
2 Tablespoons lemon rind
1/4 teaspoon sea salt

Prepare pie crust (see Pie Crust recipe choices).

Mix agar with boiling water. Let sit one minute.

Pour agar mixture into blender. **Add** remaining ingredients to blender.

Process until very smooth.

Place over heat. **Stir** constantly until thickened.

Pour into a 10-inch pie shell.

Place in refrigerator to chill.

Pumpkin Pie

Cashew Cream makes a wonderful accompaniment to this pie. (See recipe)

Crust:
3/4 cup barley flour
3/4 cup oats
1/2 cup toasted almonds, finely chopped
1/2 teaspoon cinnamon
pinch of sea salt
scant 1/8 teaspoon stevia powder
1/4 cup oil

Blend dry ingredients.

Stir in oil. **Add** 1-2 Tablespoons of water, if needed.

Press into an oiled 9-inch pie plate. **Spread** to cover all surfaces.

Pie:
2 cups cooked pumpkin, kabocha or butternut squash
1 pound firm or extra firm tofu
1/2 cup brown rice syrup
1 rounded teaspoon of cinnamon, ground
1/2 teaspoon nutmeg, ground
1/2 teaspoon ginger, ground
1/4 teaspoon allspice, ground

1/4 teaspoon cloves, ground
1/2 teaspoon sea salt
1/4 teaspoon stevia powder

Preheat oven to 375 degrees.

Combine all ingredients in blender. **Process. Add** water only if the mixture seems very thick.

Pour into pie crust. **Bake** on the middle shelf for 30 minutes.

Cool and firm up on a rack for at least 2 hours before serving.

Carob Cupcakes

1 2/3 cups barley or wheat pastry flour
1/2 cup roasted carob powder
2 Tablespoons grain coffee (preferably Pero)
3/4 teaspoon sea salt
2 teaspoons baking powder
2/3 cup brown rice syrup
1 tsp stevia leaf
1/2 cup canola oil
1 cup vegan milk
2 teaspoons vanilla
1/3 cup vegan carob chips

Preheat oven to 350 degrees.

Mix dry ingredients in one bowl and wet ingredients in another. **Add** together. **Stir** just until combined.

Pour into oiled or papered muffin tins. (*I personally like to use paper cups but oiling the muffin tins are fine as well.*)

Bake for approximately 18-20 minutes, or until a toothpick inserted in the center comes out clean.

Cool. Serve as is or with Carob Frosting (*see recipe in Desserts*).

Variations:
•*Try lightly toasted almond slivers instead of carob chips. Decrease vanilla to 1 1/2 teaspoons and add 1/2 teaspoon almond flavoring.*

•*Mix cherries into dry ingredients and omit vegan carob chips.*

Black Forest Cake

1 1/2 cups water
1 1/4 cups maple syrup
1 1/2 teaspoons vanilla
3/4 cup applesauce
3 cups flour (*spelt, wheat pastry, or combine with barley*)
1 cup carob powder
1 1/2 Tablespoons baking powder
1 1/2 teaspoons baking soda
cherries or strawberries, sliced
Carob Ganache (*see recipe in Desserts*)
1/2 Vanilla Tofu Cream (*see recipe in Desserts*)

Preheat oven to 350 degrees.

Mix liquid ingredients.

Mix dry ingredients.

Stir dry ingredients into wet.

Pour into 2 oiled and floured 9-inch cake pans.

Bake for about 35 minutes, or until done. **Cool** for 10 minutes. Remove from pans. **Invert** on cooling rack. **Cool** completely. **Split** each layer in half lengthwise with a serrated knife to form 4 round layers.

Make Ganache and Vanilla Cream (see recipes).

Place one layer of cake on a serving plate. **Spread** with 1/3 of Ganache.

Place another layer of cake on top of Ganache. **Layer** strawberries or cherries. **Place** another layer of cake on top of strawberries. **Spread** with Vanilla Cream. **Place** the last layer on top and pour the remaining Ganache over the cake, spreading it with a knife.

Cool in refrigerator until ready to serve. **Place** a few strawberries or cherries decoratively over cake, if desired.

Carrot Cake

*This is my favorite cake.
I use only fruit as a sweetener, and it is
still sinfully rich.*

2 cups finely ground carrots (*or carrot pulp from juiced carrots*)
1 cup raisins, soaked in water about 1 hour (*save soak water*)
1 cup dates
1 cup nuts (*walnuts, pecans, almonds, brazil nuts, etc.*)
2 cups oat flour
1 1/2 teaspoons cinnamon, ground
1 1/2 teaspoons nutmeg, ground
1 lemon zest
1 orange zest
1/4 cup dried pineapple, diced small
2 teaspoons vanilla
1/4 teaspoon sea salt

Frosting:
2 cups cashews
1/2 cup raisin soak water, adding more if necessary
2 Tablespoon lemon juice
pinch of stevia
2 teaspoons vanilla
1 lemon zest

Press excess liquid from carrots, if necessary. **Process** raisins, dates, and nuts in food processor until finely ground. **Combine** well with remaining ingredients.

Prepare frosting. **Process** all ingredients in blender until smooth. **Add** more raisin soak water, if necessary, to achieve desired consistency.

Line a 10-inch pie pan with plastic wrap. **Press** half of cake mixture into pan. **Turn** pan over onto serving plate. **Remove** pan and plastic wrap.

Spread half of frosting over top. **Repeat** molding with remaining mixture. **Gently** release on top of first layer. **Spread** remaining frosting on top and sides of cake.

Garnish with cinnamon and chopped nuts, if desired.

Peanut Butter Cake

Try this with my Carob Frosting recipe

3 Tablespoons flax seed
1/2 cup water
1/2 cup organic peanut butter
1/3 cup oil
3/4 cup rice syrup
1 1/2 teaspoons vanilla
1 cup vegan milk
2 cups barley or wheat pastry or spelt flour
1 teaspoon baking powder
3/4 teaspoon sea salt
1/2 teaspoon cinnamon, ground
1/2 cup vegan carob chips
1/2-3/4 cup organic peanuts, coarsely chopped (*optional*)

Preheat oven to 350 degrees.

Mix wet ingredients.

Mix dry ingredients in separate bowl.

Add wet ingredients to dry. **Combine** well.

Pour into an oiled and floured 9-inch pan.

Bake for approximately 45 minutes, or until center springs back when touched.

Strawberry Shortcake

Vanilla Tofu Cream (*see recipe in Desserts*)

Cake:
2 cups barley flour
2 cups spelt flour
4 teaspoons baking powder
2 teaspoons baking soda
2/3 cup oil
1 1/2 cups maple syrup
1 1/2 cups water
2 teaspoons apple cider vinegar
1 teaspoon salt
2 teaspoons vanilla extract

Strawberry Sauce:
1 pint strawberries, hulled and stemmed
1/2 teaspoon lemon juice
1/4 teaspoon vanilla
1 Tablespoon maple syrup
pinch of sea salt
1 pint of strawberries, sliced

Preheat oven to 350 degrees.

Sift flours, baking powder, and baking soda together in one bowl.

Whisk together remaining ingredients in another bowl.

Mix wet and dry ingredients together.

Pour into oiled pans.

Bake for approximately 25 minutes, until toothpick inserted in center comes out clean and cake is golden brown.

Cool.

Prepare sauce:
Blend all ingredients except last pint of strawberries.

Stir in sliced strawberries.

Serve shortcake with Vanilla Tofu Cream (*see recipe in Desserts*) and Strawberry Sauce.

Beverages

The average American consumes 52 gallons of soda per year for a total of approximately 65,000 empty calories. Phosphorous (the bubbly in soda) and sugar leach alkaline mineral reserves, such as calcium, from our body, and aspartame and other toxins create chemical warfare within.

Apple Milk

1 cup fresh apple juice
1 cup almond milk
1 medium banana
1/4 teaspoon cinnamon

Blend all ingredients in blender.

Coconut Milk

2 small coconuts (*make sure there are no cracks*)

Test the 3 "eyes" of the coconut with an ice pick to find the weakest one. **Pierce** it to make a hole.

Drain liquid and reserve 1/2 cup. (Add cold water to make 1/2 cup, if necessary).

Bake coconut in preheated 400 degree oven for 15 minutes. **Break** with a hammer. **Remove** flesh from the shell, taking it out carefully with the point of a strong knife.

Cut coconut meat into small pieces.

Grind coarse half the coconut meat with half the reserved coconut liquid in a food processor. Let mixture drain in a cheesecloth-lined sieve set over a bowl.

Squeeze mixture in cheesecloth to extract the thick coconut milk. **Transfer** the ground coconut from the cheesecloth to a bowl. **Reserve** it for making a batch of light coconut milk.

Repeat the procedure with the remaining coconut milk and liquid.

To make light coconut milk: **Grind** fine half the reserved ground coconut with 3/4 cups boiling water. Let mixture drain in the cheesecloth-lined sieve. **Squeeze** it in the cheesecloth to extract the thin coconut milk. **Discard** the finely-ground coconut.

Lemonade for One

juice of 1 lemon
12 ounces water
1/8-1/4 teaspoon stevia powder

Stir all ingredients.

Carob Nut Drink

2 Tablespoons cashews
2 Tablespoons almonds
1 cup soy milk
1 Tablespoon carob powder
1/4 teaspoon vanilla
1 Tablespoon grain coffee (*preferably Pero*)
1/8 teaspoon stevia

Blend all ingredients in blender until smooth.

Carob Shake

1 cup almond milk
2 teaspoons unsweetened carob powder
1 Tablespoon sweetener
1 1/2 frozen medium bananas

Blend all ingredients in blender.

Hot Carob Drink

2 cups vegan milk
1 heaping Tablespoon carob powder
1-2 Tablespoons rice syrup
1/4 teaspoon vanilla
sea salt to taste

Heat all ingredients in sauce pan. **Whisk** until frothy and free of lumps.

Blueberry, Fig, and Date Shake

2 cups almond milk
2 Tablespoons lemon juice
1 Tablespoon sweetener
1/2 teaspoon cinnamon, ground
1/2 cup pitted dates
1/4 cup figs
1 cup blueberries

Blend all ingredients in blender.

The Meeny Greeny Banana Shake

1 frozen banana
1/2-3/4 cup vegan milk
small handful of almonds
1 teaspoon spirulina or chlorella
1 teaspoon flax oil

Process in blender until smooth.

Dreamy Date Shake

1/2 banana, frozen if possible
3-4 dates, pits removed
1/4 cup almonds
1/4 teaspoon nutmeg, ground
1/4 teaspoon maple flavoring
vegan milk

Place all ingredients, except milk, in blender.

Pour milk to the 1 1/2 cup line.

Process until smooth.

Cashew/Apricot Drink

1/3 cup apricots
3 cups hot water
1/2 cup cashews
1/2 teaspoon vanilla

Soak apricots in hot water for 5 minutes.

Blend all ingredients in blender until smooth.

Just Peachy! Shake

2 medium ripe peaches
1 frozen banana
small handful almonds
small handful cashews
almond milk
1/4 teaspoon vanilla (*not needed if almond milk is flavored*)

Blend all ingredients in blender until smooth.

Fruit Smoothie

1 banana, fresh or frozen
1 cup frozen berries (*raspberries are sweetest*)
2 Tablespoons sunflower seeds
1 cup juice (*I usually dilute with water 50%*)
1/2 teaspoon spirulina (*optional*)
Acidophilus powder (*optional*)

Blend all in blender until smooth.

Cranberry Yogurt Shake

3/4 cup plain yogurt (*preferably vegan*)
1/4 cup distilled water
1/3 cup cranberries, fresh or frozen
2 Tablespoons sunflower seeds
1/8 teaspoon stevia powder
Acidophilus powder (*optional*)

Blend all ingredients in blender until smooth.

Carrot Drink

1 medium carrot
1/2 apple, quartered and cored
1/2 lemon, peel and seeds removed
1 Tablespoon flax oil (*optional*)
1 cup water

Blend all ingredients in blender until smooth.

Carrot Drink #2

1 medium carrot
1/4 beet
1/2 apple, cored and quartered
1/4 lemon, peel and seeds removed
1/4 cup parsley
1 Tablespoon Kyogreen (*or other microalgae*)
1 cup water

Blend all ingredients in blender until smooth.

Glossary of Special Ingredients

Amaranth—An extraordinarily, nutritious seed, high in protein, normally used as a side dish, though not by itself. It has quite a strong taste and so is usually added with other grains in small amounts. My family likes it in rice where I may add an additional 2-3 Tablespoons of amaranth in while cooking. Try popping it in a heavy, dry pan, it will look like miniature popcorn.

Arrowroot—Used as a thickener, it looks much like cornstarch, though it is derived from a tropical starchy tuber and is superior nutritionally to cornstarch. Use equivalent amounts.

Apple cider vinegar—Made from freshly pressed apple juice, touted as a tonic for many ailments. Purchase only organic, unfiltered, and not pasteurized to ensure purity and quality. Used in most of my recipes calling for vinegar.

Barley malt syrup—Thick, amber-colored sweetener made from sprouted barley. Not as sweet as sugar and comprised of primarily maltose, a complex sugar, less destructive on the body's mineral balance.

Bragg Liquid Aminos—A non-fermented seasoning similar to soy sauce and made with just soybeans. Highly concentrated with a high sodium content, use sparingly.

Carob—Ground and roasted pods from a tropical tree. Good source of calcium, iron, magnesium and vitamins A & B. Use in place of cocoa powder.

Flax seeds—Rich in the essential omega-3 fatty acids and vitamin E. Store in freezer and grind as you need them. Sprinkle on your hot cereal or bake into breads or muffins for a rich, nutty flavor. Three Tablespoons ground seed mixed with 1/2 cup water is equivalent to 2 eggs when replacing in quick bread recipes.

Kudzu—Used as a thickener, it can replace cornstarch or arrowroot in equal amounts. It is valued in Chinese medicine for a variety of ailments including digestive disorders, colds and headaches. Usually comes in chalky white chunks. Press with the back of a spoon to break it up before using.

Lecithin—I prefer granules over liquid variety. Extracted from soybeans, it is used extensively as a flavor enhancer and acts as a preservative. Lecithin helps to emulsify cholesterol in the body as well as aids in the utilization of fats.

Millet—A gluten-free, alkaline cereal grain with a high amino-acid profile and high iron content. May be cooked into a dry pilaf or a smoother mashed potato texture by adding more water. Dry toasting it prior to cooking gives it a richer, nuttier flavor. Its mild taste lends itself well to a myriad of different seasonings, gravies or sauces.

Microalgae—Chlorella, spirulina, and wild blue green algae are the three most widely available. These chlorophyll-rich foods enrich the blood and are higher in protein, beta carotene, and nucleic acids than any other food. These foods renew human cells and help to reverse aging.

Miso—A fermented paste made from soybeans and a grain such as rice or barley. Ranges in color from blond to brown, with the taste being stronger in the darker shades. Wonderful flavor when stirred into a soup or sauce just before serving, yet works great in dressings and some desserts as well. A concentrated protein source. Very salty and should be used in moderation.

Nut butters—Thick paste made by grinding nuts, most popular being peanut. Use organic when possible and watch for ingredients, supermarket brands usually use hydrogenated oil as an emulsifier and other ingredients which simply do not have to be there. A wide variety is available including almond, cashew, and more exotic ones like filbert.

If you have a strong blender making your own with fresh or freshly roasted nuts is best.

Nutritional yeast—Do not confuse with brewers or baking yeast. A rich source of B vitamins and protein, this is an inactive yeast and will not ferment. Adds wonderful flavor to gravies and sauces.

Quinoa—An easy to digest grain which contains the highest protein of any other grain. Also rich in iron, calcium (more than milk), phosphorous, B vitamins, and vitamin E. Easy to prepare, rinse first, cooks within 15 minutes.

Rice syrup—Like barley malt syrup, this is comprised predominantly of maltose, a slow-digesting carbohydrate. It is not as sweet as honey or sugar in baked goods, though I still like the subtle flavor and couple it with stevia powder if I want a sweeter flavor. We like rice syrup on pancakes and it makes great tasting popcorn balls!

Sea salt—Containing all trace elements, including iodine, this is superior to commercial salt which is highly refined and contains many additives. Sea salt is evaporated and impurities are removed. A much superior taste to the harsh, chemically treated brands.

Seaweed—Many varieties to explore, some of which are Dulse (my favorite), Kombu (used primarily in soups and stews, makes beans more user friendly!), Wakame, Arame, Nori (popular in sushi rolls), Hijiki, and Agar-Agar (kanten). Agar is used as a gelling agent. Sea Vegetables are extremely valuable food source with a full spectrum of minerals, rich in iodine, calcium, and iron.

Sesame butter—Less refined than tahini, this is a paste made from whole, roasted sesame seeds. If unavailable, tahini may be substituted. Because of its high Vitamin E content, it will have a longer shelf life than other nut butters.

Stevia—An herb that is 30-300x sweeter than sugar. Available in leaf form or as a clear liquid or white powder. See section on sweeteners for more info.

Soy yogurt—Available in health food stores in plain or flavored varieties. Can also be made easily at home by mixing 1 teaspoon dairy yogurt or yogurt starter into a quart of soy milk and letting it sit uncovered in a warm spot for 14-18 hours. Alternatively try boiling 1 cup of water with 1/4 cup soy powder and 2 teaspoons of rice or barley syrup and leave to sit 48 hours. Then add 1 quart soymilk and let sit an additional 14 hours.

Tempeh—A traditional Indonesian food made by splitting, cooking and fermenting soybeans, Fresh is best and easy to make, though it takes 30 hours to incubate. Inoculated by a culture which forms fuzzy white/gray/black mycelium enzymes which bind the beans together creating a hardy, meaty, texture. When homemade it is rich in vitamin B12 and contains high amounts of protein which is easy to assimilate. My family loves the flavor and the versatility of this wonderful and nutritious food. Check out The Tempeh Cookbook by Dorothy R. Bates for making your own. I double my recipes and freeze them to always have some on hand. Do not eat raw.

Toasted sesame oil—Highly aromatic and intensely flavored oil made from toasted sesame seeds. Not used as a cooking oil. You only need a few drops to flavor grains, beans, or stir fries.

Vogue Vege Base—A great product made from dehydrated vegetables. Adds depth of flavor to many recipes. Use for broth.

Dietary Changes

1. Go slowly! Changing too much too quickly sets you up for failure.

2. Eliminate beverages such as coffee and soda.

3. Lower the concentrated protein portions on your plate and raise the vegetable portions.

4. Never drink water (or other beverage) with meals. This dilutes digestive enzymes, thus diminishing or halting the digestive process.

5. Man does not live on rice, beans, and green salads alone. Be creative. Use a wide range of cookbooks, experiment, and have fun.

6. Changing the way you eat is more difficult than changing religions or learning a new language. Not because a healthier diet is any harder to follow, but because we have to unlearn certain behaviors and beliefs at the same time, most of which have been with us since birth. Patience and a willingness to learn in time will enable you to nourish yourself and your family in a manner that is second nature.

7. Eliminate cookies, cakes, chips, pretzels, etc. If they are not in your house, you and your family will not be tempted. Always have a variety of healthier options available.

8. Eating healthy in our society today, sadly, is a learned behavior. There are no short cuts. Do not be tempted to buy boxed or prepared "healthier" foods because it is easier. Otherwise, you will still have to train yourself to a whole foods diet.

9. Plan and organize! Plan weekly menus and stick with them. This makes shopping easier and supports your efforts in remaining on this new road you are traveling. Experts say it takes three weeks to change a

learned behavior. Give yourself at least a month to see how much easier it is to live and eat in this healthier way.

10. Change the way you perceive food. So many times we make food selections based on emotions. An interesting exercise is to keep a food diary and write down how you feel prior to eating. Awareness is the first step to a healthier diet. Being conscious of our choices makes us less a victim and more responsible for our actions. Nourishment is a gift of love, whether to oneself or to ones family. Each and every one of us deserves this gift.

The Natural Home

Using chemical cleansers in my home is not an option. I believe there are safer, less expensive, and easier ways to make cleaners that are just as effective. For anyone who is concerned about the toxic effects of chemicals on their family, pets, and environment, try these out!

White vinegar and lemon juice are fabulous cleansers to use for refrigerators, cupboards and countertops. It has the added benefit of repelling ants. Simply dilute with water (1/2 lemon or splash of vinegar).

To wash floors, I add 1 Tablespoon of castile soap and five drops each of the following essential oils: clove, thyme, lavender, peppermint, and tea tree, to a bucket of water. It is highly aromatic, but diminishes quickly. The benefits are that they work as a wonderful disinfectant. Research has found that molds, staphylococci, several bacillus strains, and other detrimental microorganisms are wiped out with applications of these oils.

Baking soda straight out of the box is wonderful for scrubbing pots and stovetops. It will not dissolve build up as easily as some of the chemical brands, so a little elbow grease it needed—but it works! We purchased a 30-some-odd-year-old house from a sweet old lady who fried all her food. There was tremendous build up on the hood of the stove, as well as on the surrounding cabinets. The baking soda worked like a charm.

One-half cup of baking soda poured into the sink, followed by a 1/2 cup of vinegar, covered for a minute, will usually take care of minor pipe blockages. Use on a weekly basis to keep your pipes clean.

Vinegar diluted in water is my window and mirror cleaner of choice.

Insect repellents are also easy to make. Citronella, geranium (especially good), peppermint, eucalyptus, cloves, and rosemary may repel mosquitoes. Choose two or three of these. Add 1-2 drops of each into a tablespoon of lotion and rub onto skin. Experiment to find which ones work best for you. If you do get bit, add a drop of lavender directly on the bite or salt mixed with a touch of water, patted on like a poultice. For several bites from mosquitoes or "no-see-ums" (those irritating invisible attackers), try soaking in a bath with epsom or sea salt for 15 minutes or more.

Pennyroyal is a common sight around my home. I toss the dried form (fresh is good too) into every corner, under the beds and couch, etc., to deter fleas. Smells nice. Lightly minty.

A flea comb is another product I would highly recommend for your animals. Combining that with frequent vacuuming controls fleas. For additional help, try a citrus-based flea dip and/or flea collar.

Diatomaceous earth is what I use for the creepy crawlies. This fine, gray powder acts on a mechanical, not a chemical, level. It is completely safe around small pets and children. It can usually be found in natural food markets and some garden stores.

If cockroaches are a problem, try this simple recipe. Mix equal parts flour, sugar, boric acid, mixed with a little oil until it forms a paste. Roll into balls and tuck away into cupboard corners, under the sink, behind appliances, etc. Keep this away from children and pets.

Do not under estimate the power of the sun and fresh air! Opening windows daily for short periods of time (even in the winter) will rid your home of many contaminants and bring in a new supply of much needed nutrients. The sun will correct many of the mold problems you may have.

Plants are wonderful pollutant fighters, as well as oxygen recyclers. Some of the chemicals that come up in a typical American home include benzene, trichlorothylene, and formaldehyde. Plants will absorb and transform them into nutrients that they can use. Nervous disorders, anemia, nausea, headaches, etc., are just some of the symptoms. My husband and then five-month-old daughter were greatly affected by the outgassing from new carpets and the fresh paint on the walls of an apartment we rented while we looked for a home. Both had severe allergic reactions, swelling, dark circles under the eyes, and inflammation of the mucous membranes of their mouth, eyes, and throat. We immediately went out and purchased spider plants, heartleaf philodendron, golden pothos, and a few other species, and hung them in every room. Daily vacuuming and open windows helped until we were able to move out.

Detergents, plastics, inks, synthetic fibers, wood finishes, dry cleaning, plywood, natural gas, and much more are also toxic. Plants can help. Limit or eliminate the use of these products. Conventional dishwashing detergents often contain phosphates, which rob our waters of oxygen, suffocating aquatic animals and plants.

We use laundry discs instead of detergent, do not dry clean, turn off the gas to our stove to prevent small leaks from escaping, and recommend the use of "chemically responsible" paints and varnishes such as those sold through Safecoat, who can be reached at 800-239-0321, or www.afmsafecoat.com.

There are many brands of cleansers available in your natural foods market from dish soap to toilet cleansers to hydrogen peroxide-based bleaching solutions. Though I prefer to make my own, usually for a fraction of the price, these are excellent alternatives.

For more ideas and recipes, pick up Casey Kellars' book, Natural Cleaning for your home: 95 pure and simple recipes.

Co-Creation

We are all co-creating our reality. When our soul entered our body and became earth bound, there were certain responsibilities that went along with it. First and foremost is to revere life in all forms, beginning with ourselves. Many of use have deviated from this simple rule. It is evident by the atrocities that we inflict upon our physical and spiritual being. The road back to reverence is one of the most challenging and greatest acts of love that there is. It takes discipline and courage.

Once back on that path, though, we learn compassion for ourselves and in turn we learn compassion for others. The gentle waves of awareness that originate from our new understanding lap at the consciousness of everyone we come in contact with. For those who are ready to hear, their hearts and souls will be awakened and they will bring along their gifts.

For this is the beauty of life. Each and every one of us has a unique gift to give. It is our purpose for living. We were born with certain goals to accomplish, whether it be raising a family or raising the consciousness of others. How do we know our goals? By how your heart responds to what you do. When I saw my midwife's face light up with joy and wonderment each time she touched my womb and connected with my then unborn child, I knew she was living her soul's task. When what you do is so deeply gratifying, that you wake up each day with the anticipation of service to others, you are doing what you were meant to be doing.

There is a fine line between service to others and martyrdom though. It has to be a genuine love that you give to others with no strings attached.

This can only happen if you love yourself. Loving yourself means keeping each part of you—emotional, spiritual, and physical—healthy. If one is out of balance it throws everything else out of balance too. You see many healers, for example, who focus and work on one aspect of being and forsake others. It is difficult to accept advise from a therapist with apparent unresolved issues or to follow the suggestions of an overweight healthcare practitioner in the proper way to eat or exercise. People can tell if you are a believable person by the way you take care of yourself. More importantly, you will believe in yourself if everything in your house is in order. No one is perfect, but striving for perfection (balance) is a noble pursuit. True love of self is not neglectful.

Feeding the body correctly then seems to be of monumental importance. To do so will make it easier for the mental, emotional, and spiritual aspects of ourselves to grow and express themselves.

Looking at impoverished families in this way enhances an already disturbing picture. How many great minds and spiritual leaders lay wasting away behind crumbling, stench-filled walls, their bodies degenerating with each mouthful of the denatured foods of commerce?

Poor nutrition breeds confusion, bitterness, despair and finally apathy.

There are a few noble souls who recognize this and try to make a difference with certain educational programs geared for the poor.

Educating the middle class is important too, for poor diet is an insidious evil influenced heavily by the money food manufacturers place into advertising. The emphasis always on convenience and immediate gratification. These are poor standards to expose our children to. The effects are being seen in more frequent episodes of violence, many of which take place in nice communities, nice schools, by nice children. We need to understand and teach our children how nutrition affects the way we think, feel, and react.

A tremendous amount of research shows how food affects us on a chemical level and how easy it is to keep our bodies running at its optimum. There is some margin for error, but not for continual abuse. And abuse is what it is, making us self-destructive perpetrators.

If there is no effort to change, then the frequent episodes of violence will escalate into an epidemic of fear-based mayhem. Fear is the most basic negative emotion from which all other negative emotions stem. But, by diminishing our own fear, we diminish it in our world. All it takes is the realization of just how remarkable each of us is. Realization occurs when clarity is restored. Clarity is restored by removing as many toxins as possible, creating the climate for recovery of our consciousness and the remembrance of our life's work.

References and Resources

My search for answers to my health questions, has led me on an extraordinary journey of discovery. I am constantly looking for new sources of information. In this section, I have included a partial list of books, periodicals, and organizations which I have found very helpful. I urge anyone who wants to make changes in their lives to obtain as much knowledge as possible. It is the only way to break from a victimized stance to one of self-worth and confidence. Being aware gives us back the power to make the important decisions in our own life, and the realization of the consequences of our actions. This, in turn, will create a more responsible family and community-minded individual.

Cookbooks:
The Uncheese Cookbook, by JoAnne Stepaniak.

The Tempeh Cookbook, by Dorothy R. Bates

Ten Talents, by Frank and Rosalie Hurd

Recipes from an Ecological Kitchen, by Lorna J. Sass

The American Vegetarian Cookbook from the Fit for Life Kitchen, by Marilyn Diamond.

Books and Periodicals:
Food and Water, 398 Vermont Route 215, Walden, Vermont, 05873.

Environmental Research Foundation, *Rachel's Environment and Health Weekly*, PO Box 5036, Annapolis, MD, 21403-7036, 410-263-1584, erf@rachel.org.

Natural Health Magazine, PO Box 7442, Red Oak, IA, 51591-0440, 800-526-8440.

Organic Gardening, 33 East Minor Street, Emmaus, PA, 18098, 610-967-5171, www.organicgardening.com.

Vegetarian Times, 4 Highridge Park, Stamford, CT, 06909, 800-829-3340, www.vegetariantimes.com.

Diet for a small Planet, by Frances Moore Lappe.

Silent Spring, by Rachel Carson.

Prescription for Nutritional Healing, by James F. Balch, M.D., and Phyllis A. Balch, C.N.C.

The New Our Bodies, Ourselves, by the Boston Women's Health Book Collective.

Diet for a New America and May All be Fed, by John Robbins.

Healing with Whole Foods, by Paul Pitchford.

The Environmental Magazine, 28 Knight Street, Norwalk, CT, 06851, 203-854-5559, www.emagzine.com.

Living Downstream, by Sandra Steingraver.

Hormonal Chaos, The scientific and social origins of the environmental endocrine hypothesis, by Sheldon Krimsky.

Farmageddon

The Nutrition Bible: A comprehensive, No-Nonsense Guide to Foods, Nutrients, Additives, Preservatives, Pollutants and everything else we eat and drink, by Jean Anderson and Barbara Deskins

Food and Healing , by Annemarie Colbin

Fats that heal, fats that kill: the complete guide to fats, oils, cholesterol and human health , by Udo Erasmus

The Body Ecology Diet: Recovering your health and rebuilding your immunity, by Donna Gates

Foods that heal: A guide to Understanding and using the healing powers of Natural foods , by Bernard Jensen

Spontaneous Healing: how to discover and enhance your body's natural ability to maintain and heal itself , by Andrew Weil

How to Grow Fresh Air: 50 houseplants to purify your home or office, by B.C. Wolverton

Natural Cleaning For Your Home: 95 Pure and Simple Recipes, by Casey Kellars

Organizations:

American Natural Hygiene Society, PO Box 30630, Tampa, FL, 33630, 813-855-6607.

Price-Pottenger, Nutrition Foundation, PO Box 2614, La Mesa, CA, 91943-2614, 800-366-3748, price-pottenger.org.

Natural Law Party, PO Box 1900, Fairfield, IA, 52556, 515-472-2040, www.natural-law.org.

Greenpeace, 1611 Connecticut Avenue, NW., Washington, DC, 20009, 202-462-1177.

Sierra Club, PO Box 7603, San Francisco, CA, 94120-9826, 415-776-2211.

Center for Science in the Public Interest/Americans for Safe Food, 1501 16th Street, NW, Washington, DC, 20036, 202-332-9110.

American Vegan Society, 501 Old Harding Highway, Malaga, NJ, 08328.

North American Vegetarian Society, PO Box 72, Dolgeville, NY, 13329.

Index

Agar Fruit Gel, 394
Almond Balls, 405
Almond Clusters, 408
Almonnaise, 82, 152, 194-195, 206, 210, 281-282
Appetizers, Dips, and Spreads,
Babaghanoush, 68
Banana-Miso-Sesame Spread, 69
Brilliant Green Dip, 79
Carrot Butter, 18, 80
Cheddar, Sunflower Seed, and Olive Spread, 70
Guacamole, 71, 344
Lentil Spread, 72
Quick and Easy Hummus, 18, 75
Roasted Garlic and Mushroom Spread, 74
Seed Spread, 76
Spinach Cheese Logs, 73
Spinach-Mushroom Dip, 77
Tzatziki, 78, 341
Yogurt, Cucumber, and Garlic Dip, 78
Apple and Potato Salad, 148
Apple Milk, 446

Apple, Apricot, and Raisin Muffins, 226
Arame-Zucchini Sesame Toss, 170
Asian Spring Rolls, 19, 306
Asparagus-Tofu Stir Fry, 289
Autumnal Glory, 105
Babaghanoush, 68
Baked Polenta with Shiitake Ragout, 318
Baked Tofu with Cabbage and Wild Rice, 371
Baked Tomatoes, 248
Banana Chipsicle, 424
Banana Date Muffins, 229
Banana Muffins, 228
Banana Raisin Ice Cream, 423
Banana Spice Bars, 401
Banana-Miso-Sesame Spread, 69
Basic Cream Sauce for Steamed Vegetables, 101
Basic Vinaigrette Dressing, 200
Basil Dressing, 185, 203
Basil, Mint, and Orange Vinaigrette, 204
BBQ Style Tempeh, 376

479

Bean Croquettes, 19, 296
Bean Salad, 180
Beans, 3, 19, 30, 63, 75, 104-105, 155, 163, 178, 180, 184, 196, 255, 258, 281, 285, 295-296, 298, 302, 316-317, 330-331, 345, 355-358, 381, 391, 463-465
Bean Croquettes, 19, 296
Bean Salad, 180
Chickpea, Eggplant, and Tomato Stew, 361
Chili Slaw, 155
Chipotle and White Bean Pasta, 298
Corn, Kidney, and Cucumber Salad, 163
Curried Sprouted Lentil Stew, 119
Daddy's Favorite Salad, 196
Enchilada Pie, 355
Italian Beans 'n Greens Over Polenta, 316
Lentil and Brown Rice Soup, 128
Lentil Spread, 72
Lentil-Tomato Loaf, 297
Mexican Pasta Salad, 184
Pine Nut, Pinto Bean, and Scallion Pilaf, 258
Quick and Easy Soft Tacos, 357
Rio Grande Tempeh, 86, 381
Spaghetti Squash and Green Beans, 19, 285
Spicy Chickpea Salad, 179

Spicy Kale and Chickpea Stew, 136
Squash and Bean Casserole, 19, 330
Squash, Aduki, Corn Chowder, 105
Tempeh Skillet Dinner, 391
Veggie and Black Bean Tacos, 358
White Beans with Tomato and Sage, 19, 295
Beverages
Apple Milk, 446
Blueberry, Fig, and Date Shake, 452
Carob Nut Drink, 449
Carob Shake, 450
Carrot Drink, 459-460
Carrot Drink #2, 460
Cashew/Apricot Drink, 455
Coconut Milk, 2, 117, 310, 314, 447
Cranberry Yogurt Shake, 458
Dreamy Date Shake, 454
Fruit Smoothie, 457
Hot Carob Drink, 451
Just Peachy! Shake, 456
Lemonade for One, 448
Meeny Greeny Banana Shake, 453
Black Forest Cake, 437
Blueberry, Fig, and Date Shake, 452
Breads, 6, 40, 222-223, 462

Apple, Apricot, and Raisin Muffins, 226
Banana Date Muffins, 229
Banana Muffins, 228
Carrot-Date Muffins, 231
Corn Cakes, 243
Date and Oatmeal Yogurt Muffins, 233
Lemon Cranberry Muffins, 235
Oatcakes, 245
Pumpkin-Apricot Bread, 224
Sesame Biscuits, 242
Squash-Corn Muffins, 237
Wheat-Free Muffins, 240
Zucchini Muffins, 238
Breakfast, 17, 272
Brilliant Green Dip, 79
Broccoli, 18, 30, 35, 87, 106, 116, 167-169, 178, 249, 255, 263-264, 302, 305, 358, 378-379
Broccoli Salad Italiano, 168
Broccoli Soup, 18, 106
Broccoli Stuffed Tomatoes, 249
Broccoli with Cheddar Vinaigrette, 167
Curried Broccoli, Watercress, and Spinach Soup, 116
Hot and Pungent Tempeh with Broccoli, 378
Italian Chopped Salad, 178, 348
Oriental Noodles with Spicy Ginger and Peanut Sauce, 305
Rice and Broccoli Salad with Sunflower Seed Dressing, 169
Spinach and Broccoli, 263
Veggie and Black Bean Tacos, 358
Broccoli Salad Italiano, 168
Broccoli Soup, 18, 106
Broccoli Stuffed Tomatoes, 249
Broccoli with Cheddar Vinaigrette, 167
Butter, 3, 6, 8, 18, 35, 57, 68-69, 75, 77, 79-80, 84, 87, 99, 102, 104, 106, 109, 114, 138, 154, 212-213, 259, 266-267, 278, 282, 305, 337, 366, 368, 370, 380, 395-396, 399, 403, 405-406, 408, 410, 412, 414, 422, 424, 441, 463
Cabbage, 122, 141, 153-155, 157, 176, 178, 196, 211, 281, 283, 291, 306-307, 350-351, 371-372
Asian Spring Rolls, 19, 306
Baked Tofu with Cabbage and Wild Rice, 371
Chili Slaw, 155
Chopped Main Salad, 19, 176
Cole Slaw, 153
Daddy's Favorite Salad, 196
Far East Coleslaw, 154
Fragrant Oriental Soup, 122
Italian Chopped Salad, 178, 348
O Konomi Yaki, 291
Reubens, 283
Stuffed Cabbage Stroganoff, 350

Sweet Potato Slaw, 157
Carbohydrates, 21, 32, 39-40
Carob Chews, 406
Carob Cupcakes, 412, 435
Carob Dessert Fondue, 411
Carob Frosting, 412, 435, 441
Carob Ganache, A Pourable Icing, 414
Carob Nut Drink, 449
Carob Pudding, 396, 415
Carob Shake, 450
Carrot Butter, 18, 80
Carrot Cake, 439
Carrot Drink, 459-460
Carrot-Date Muffins, 231
Carrots, 80, 85, 107-108, 114, 119, 122, 128, 130, 134, 139-141, 144, 154, 165, 185, 231, 250-251, 255, 293, 303-304, 336, 339, 364, 376-377, 386-387, 439-440
BBQ Style Tempeh, 376
Butter, 3, 6, 8, 18, 35, 57, 68-69, 75, 77, 79-80, 84, 87, 99, 102, 104, 106, 109, 114, 138, 154, 212-213, 259, 266-267, 278, 282, 305, 337, 366, 368, 370, 380, 395-396, 399, 403, 405-406, 408, 410, 412, 414, 422, 424, 441, 463
Carrot Butter, 18, 80
Carrot Cake, 439
Carrot Drink, 459-460
Carrot-Date Muffins, 231

Carrots in Orange Sauce, 250
Cashew Nut Casserole, 323
Chilled Curried Carrot Soup, 108
Creamy Mushroom Soup, 114
Curried Sprouted Lentil Stew, 119
Deli Style Tempeh, 377
Fragrant Oriental Soup, 122
Ginger Carrots, 251
Lentil and Brown Rice Soup, 128
Noodles in Green Sauce, 303
Pasta and Vegetable Salad with Basil Dressing, 185
Pea and Carrot Soup, 18, 130
Sesame Carrot Salad, 19, 165
Soba Soup with Spinach, Tofu, and Arame, 134
Squash and Sweet Potato Chowder, 139
Tempeh in Red Wine Sauce, 387
Tomato Carrot Soup, 18, 140
Carrots in Orange Sauce, 250
Cashew Burgers, 19, 364-365
Cashew Cream, 6, 303, 385, 413, 427, 433
Cashew French Toast, 18, 275
Cashew Nut Casserole, 323
Cashew/Sunflower Mayonnaise, 83
Cauliflower, 166, 281-282, 314-315
Cauliflower Salad, 166
Cauliflower Salad, 166
Celery, 76, 106-107, 114, 116, 119, 123, 125, 128, 131-132, 142, 148,

152, 155, 158, 176, 181-182, 188-190, 193-196, 211, 259, 297, 323, 337-338, 354, 366, 375-376, 387
Celery Soup, 107
Celery and Apple Salad, 158
Celery Soup, 107
Changing Our Perception of Food, 9
Chard, 144, 171
Moroccan Swiss Chard Salad, 171
Winter Greens Soup, 144
Cheddar, Sunflower Seed, and Olive Spread, 70
Chestnut, Apple, and Cornbread Stuffed Squash, 337
Chickpea, Eggplant, and Tomato Stew, 361
Children's Food List, 17
Chili and Corn Filled Zucchini, 344
Chili Slaw, 155
Chilled Curried Carrot Soup, 108
Chipotle and White Bean Pasta, 298
Chopped Main Salad, 19, 176
Cilantro Soup, 110
Citrus Spaghetti Squash Noodles, 252
Coconut and Cashew Veggies with Tofu and Orange Sauce, 293
Coconut Curry Melange, 314
Coconut Macaroons, 417

Coconut Milk, 2, 117, 310, 314, 447
Co-Creation, 0, 471
Cold Zucchini and Red Bell Pepper Soup with Cumin, 111
Cole Slaw, 153
Collard Potato Salad with Mustard Dressing, 150
Collards, 35, 150, 265, 286, 295, 377
Collard Potato Salad with Mustard Dressing, 150
Deli Style Tempeh, 377
Mediterranean Stuffed Collard Greens, 19, 341
Spaghetti Squash with Greens, 286
Sprouted Wheat and Veggie Bowl, 181
Stuffed Cabbage Stroganoff, 350
White Beans with Tomato and Sage, 19, 295
Condiments, 0, 74, 100, 109, 132, 138, 152, 160, 178, 184, 192, 194-195, 206, 210-211, 259, 278, 281-282, 287, 313, 322, 337, 348, 357-359, 375, 390, 414
Almonnaise, 82, 152, 194-195, 206, 210, 281-282
Basic Cream Sauce for Steamed Vegetables, 101
Butter, 3, 6, 8, 18, 35, 57, 68-69, 75, 77, 79-80, 84, 87, 99, 102, 104, 106,

109, 114, 138, 154, 212-213, 259, 266-267, 278, 282, 305, 337, 366, 368, 370, 380, 395-396, 399, 403, 405-406, 408, 410, 412, 414, 422, 424, 441, 463
Corn and Sun-Dried Tomato Relish, 86, 381
Cranberry Chutney, 88
Cranberry, Orange, and Ginger Relish, 89
Creamy
Dulse Gomacio, 18-19, 85, 357
Eggplant, Tomato, and Bell Pepper Relish, 90
Fresh Tomato Sauce, 18, 92, 313, 322
Garam Masala, 94, 120, 263, 308-309
Mushroom-Onion Gravy, 96, 375, 390
Orange, Fig, and Pine Nut Relish, 98
Roasted Garlic, 74, 95, 100, 132-133, 178, 211, 259, 287, 321
Sesame Sauce, 87
Tofu Sour Cream, 6, 97, 160, 184, 192, 359
Tomato Salsa, 93, 184, 344
Corn, 2, 7, 19, 43, 45, 55-56, 86, 105, 113, 149, 155, 163, 176, 178, 181, 184-185, 192, 194, 199, 243, 281, 298, 316, 321, 330, 332-333, 344, 355-357, 371, 381, 383-384, 408
Chili and Corn Filled Zucchini, 344
Chipotle and White Bean Pasta, 298
Chopped Main Salad, 19, 176
Corn and Rice Soup, 113
Corn and Sun-Dried Tomato Relish, 86, 381
Corn Cakes, 243
Corn, Kidney, and Cucumber Salad, 163
Italian Chopped Salad, 178, 348
Mexican Pasta Salad, 184
Pasta and Vegetable Salad with Basil Dressing, 185
Potato, Corn, and Cherry Tomato Salad, 19, 149
Quick and Easy Soft Tacos, 357
Sprouted Wheat and Veggie Bowl, 181
Squash, Aduki, Corn Chowder, 105
Squash-Corn Muffins, 237
Tri-Grain Hash, 384
Corn and Rice Soup, 113
Corn and Sun-Dried Tomato Relish, 86, 381
Corn Cakes, 243
Corn, Kidney, and Cucumber Salad, 163

Cranberries, 88-89, 235, 458
Cranberry Chutney, 88
Cranberry, Orange, and Ginger Relish, 89
Cranberry Chutney, 88
Cranberry Yogurt Shake, 458
Cranberry, Orange, and Ginger Relish, 89
Cream of Rice Cereal, 273
Creamy Eggplant Casserole, 325
Creamy Fruit Pudding, 397
Creamy Mushroom Soup, 114
Crepes, 306-307, 425-427
Cucumber Dill Sour Cream Dressing, 205
Cucumber, Dill, and Wakame Salad, 161
Cucumber, Orange, and Aniseed Salad, 162
Cucumbers, 78, 160-161
Cucumber, Dill, and Wakame Salad, 161
Cucumbers with Tofu Sour Cream, 160
Curried , 195
Curried Broccoli, Watercress, and Spinach Soup, 116
Curried Coconut Noodle Soup, 117
Curried Sprouted Lentil Stew, 119
Daddy's Favorite Salad, 196

Dairy, 0-1, 5, 29, 31, 34-35, 39, 48, 57, 62, 464
Dal, 120-121
Dal Soup, 120
Dal Soup, 120
Date and Oatmeal Yogurt Muffins, 233
Deli Style Tempeh, 377
Desserts, 62-63, 425, 435, 437, 442-443, 462
Agar Fruit Gel, 394
Almond Balls, 405
Almond Clusters, 408
Banana Chipsicle, 424
Banana Raisin Ice Cream, 423
Banana Spice Bars, 401
Black Forest Cake, 437
Carob Chews, 406
Carob Cupcakes, 412, 435
Carob Dessert Fondue, 411
Carob Frosting, 412, 435, 441
Carob Ganache, A Pourable Icing, 414
Carob Pudding, 396, 415
Carrot Cake, 439
Cashew Cream, 6, 303, 385, 413, 427, 433
Coconut Macaroons, 417
Creamy Fruit Pudding, 397
Crepes, 306-307, 425-427
Double Dip Fruit Bits, 404
Fruit and Nut Balls, 407

Fruit Mousse Pie, 430
Ginger Cookies, 418
Lemon Mousse, 399
Lemon Pie, 432
Oatmeal Date Cookies In-The-Raw, 419
Peanut Butter Cake, 412, 441
Pie Crust, 428-429, 431-432, 434
Pie Crust #2, 429
Pumpkin Pie, 433
Quick and Easy Oatmeal Cookies, 420
Sesame Crunch Cookies, 421
Sesame Crunchies, 403
Sesame Custard, 395
Sesame Millet Cookies, 422
Sprouted Wheat Surprises, 410
Strawberry Mousse, 400
Strawberry Shortcake, 442
Sunflower-Apricot Patties, 409
Tapioca Pudding, 398
Vanilla Tofu Cream, 415, 425, 437, 442-443
Dietary Changes, 465
Double Dip Fruit Bits, 404
Dreamy Date Shake, 454
Dried Tomato, Caper, and Olive Dressing, 181, 206
Dulse Gomacio, 18-19, 85, 357
Earth Burgers, 19, 365
Egg Salad with Jalapeno and Cumin, 194

Eggplant, 68, 90-91, 262, 267-268, 287-288, 325-326, 334, 336, 361-362
Babaghanoush, 68
Chickpea, Eggplant, and Tomato Stew, 361
Creamy Eggplant Casserole, 325
Eggplant, Tomato, and Bell Pepper Relish, 90
Ratatouille, 262
Tender Thai Vegetables, 267
Ultimate Sandwich with Creamy Mozzarella, 287
Eggplant, Tomato, and Bell Pepper Relish, 90
Enchilada Pie, 355
Entrees, 271
Asian Spring Rolls, 19, 306
Asparagus-Tofu Stir Fry, 289
Baked Polenta with Shiitake Ragout, 318
Baked Tofu with Cabbage and Wild Rice, 371
BBQ Style Tempeh, 376
Bean Croquettes, 19, 296
Breakfast, 17, 272
Cashew Burgers, 19, 364-365
Cashew French Toast, 18, 275
Cashew Nut Casserole, 323
Chestnut, Apple, and Cornbread Stuffed Squash, 337

Chickpea, Eggplant, and Tomato Stew, 361
Chili and Corn Filled Zucchini, 344
Chipotle and White Bean Pasta, 298
Coconut and Cashew Veggies with Tofu and Orange Sauce, 293
Coconut Curry Melange, 314
Cream of Rice Cereal, 273
Creamy Eggplant Casserole, 325
Deli Style Tempeh, 377
Earth Burgers, 19, 365
Enchilada Pie, 355
Hot and Pungent Tempeh with Broccoli, 378
Italian Beans 'n Greens Over Polenta, 316
Lentil-Tomato Loaf, 297
Lettuce Wrapped Tempeh Meatballs, 380
Matar Paneer, 308
Mediterranean Stuffed Collard Greens, 19, 341
Millet Nut and Seed Balls, 20, 370
Millet Seed Patties, 368
Millet Stuffed Zucchini, 346
My Favorite Scrambler, 277
Noodles in Green Sauce, 303
Nut Burgers In-The-Raw, 366
O Konomi Yaki, 291
Oriental Noodles with Spicy Ginger and Peanut Sauce, 305
Pancakes, 18, 222, 279-280, 463
Pancakes #2, 280
Pecan Patties, 369
Polenta Pizza, 19, 321
Portabello Casserole, 327
Primavera Pasta, 300, 302
Primavera Pasta #2, 302
Quick and Easy Soft Tacos, 357
Quicky Oats, 18, 274
Reubens, 283
Rio Grande Tempeh
Rosemary Tofu Sauté, 20, 373
Salisbury Steaks, 98, 375
Sandwich Suggestions, 281
Sausage and Potato Skillet, 363
Savory Stuffed Portabellos, 348
Spaghetti Squash and Green Beans, 19, 285
Spaghetti Squash with Greens, 286
Spicy Thai Noodles, 311
Spinach and Rice Casserole with Toasted Almonds, 19, 328
Spinach Fritters, 92, 313
Squash and Bean Casserole, 19, 330
Squash and Leek Turnovers, 19, 352
Stuffed Cabbage Stroganoff, 350
Sweet Squash Stuffed with Wild Rice, 354

Tempeh Hash, 383
Tempeh in Red Wine Sauce, 387
Tempeh in Shiitake Cream Sauce, 385
Tempeh Millet Loaf, 20, 389
Tempeh Sausage Patties, 367
Tempeh Skillet Dinner, 391
Tempeh with Lemon Ginger Glaze, 392
Thai Stir Fry, 310
Tri-Grain Hash, 384
Ultimate Sandwich with Creamy Mozzarella, 287
Vegetable Enchilada Casserole, 332
Vegetable Lasagna, 334
Veggie and Black Bean Tacos, 358
Veggie Rolls, 19, 339
Waffles, 18, 278
White Beans with Tomato and Sage, 19, 295
Eric's Favorite Dressing, 208
Escarole, Spinach, Hijiki, and Red Onion Salad, 172
Far East Coleslaw, 154
Fats, 14, 21-23, 33, 35, 104, 222, 462, 477
Feeding Your Children, 13
Fennel, 3, 94, 107, 131, 164, 174, 300, 367
Spinach, Fennel, and Pink Grapefruit Salad, 164

Fragrant Oriental Soup, 122
Fresh Tomato Sauce, 18, 92, 313, 322
Fresh Tomato Soup, 18, 109
Fruit and Nut Balls, 407
Fruit Mousse Pie, 430
Fruit Smoothie, 457
Garam Masala, 94, 120, 263, 308-309
Garlic Mint Dressing, 209
Gazpacho, 123, 125
Genetically Engineered Foods, 55, 57
Ginger Carrots, 251
Ginger Cookies, 418
Ginger Mint , 197
Gingered Butternut Squash Soup, 126
Glossary of Special Ingredients, 461
Grapefruit, 164
Spinach, Fennel, and Pink Grapefruit Salad, 164
Green Goddess Dressing, 210
Guacamole, 71, 344
Herbed Vinaigrette Dressing, 201
Hot and Pungent Tempeh with Broccoli, 378
Hot Carob Drink, 451
How to Sprout, 64
Insalata Caprese, 175
Introduction, xiii

Irradiated Foods, 59
Italian Beans 'n Greens Over Polenta, 316
Italian Chopped Salad, 178, 348
Jicama, 159
South American Jicama and Orange Salad, 159
Kale, 29-30, 35, 136-137, 144, 150-151, 157, 181, 265, 286, 300, 316-317, 370, 373-374
Spicy Kale and Chickpea Stew, 136
Sweet Potato Slaw, 157
Warm Potato-Kale Salad, 151
Winter Greens Soup, 144
Lemon Bulgur Mounds with Chives, 254
Lemon Cranberry Muffins, 235
Lemon Mousse, 399
Lemon Pie, 432
Lemon Soup, 18, 115
Lemonade for One, 448
Lemon-Sesame Dressing, 181, 212
Lentil and Brown Rice Soup, 128
Lentil Spread, 72
Lentil-Tomato Loaf, 297
Lettuce Wrapped Tempeh Meatballs, 380
Living Foods, 61
Marinated Mushroom Salad, 177
Matar Paneer, 308
Mediterranean Stuffed Collard Greens, 19, 341

Mexican Pasta Salad, 184
Milk Alternatives, 37
Millet, 3, 7, 18, 20, 29-30, 101, 182, 228, 272, 278, 291, 293, 346-347, 364, 368, 370, 375, 384, 387, 389, 403, 422, 462
Cashew Burgers, 19, 364-365
Millet Nut and Seed Balls, 20, 370
Millet Salad with Apricots, Pine Nuts, and Ginger, 182
Millet Seed Patties, 368
Millet Stuffed Zucchini, 346
Salisbury Steaks, 98, 375
Sesame Millet Cookies, 422
Tempeh Millet Loaf, 20, 389
Tri-Grain Hash, 384
Millet Nut and Seed Balls, 20, 370
Millet Salad with Apricots, Pine Nuts, and Ginger, 182
Millet Seed Patties, 368
Millet Stuffed Zucchini, 346
Miso Vinaigrette Dressing, 202
Mock Chicken, 189, 191-193
Mock Chicken Salad, 189
Mock Chicken Taco Salad, 192
Mock Chicken with Spicy Fruit Salad, 193
Mock Egg Salad, 190
Moroccan Swiss Chard Salad, 171
Muligatawny, 129
Mushroom-Onion Gravy, 96, 375, 390

Mushrooms, 74, 77, 96, 101, 114, 122, 132, 142, 177, 198, 267, 277, 288, 291, 293, 304, 306, 310, 318-319, 321, 325, 327, 333, 335-336, 339, 348, 350-351, 354, 372, 375, 385
Asian Spring Rolls, 19, 306
Baked Polenta with Shiitake Ragout, 318
Creamy Eggplant Casserole, 325
Creamy Mushroom Soup, 114
Fragrant Oriental Soup, 122
Marinated Mushroom Salad, 177
Mushroom-Onion Gravy, 96, 375, 390
O Konomi Yaki, 291
Oriental Salad with Smoked Tofu, 198
Portabello Casserole, 327
Roasted Garlic and Mushroom Soup, 132
Roasted Garlic and Mushroom Spread, 74
Savory Stuffed Portabellos, 348
Spinach-Mushroom Dip, 77
Tender Thai Vegetables, 267
Thai Stir Fry, 310
Ultimate Sandwich with Creamy Mozzarella, 287
Vegetable Enchilada Casserole, 332
Vegetable Lasagna, 334

Wild Rice and Shiitake Mushroom Soup, 142
Mustard Cream Dressing, 148, 217
Mustard Dressing, 150, 216
Mustard Garlic Dressing, 218
My Favorite Scrambler, 277
Noodles, 4, 40, 90, 92, 117-118, 135, 184-185, 252, 299-305, 311-312, 334, 359-360
Curried Coconut Noodle Soup, 117
Mexican Pasta Salad, 184
Noodles in Green Sauce, 303
Oriental Noodles with Spicy Ginger and Peanut Sauce, 305
Spicy Sausage and Soba Noodles in Paprika Sauce, 359
Spicy Thai Noodles, 311
Vegetable Lasagna, 334
Noodles in Green Sauce, 303
Nori Rolls, 19, 255
Nut Burgers In-The-Raw, 366
O Konomi Yaki, 291
Oatcakes, 245
Oatmeal Date Cookies In-The-Raw, 419
Orange, Fig, and Pine Nut Relish, 98
Oranges, 98, 159
Carrots in Orange Sauce, 250
Cranberry, Orange, and Ginger Relish, 89

Cucumber, Orange, and Aniseed Salad, 162
Orange, Fig, and Pine Nut Relish, 98
South American Jicama and Orange Salad, 159
Organic Foods, 47
Oriental Dressing, 219
Oriental Gazpacho, 123
Oriental Noodles with Spicy Ginger and Peanut Sauce, 305
Oriental Quinoa Pilaf, 256
Oriental Salad with Smoked Tofu, 198
Pancakes, 18, 222, 279-280, 463
Pasta, 4, 56-57, 104, 184-185, 298, 300, 302
Chipotle and White Bean Pasta, 298
Mexican Pasta Salad, 184
Oriental Noodles with Spicy Ginger and Peanut Sauce, 305
Pasta and Vegetable Salad with Basil Dressing, 185
Primavera Pasta, 300, 302
Spicy Sausage and Soba Noodles in Paprika Sauce, 359
Spicy Thai Noodles, 311
Vegetable Lasagna, 334
Pasta and Vegetable Salad with Basil Dressing, 185
Pea and Carrot Soup, 18, 130

Peanut Butter Cake, 412, 441
Peas, 3, 79, 130, 152, 172, 176, 185, 188, 195, 308-309, 314-315, 354, 383
Pea and Carrot Soup, 18, 130
Pecan Patties, 369
Pesto Dressing, 100, 178
Pie Crust, 428-429, 431-432, 434
Pie Crust #2, 429
Pine Nut, Pinto Bean, and Scallion Pilaf, 258
Polenta, 19, 316-321, 330-331
Baked Polenta with Shiitake Ragout, 318
Italian Beans 'n Greens Over Polenta, 316
Polenta Pizza, 19, 321
Polenta Pizza, 19, 321
Portabello Casserole, 327
Potato, 6, 10, 19, 23, 57, 104, 106, 132, 139, 144, 148-150, 152, 157, 259, 293, 314-315, 333, 363, 384, 462
Sweet Potato Slaw, 157
Potato Salad, My Way, 152
Potato, Corn, and Cherry Tomato Salad, 19, 149
Potatoes, 17, 55, 57, 96-97, 110, 114, 119, 131, 138-139, 144, 148-152, 178, 259-260, 266, 333, 348, 363, 371, 383, 387, 391

Apple and Potato Salad with Mustard Cream Dressing, 148
Cilantro Soup, 110
Collard Potato Salad with Mustard Dressing, 150
Potato Salad, My Way, 152
Potato, Corn, and Cherry Tomato Salad, 19, 149
Special Mashed Potatoes, 259
Suzhou Potatoes, 260
Warm Potato-Kale Salad, 151
Winter Vegetables with Horseradish Dill Sauce, 266
Primavera Pasta, 300, 302
Primavera Pasta #2, 302
Proteins, 14, 27, 50
Pumpkin Pie, 433
Pumpkin-Apricot Bread, 224
Quick and Easy Hummus, 18, 75
Quick and Easy Oatmeal Cookies, 420
Quick and Easy Soft Tacos, 357
Quicky Oats, 18, 274
Quinoa, 3, 19, 29-30, 173, 183, 185, 222, 256-257, 357, 384, 463
Oriental Quinoa Pilaf, 256
Quick and Easy Soft Tacos, 357
Quinoa Salad with Sun-Dried Tomatoes, 183
Tabbouleh, 19, 173
Tri-Grain Hash, 384

Quinoa Salad with Sun-Dried Tomatoes, 183
Raspberry, Orange, and Lemon Dressing, 215
Ratatouille, 262
Red Bell and Fennel Soup, 131
References and Resources, 475
Reubens, 283
Rice, 2-4, 7-8, 18-19, 37, 40, 45, 69, 97-98, 101, 104, 113, 115, 117, 128, 134, 141-143, 145, 169, 183, 185, 187-188, 193, 198, 209, 219, 222, 228, 237, 240, 243, 250, 252, 255, 258, 269, 273, 275, 278, 281-282, 287-288, 291, 293, 305-306, 311, 313, 328, 354-355, 364, 368, 371, 375, 378, 392, 395-397, 399, 401, 403, 405-406, 408, 412, 414, 417-418, 426, 430, 432-433, 435, 441, 451, 461-465
Baked Tofu with Cabbage and Wild Rice, 371
Cashew Burgers, 19, 364-365
Corn and Rice Soup, 113
Lentil and Brown Rice Soup, 128
Nori Rolls, 19, 255
Oriental Salad with Smoked Tofu, 198
Pine Nut, Pinto Bean, and Scallion Pilaf, 258
Rice and Broccoli Salad with Sunflower Seed Dressing, 169

Salisbury Steaks, 98, 375
Spanish Rice, 269
Spinach and Rice Casserole with Toasted Almonds, 19, 328
Sweet Squash Stuffed with Wild Rice, 354
Wild Rice and Shiitake Mushroom Soup, 142
Wild Rice Salad, 187-188
Wild Rice Salad #2, 188
Rice and Broccoli Salad, 169
Rio Grande Tempeh
Roasted Garlic, 74, 95, 100, 132-133, 178, 211, 259, 287, 321
Roasted Garlic and Mushroom Soup, 132
Roasted Garlic and Mushroom Spread, 74
Roasted Shallot Vinaigrette Dressing, 211
Rosemary Tofu Sauté, 20, 373
Salad Dressings, 181
Basic Vinaigrette Dressing, 200
Basil Dressing, 185, 203
Basil, Mint, and Orange Vinaigrette, 204
Cucumber Dill Sour Cream Dressing, 205
Dried Tomato, Caper, and Olive Dressing, 181, 206
Eric's Favorite Dressing, 208
Garlic Mint Dressing, 209

Green Goddess Dressing, 210
Herbed Vinaigrette Dressing, 201
Lemon-Sesame Dressing, 181, 212
Miso Vinaigrette Dressing, 202
Mustard Cream Dressing, 148, 217
Mustard Dressing, 150, 216
Mustard Garlic Dressing, 218
Oriental Dressing, 219
Pesto Dressing, 100, 178
Raspberry, Orange, and Lemon Dressing, 215
Roasted Shallot Vinaigrette Dressing, 211
Spiced Sesame Dressing, 213
Spicy Dressing, 214
Sunflower Seed Dressing, 169, 207
Salads, 19, 192-193, 465
Apple and Potato Salad with Mustard Cream Dressing, 148
Arame-Zucchini Sesame Toss, 170
Bean Salad, 180
Broccoli Salad Italiano, 168
Broccoli with Cheddar Vinaigrette, 167
Cauliflower Salad, 166
Celery and Apple Salad, 158
Chili Slaw, 155
Chopped Main Salad, 19, 176
Cole Slaw, 153
Collard Potato Salad with Mustard Dressing, 150

Corn, Kidney, and Cucumber Salad, 163
Cucumber, Dill, and Wakame Salad, 161
Cucumber, Orange, and Aniseed Salad, 162
Cucumbers with Tofu Sour Cream, 160
Curried , 195
Daddy's Favorite Salad, 196
Egg Salad with Jalapeno and Cumin, 194
Escarole, Spinach, Hijiki, and Red Onion Salad, 172
Far East Coleslaw, 154
Ginger Mint
Insalata Caprese, 175
Italian Chopped Salad, 178, 348
Marinated Mushroom Salad, 177
Mexican Pasta Salad, 184
Millet Salad with Apricots, Pine Nuts, and Ginger, 182
Mock Chicken, 189, 191-193
Mock Chicken Salad, 189
Mock Chicken Taco Salad, 192
Mock Chicken with Spicy Fruit Salad, 193
Mock Egg Salad, 190
Moroccan Swiss Chard Salad, 171
Oriental Salad with Smoked Tofu, 198

Pasta and Vegetable Salad with Basil Dressing, 185
Potato Salad, My Way, 152
Potato, Corn, and Cherry Tomato Salad, 19, 149
Quinoa Salad with Sun-Dried Tomatoes, 183
Rice and Broccoli Salad, 169
Sesame Carrot Salad, 19, 165
South American Jicama and Orange Salad, 159
Spicy Chickpea Salad, 179
Spinach, Fennel, and Pink Grapefruit Salad, 164
Sprouted Wheat and Veggie Bowl, 181
Sweet Potato Slaw, 157
Tabbouleh, 19, 173
Tomato and Fennel Salad, 174
Warm Potato-Kale Salad, 151
Wild Rice Salad, 187-188
Wild Rice Salad #2, 188
Salisbury Steaks, 98, 375
Sandwich Suggestions, 281
Sausage and Potato Skillet, 363
Savory Stuffed Portabellos, 348
Seed Spread, 76
Sesame Biscuits, 242
Sesame Carrot Salad, 19, 165
Sesame Crunch Cookies, 421
Sesame Crunchies, 403
Sesame Custard, 395

Sesame Millet Cookies, 422
Sesame Sauce, 87
Side Dishes
Baked Tomatoes, 248
Broccoli Stuffed Tomatoes, 249
Carrots in Orange Sauce, 250
Citrus Spaghetti Squash Noodles, 252
Ginger Carrots, 251
Lemon Bulgur Mounds with Chives, 254
Nori Rolls, 19, 255
Oriental Quinoa Pilaf, 256
Pine Nut, Pinto Bean, and Scallion Pilaf, 258
Ratatouille, 262
Spanish Rice, 269
Special Mashed Potatoes, 259
Spinach and Broccoli, 263
Suzhou Potatoes, 260
Tender Thai Vegetables, 267
Wilted Spinach, 19, 265
Winter Vegetables with Horseradish Dill Sauce, 266
Soba Soup with Spinach, Tofu, and Arame, 134
Soups, 17, 57, 63, 104, 463
Autumnal Glory, 105
Broccoli Soup, 18, 106
Celery Soup, 107
Chilled Curried Carrot Soup, 108
Cilantro Soup, 110

Cold Zucchini and Red Bell Pepper Soup with Cumin, 111
Corn and Rice Soup, 113
Creamy Mushroom Soup, 114
Curried Broccoli, Watercress, and Spinach Soup, 116
Curried Coconut Noodle Soup, 117
Curried Sprouted Lentil Stew, 119
Dal Soup, 120
Fragrant Oriental Soup, 122
Fresh Tomato Soup, 18, 109
Gazpacho, 123, 125
Gingered Butternut Squash Soup, 126
Lemon Soup, 18, 115
Lentil and Brown Rice Soup, 128
Muligatawny, 129
Oriental Gazpacho, 123
Pea and Carrot Soup, 18, 130
Red Bell and Fennel Soup, 131
Roasted Garlic and Mushroom Soup, 132
Soba Soup with Spinach, Tofu, and Arame, 134
Spicy Kale and Chickpea Stew, 136
Spinach, 18-19, 30, 73, 77, 92, 115-116, 119, 134, 138, 144, 164, 172, 263-265, 277, 303, 313, 328-329, 335-336, 373-374
Squash and Sweet Potato Chowder, 139

Squash, Aduki, Corn Chowder, 105
Tomato Carrot Soup, 18, 140
Wild Rice and Shiitake Mushroom, 142
Winter Greens, 144
Zucchini Basil, 145
South American Jicama and Orange Salad, 159
Spaghetti Squash and Green Beans, 19, 285
Spaghetti Squash with Greens, 286
Spanish Rice, 269
Special Mashed Potatoes, 259
Spiced Sesame Dressing, 213
Spicy Chickpea Salad, 179
Spicy Dressing, 214
Spicy Kale and Chickpea Stew, 136
Spicy Sausage and Soba Noodles in Paprika Sauce, 359
Spicy Thai Noodles, 311
Spinach, 18-19, 30, 73, 77, 92, 115-116, 119, 134, 138, 144, 164, 172, 263-265, 277, 303, 313, 328-329, 335-336, 373-374
Broccoli, Watercress, and Spinach Soup, 116
Curried Broccoli, Watercress, and Spinach Soup, 116
Curried Sprouted Lentil Stew, 119
Escarole, Spinach, Hijiki, and Red Onion Salad, 172
Lemon Soup, 18, 115
Noodles in Green Sauce, 303
Soba Soup with Spinach, Tofu, and Arame, 134
Spinach and Broccoli, 263
Spinach and Rice Casserole with Toasted Almonds, 19, 328
Spinach Cheese Logs, 73
Spinach Soup, 18, 116, 138
Spinach, Fennel, and Pink Grapefruit Salad, 164
Spinach-Mushroom Dip, 77
Vegetable Lasagna, 334
Wilted Spinach, 19, 265
Winter Greens Soup, 144
Spinach and Broccoli, 263
Spinach and Rice Casserole with Toasted Almonds, 19, 328
Spinach Cheese Logs, 73
Spinach Fritters, 92, 313
Spinach Soup, 18, 116, 138
Spinach, Fennel, and Pink Grapefruit Salad, 164
Spinach-Mushroom Dip, 77
Sprouted Wheat and Veggie Bowl, 181
Sprouted Wheat Surprises, 410
Sprouting, 45, 63-64, 136
Squash, 19, 90, 105, 126, 139, 237, 252, 285-286, 300, 303, 305, 327, 330-331, 337-338, 352-354, 433
Arame-Zucchini Sesame Toss, 170

Chestnut, Apple, and Cornbread Stuffed Squash, 337
Chili and Corn Filled Zucchini, 344
Citrus Spaghetti Squash Noodles, 252
Cold Zucchini and Red Bell Pepper Soup, 111
Gingered Butternut Squash Soup, 126
Millet Stuffed Zucchini, 346
Primavera Pasta, 300, 302
Spaghetti Squash and Green Beans, 19, 285
Spaghetti Squash with Greens, 286
Squash and Bean Casserole, 19, 330
Squash and Leek Turnovers, 19, 352
Squash and Sweet Potato Chowder, 139
Squash, Aduki, Corn Chowder, 105
Sweet Squash Stuffed with Wild Rice, 354
Vegetable Enchilada Casserole, 332
Zucchini Basil Soup, 145
Zucchini Muffins, 238
Squash and Bean Casserole, 19, 330

Squash and Leek Turnovers, 19, 352
Squash and Sweet Potato Chowder, 139
Squash, Aduki, Corn Chowder, 105
Squash-Corn Muffins, 237
Strawberry Mousse, 400
Strawberry Shortcake, 442
Stuffed Cabbage Stroganoff, 350
Substitutions, 5
Suggested Staple List, 0-1
Sun-dried Tomatoes, 86, 119, 132, 168, 183, 187, 206, 283, 298, 316, 323, 327, 335, 346
Corn and Sun-Dried Tomato Relish, 86, 381
Sunflower Seed Dressing, 169, 207
Sunflower-Apricot Patties, 409
Suzhou Potatoes, 260
Sweet Potato Slaw, 157
Sweet Squash Stuffed with Wild Rice, 354
Sweeteners, 0-1, 8, 43-45, 56, 222, 394, 463
Tabbouleh, 19, 173
Tapioca Pudding, 398
Tempeh, 4, 20, 30, 86, 189, 195, 283-284, 335, 359, 363, 367, 371-372, 375-381, 383, 385-389, 391-392, 464, 475

Baked Tofu with Cabbage and Wild Rice, 371
BBQ Style Tempeh, 376
Curried , 195
Deli Style Tempeh, 377
Hot and Pungent Tempeh with Broccoli, 378
Lettuce Wrapped Tempeh Meatballs, 380
Mock Chicken Salad, 189
Reubens, 283
Rio Grande Tempeh Salisbury Steaks, 98, 375
Tempeh Hash, 383
Tempeh in Red Wine Sauce, 387
Tempeh in Shiitake Cream Sauce, 385
Tempeh Millet Loaf, 20, 389
Tempeh Sausage Patties, 367
Tempeh Skillet Dinner, 391
Tempeh with Lemon Ginger Glaze, 392
Tempeh Hash, 383
Tempeh in Red Wine Sauce, 387
Tempeh in Shiitake Cream Sauce, 385
Tempeh Millet Loaf, 20, 389
Tempeh Sausage Patties, 367
Tempeh Skillet Dinner, 391
Tempeh with Lemon Ginger Glaze, 392
Tender Thai Vegetables, 267

Thai Stir Fry, 310
The Meeny Greeny Banana Shake, 453
The Natural Home, 467
Tofu, 4, 6, 20, 30, 56, 70, 97, 104, 115, 117-118, 122, 134, 152, 160, 184, 190-192, 194, 196-198, 208, 213, 255, 277, 281, 289, 291-294, 308-315, 328, 334, 359, 363, 371-373, 375, 381, 396, 399-400, 415, 425-427, 430, 433, 437, 442-443
Asparagus-Tofu Stir Fry, 289
Baked Tofu with Cabbage and Wild Rice, 371
Carob Pudding, 396, 415
Cheddar, Sunflower Seed, and Olive Spread, 70
Coconut and Cashew Veggies with Tofu and Orange Sauce, 293
Coconut Curry Melange, 314
Crepes, 306-307, 425-427
Cucumbers with Tofu Sour Cream, 160
Curried Coconut Noodle Soup, 117
Daddy's Favorite Salad, 196
Egg Salad with Jalapeno and Cumin, 194
Fragrant Oriental Soup, 122
Fruit Mousse Pie, 430
Lemon Mousse, 399
Lemon Soup, 18, 115

Matar Paneer, 308
Mock Chicken, 189, 191-193
Mock Chicken with Spicy Fruit Salad, 193
Mock Egg Salad, 190
My Favorite Scrambler, 277
Nori Rolls, 19, 255
O Konomi Yaki, 291
Oriental Salad with Smoked Tofu, 198
Potato Salad, My Way, 152
Pumpkin Pie, 433
Rosemary Tofu Sauté, 20, 373
Salisbury Steaks, 98, 375
Sandwich Suggestions, 281
Sausage and Potato Skillet, 363
Soba Soup with Spinach, Tofu, and Arame, 134
Spicy Thai Noodles, 311
Spinach and Rice Casserole with Toasted Almonds, 19, 328
Spinach Fritters, 92, 313
Strawberry Mousse, 400
Thai Stir Fry, 310
Tofu Sour Cream, 6, 97, 160, 184, 192, 359
Vanilla Tofu Cream, 415, 425, 437, 442-443
Vegetable Lasagna, 334
Tofu Sour Cream, 6, 97, 160, 184, 192, 359
Tomato and Fennel Salad, 174

Tomato Carrot Soup, 18, 140
Tomato Salsa, 93, 184, 344
Tomatoes, 2, 57, 86, 90, 92-93, 109, 113, 119, 123, 125, 128, 132-133, 136-137, 140-141, 149, 168, 174-175, 178, 183, 187, 206, 248-249, 262, 283, 285, 295, 297-298, 300-301, 316-317, 323, 327, 332, 335, 346, 355, 357-358, 361-363, 391
Baked Tomatoes, 248
Broccoli Stuffed Tomatoes, 249
Eggplant, Tomato, and Bell Pepper Relish, 90
Fresh Tomato Sauce, 18, 92, 313, 322
Fresh Tomato Soup, 18, 109
Insalata Caprese, 175
Lentil-Tomato Loaf, 297
Potato, Corn, and Cherry Tomato Salad, 19, 149
Quinoa Salad with Sun-Dried Tomatoes, 183
Tomato and Fennel Salad, 174
Tomato Carrot Soup, 18, 140
Tomato Salsa, 93, 184, 344
Tri-Grain Hash, 384
Tzatziki, 78, 341
Ultimate Sandwich with Creamy Mozzarella, 287
Vanilla Tofu Cream, 415, 425, 437, 442-443

Vegetable Enchilada Casserole, 332
Vegetable Lasagna, 334
Veggie and Black Bean Tacos, 358
Veggie Rolls, 19, 339
Waffles, 18, 278
Warm Potato-Kale Salad, 151
Wheat-Free Muffins, 240
White Beans with Tomato and Sage, 19, 295
Wild Rice and Shiitake Mushroom Soup, 142
Wild Rice Salad, 187-188
Wild Rice Salad #2, 188
Wilted Spinach, 19, 265
Winter Greens Soup, 144
Winter Vegetables with Horseradish Dill Sauce, 266
Yogurt, Cucumber, and Garlic Dip, 78
Zucchini Basil Soup, 145
Zucchini Muffins, 238

9 780595 096619